*The Consolations of Autumn*

# Table of Contents

# The Consolations of Autumn

*Sages in Hard Times*

# Hazhir Teimourian

PEACH PUBLISHING

ISBN 978-1-78036-268-7

Published by
Peach Publishing

To all my loved ones. Non nova, sed nove! May it amuse – and enthuse –
them, when they are my age.


In good times, philosophers' interests are more purely intellectual;
in bad times, they invent consolations!

Bertrand Russell

# Prologue

And this is the kind of thing we should say to one another by the fireside in winter-time, as we lie on soft couches, after a good meal, sipping sweet wines and crunching chickpeas: 'Of what land are you, and how old are you, good Sir? And how old were you when the Mede appeared?'

Xenophanes, 6th century BC Greek refugee

How did the great sages of the past try to remain functional human beings in the face of misfortune or even calamity, the lonely battles that we shall all have to fight at one or other stage of our lives? How did their particular experience of life equip them for those battles? To what extent did the wisest of them succeed? Was it hard to lead a semblance of a good life when afflicted by loss or frailty? Could they justify it when civilisation itself seemed to have collapsed all around them?

As the year 2015 and with it, my 75th birthday, came into view and I also saw chunks of the world seemingly descend into Malthusian turmoil, even barbarism in places, I needed hope. I decided to seek it in the lives of the philosophers, artists and scientists I had admired for so long. I found that for some, the challenge to be confronted was almost continuous. That group included Socrates, Darwin and Pasternak. For a few, such as Boethius and Beethoven, darkness fell early. For yet others, such as Seneca, the great Stoic statesman of the Roman Empire, the end arrived reasonably late, but it did so suddenly and brutally. Bertrand Russell sought refuge from depression during the First World War in work and by throwing himself into public affairs.

In writing this book, however, I feel that I owe the reader an explanation, for except in the case of Omar Khayyām and, possibly, Bertrand Russell, I cannot pronounce with any authority on any of the sages I have chosen to discuss here. Perhaps how the idea of the book came about will excuse my boldness.

The genesis of this book lies in two events six years apart. The earlier spur occurred in the late spring of 2003, when my wife and I were taking a short holiday abroad. After an intense bout of activity which had sometimes meant my giving 30 or even more interviews a day to broadcasters all over the world on the American-led invasion of Iraq, I needed a rest, and so we flew to the Mani region of Greece, that ancient, well-trodden land of the southern Peloponnese. But even there, I could not be quite idle. The editor of the Literary Review in London had asked me to assess a new book by the philosopher A. C. Grayling and so I had thrown that book into the holiday luggage. The extent to which I fell under the spell of What is Good: The search for the best way to live may perhaps be gleamed from the opening paragraph of my review which appeared in the August edition of the magazine:

> How appropriate that I should be reading this survey of ideas about 'the good life' here in Greece, where the everyday philosophising of homo sapiens was first raised to the level of formal discussion in academies and given the name of philosophy. Furthermore, as you watch the local people with their relaxed lifestyles, you cannot help but wonder on the qualities of the ideal life yourself. In the hot afternoons, under the canopies of vines and mulberry trees, young people whisper their own versions of eternal truths to each other over glasses of beer and Kalamata olives (favourites of Herodotus), before going for a long splash in the clear waters, while their elders take a snooze on a shaded balcony or play backgammon (a Persian borrowing) in the alleyways.

The notes I made for the review, which remain lodged in the review copy, have a question, or rather two, jotted down towards the end: Is it possible to have a reasonably good life in the face of misfortune, loss or ill health, and is living a modestly good life justifiable if the society around one is threatened by disaster? For 'the good life' has meant much more to good men than 'A flask of wine, a book of verse, and thou'.

Those two questions have always preoccupied me, right from my early schooldays in a remote corner of Kurdish western Iran (coincidentally, wherefrom Xenophanes's Medes had hailed). In recent years, the latter question concerning society has grown to haunt and torment me, often causing me sleepless nights, and I know that I am not alone in such a predicament. Far from it. There must be hundreds of millions of us watching our rudderless world drifting towards great new calamities. Our increasing numbers put unprecedented pressure on the globe's fragile eco-system, and, closer to home, our most advanced, liberal societies become less liberal to protect themselves against terrorists, within and without. It is easy to despair.

Under such circumstances, we may ask whether it is permissible morally to seek a reasonably fulfilled personal life? The answer has to be 'Yes', and that, in fact, we have a duty to pursue fulfilled lives. If we do not do so, if we do not have functional private lives, how could we act in our public persona to combat those threats? The question that arises next is: What kind of life could we permit ourselves under the new circumstances of scarcity of resources. It could certainly not be one of rampant consumerism.

The second spur came in 2009, when BBC Radio 4 asked me to write and present an episode of a philosophical/spiritual programme that is broadcast on Sunday mornings. The series is called Something Understood and has, under my old colleague in the World Service of the BBC, Sir Mark Tully, become almost cult listening to early risers. But Mark needs a rest every now and then and hence the temporary need for second-bests.

They asked what subject I wished to address and, as my episode was going to be broadcast in October, I chose to indulge in the metaphor of the fading light to speak of the peace of mind that can be the fortune of most people in the autumn of their lives. I had entered my 70th year by then and so, with the aid of an anthology of poems and songs, the programme reflected merely my own state of mind as I looked back on an eventful journey in a turbulent world.

It has to be said that the programme, which I subtitled The Consolations of Autumn, did not quite achieve the effect intended. I wished it to lift the mood of the older listener and lessen the fright of the younger as they contemplated their own autumns. But some listeners, including a professor of international relations, wrote to say that it had made them cry. I had made them think of the glory of their youths, they said, and reminded them of the loss of their loved ones.

Looking back, this was perhaps inevitable. Despite my trying to be a rabble-rouser, I had had to be realistic to be credible, and you cannot fool people into believing that they can ignore completely the moaning and creaking of their ageing limbs in later life. The most that can be achieved in the last third of our lives is aptly described by Wordsworth:

Though nothing can bring back the splendour in the grass,
The glory to the flower,
We shall grieve not,
Rather find strength in what remains behind.

But what remains behind can still be worthy of celebration, both to the individual and to his society. In fact, according to evolutionary psychologists, it explains the longevity of us humans. The greater wisdom that has come to the old shields society from the rushed judgements of its younger members. At the level of the individual, too, the old sympathise more, condemn less, sparing them some of the stress to which the young are subject. In the words of one of the heroes of this book, the great philosopher and humanist Bertrand Russell, with whom I had the honour of a little correspondence a few years after my arrival in Britain in 1959, an individual human life ought to be like a river:

... small at first, narrowly contained within its banks, rushing
passionately past boulders and over waterfalls. Gradually the river
grows wider, the banks recede, the waters flow more quietly and, in

3

the end, without any visible break, they become merged in the sea and painlessly lose their individual being.[1]

Furthermore, we live far longer lives now, and remain healthier in our last decades. In 1982, for example, there were 2560 centenarians in England and Wales. Thirty years later in 2012, their number had more than quadrupled to 12,320. Such startling changes in demographics almost never occurred before modern times.

Perhaps I should tell a personal story here to illustrate the point. In my village of Wadhurst in Sussex, south-eastern England, I formed a deep bond of friendship with a neighbour by the name of Frank Bishop. He and I had seemingly little in common. He was a retired builder who did not really enjoy leaving the village, except for occasional flights to his seaside apartment in Minorca. I, on the other hand, had been brought up far away and nowadays raised hats each week with Nobel laureates at my club in Pall Mall, was a habitué of the National Theatre and dined regularly at the House of Lords – was in fact on a committee there with former cabinet ministers and archbishops of Canterbury. But we found that planning what vegetables to grow in the next season or inspecting his hatchling chicks in the incubator he kept in his bedroom brought us together as if we were two young boys.

Frank's stooping, but always cheerful, figure was an inspiration to many in his dear 'Wodderst' and he took pride in the quality of his former work. As we walked to the shops, or more rarely, whenever I drove him to our nearest town for a restaurant meal, he pointed to a handsome house here or there. 'We done it', he would say, with a great smile on his face. He knew he was lucky to be alive, too. He had served as a gunner in the freezing rear turrets of Wellington bombers in World War II and had mourned many of his young comrades who did not return.

This idyll continued till April 2011, when, one day, I put together a tray of fresh bread and cheeses with half a bottle of wine to take over to his house to share with him for lunch. I also wanted to tell him that we planned a dinner for him and his companion, Ann, to celebrate his coming 90th birthday. But I could not find him in the house and gave up, assuming that he had gone to the chicken enclosure at the bottom of his three-acre garden to collect the morning's eggs. Several hours late, when I went over again and he would not answer my calls, I found him dead in one of the rooms.

Now, Frank would normally have died a dozen years earlier. He had had a heart attack and doctors had inserted a simple pace-maker in his chest. As a result, he had a full life as an individual and brought great happiness to his children and grandchildren, as well as to his friends. Indeed, the legacy of his good life continues. Ann and his son Roger and his family have all become good friends of ours and I do not mind admitting that when I go for an occasional visit to his grave in the village cemetery, where he is buried beside his parents and siblings, I talk to him. I tell him, for example, how our fig trees are performing, or of the health of his bees which continue to give us a wonderful harvest of golden honey each year.

The fact alone, that Frank's long and fulfilled life is no longer a rarity, is one good reason to be grateful for the scientific, social and political progress that some parts of the world have achieved in recent times. Most of us can look forward to several more decades of active life, when the great majority of even the most recent of our ancestors could not.

The examples of sages I have chosen to illustrate the debate about the good life from the early classical times to the present are almost exclusively secular freethinkers. This is for the obvious reason that men of strong faith – at least in those faiths that are centred on a personal creator – are not particularly preoccupied by life as we know it. They are lucky. They believe, as my own late father did, that a better life awaits them after death. Furthermore, had I chosen any men and women who were primarily motivated by their creeds, even secular creeds such as communism, the result would have been of less interest to the average citizen of the liberal societies of the West today, precisely the kind of people who might come across this book. Our age is one of widespread doubt, so much so that the churches have reformed some of their core doctrines – such as Creation – not to appear at odds with the findings of scientists, especially geologists, biologists, physicists and astronomers.

The examples I have chosen were also, more or less, involved in the public affairs of their communities. Hedonists are deeply alien to the innate social nature of the great bulk of humanity and, for that reason, they usually sink into obscurity when their parasitic lives come to an end, leaving them not to be missed even by their relatives. One reason why I spent years researching the life of Omar Khayyām, the eleventh century poet, scientist and deeply serious thinker, was to rescue him from the undeserved reputation that a selective – though wonderful – translation of his tavern poems had acquired for him here in the West. The same reasoning explains my inclusion of Epicurus among my luminaries here. He has had his image distorted even more radically than has poor Khayyām.

It may well be asked what possible benefit could we derive in this scientific age from 'the wisdom' of ancient men whose thinking could be described as leaping in the dark. Without any doubt, some of that 'wisdom' would cause laughter among today's primary school children. Some, such as the great Socrates, seeing the contradictory claims of their 'natural philosophy' colleagues, denounced science as useless to the serious problem of living, while others, such as Epicurus, made new claims of their own regarding the natural

5

world. But it remains true that they were among the greatest minds who have ever walked upon the surface of this wonderful planet of ours and they were brilliant observers of human behaviour. Their ethics have thus volumes to teach us, and their valiant efforts to keep themselves and those around them sane in the face of general ignorance, war and pestilence can still inspire us. That is why I have chosen them. We can make allowances for their believing, for example, that the sun was a hot rock the size of mainland Greece, while benefiting from their thinking regarding the good life.

I have given the middle section of the book over to an anthology of poems to console us for loss, and to remind us that great good can still lie ahead.

Poems can convey, even if indirectly, a philosophy of life in miniature, with the additional attraction of invoking beauty, love, longing, etc, to speak to our hearts. The rational half of our brains is only half of our story. The other part, the sentimental half, needs to be nurtured just as fully to make what remains of our tenure of consciousness worthwhile. In the poets, in the best of the poets, cold, reasoned philosophy combines with passionate love to take us closer to the sense of the divine that most of us have now lost. I have arranged this selection of distilled wisdom according to their theme for easier navigation in future returns to them.

Part three of the book is a brief meditation on the possessions, mental and physical, that enable me to live what I believe to be a fortunate existence. It is not an extravagant list. In the affluent societies of the industrialised world, most people can afford a variance of it to satisfy their own particular needs and preferences. What is not in doubt is that for us to have peace of mind and enjoy our later years requires a certain minimum standard of material comfort, companionship, culture and entertainment, as well as, of course, a reasonably good health. The good life has never, in the opinion of the wisest sages, been about hair shirts and penance.

Finally, in an appendix, I have included a series of autobiographical talks, originally entitled Kurd's Eye View that BBC Radio 4 asked me to broadcast in 1998. I should normally have been reluctant to speak about myself. I am particularly so now, now that I am older and no-longer enamoured of praise and fame. But the talks are largely about public affairs and about a rare and unexpected journey from a remote agricultural backwater to the heart of London, arguably the most influential city in all history. When the talks were first broadcast, the newspapers assessed them generously, and so they may be of amusement to readers today. Furthermore, they shed a little light on the man who has put the selection together. It is always useful to know from where the teller of a particular story hails. In this case, he hails from ancient Media.

# Part One

# Beacons for Autumn

# Socrates

*The barefoot inquisitor who became the father of all sages*

Men of Athens, I honour you and love you, but I shall obey God rather than you. And as long as I have life and strength in my body, I shall not stop pursuing knowledge or urging others to tread in the same path

DISCIPLE: Lately a flea bit Chaerephon on the forehead and then jumped on to Socrates's head. Socrates asked Chaerephon: How many times the length of its shin can a flea jump? Chaerephon didn't know, of course.

STREPSIADES: How could anyone know?

DISCIPLE: Oh, Socrates had no problem at all with that. It numbs your mind, as you'd expect of him. He caught a flea and melted some wax. He dipped the flea's legs in the wax. Now. When the wax cooled, the little beast had boots on, made of wax, knee-high, like Persian boots. All that Socrates had to do now, was to measure the height of one boot and calculate the rest.

STREPSIADES: Ah, great Zeus. What a genius. What a subtle mind.

DISCIPLE: And what would you say if I told you another story?

STREPSIADES: Oh, yes, please. Go on. Tell me.

DISCIPLE: Chaerephon asked the Master whether the mosquito buzzes through its mouth or its bum.

STREPSIADES: And what did he say?

DISCIPLE: The Master said that it was simple. Through the bum. The little insect has a very narrow gut, as you can imagine. When air is pushed through it, it wants to escape. But first it has to pass through the rump, which is wide and can inflate further under pressure. So, the air resonates, loudly, as it escapes.

STREPSIADES: Great Zeus, again. This is wonderful. Thank you, thank you. How can I possibly lose my case if I tell the jury that the arse of a mosquito is really a trumpet.[3]


There are many reasons why this passage from Aristophanes' comedy, The Clouds, elates us more than twenty-four centuries later. It occurs to us first that such a fragile treasure, recorded on perishable material, has survived almost two-and-a-half millennia of wars, plagues, neglect, damp and the teeth of young mice needing exercise. How grateful we ought to be, therefore, to the myriad numbers of scholars and scribes who copied the hand-written scripts of their predecessors, often with failing eyes in the light of dim candles, to preserve them for their heirs or to duplicate them for sale to landowners' private libraries, princely mansions and temples, from the time of the old Greeks themselves, through the dominion of their great admirers, the Romans, to reach the much maligned, Greek-speaking Byzantines. In the early fifteenth century, as it became clear that Constantinople was in danger of falling to the uncaring Turks, there was a rush in the smuggling of the ancient manuscripts to Italy and beyond in the heart of Europe for safer keeping. Had it not been for the foresight and valour of such heroes, it is most unlikely that we would now be in possession of a single play by the Greek ancients.

The second reason, just as astonishing, is that we see how advanced the theatre had already become by the time of young Aristophanes in 423 BC, when The Clouds was first performed at the temple of Dionysus in Athens. We notice a sparsity of stage direction, and there is no interval. Changes of scene and location are implied, rather than pronounced. But the manuscript reads as any modern play does and reveals that all the tricks of the modern comic actor's trade have already been developed . We also see that the Greek tongue has already risen to the level of a sophisticated national language capable of expressing the most sublime of notions.

Socrates was 46 years old at the time and such a well-known figure on the streets of that sophisticated, chaotically democratic city state that he could be brought into the script of a play without prior explanation as to who he was.

Even his friend and associate, Chaerephon, was known to most people. We shall see why, a little later.

Socrates was particularly loved by the young. Despite his mature age for those times, he adopted no airs and graces with them and made them laugh readily. With their elders, also, he was popular. He was known to them as a respected teacher who had no regard for wealth and seemed devoted to the improvement of society. His wit and wisdom had almost acquired the status of legend, which meant, of course, that he had enemies far and wide. These were, especially, the men behind the lucrative businesses and political power houses of the temples who did not wish to see the young encouraged to think for themselves. There were similarly those pompous old men, particularly politicians, whose pride and social standing he had injured by his habit of challenging their views wherever he met them.

As such, as a public-spirited man who was at the heart of most events, we can assume that on that particular day, for the staging of a new comedy, he would sit in the audience, for such temple plays were almost never repeated. He would also have had reason to be anxious. He would have heard that the farce had him as its central character, and that it would not depict him affectionately. Thus he would have prepared himself to be shocked and he would have determined to dismiss it, if he could, as harmless fun. The young playwright would have, most probably, been known to him, as most such aspiring young men sought his company eagerly.

The plot involves a minor landowner, Strepsiades, who faces ruin due to the obsession of his dissolute son with chariots and thoroughbred horses. He knows that a new breed of wise men, known as the Sophists, have set up 'logic factories' where they teach rhetoric to students, and such is their knowledge and the ingenious trickery of their advocacy that their pupils never lose a law suit in the courts. They overwhelm and confuse juries so thoroughly that they end up sympathising with the vilest of criminals, instead of sending them to the gallows. Thus Strepsiades resolves to enrol at the most famous of such schools, the one run by Socrates. There, he is somehow allowed into the presence of the master himself, who sits in a basket suspended in the air, for his feet must not touch the ground if he is to think most clearly.

This suspension in the air is also a hint to the audience that Socrates believes, as his late teacher Archelaus had done, that everything in the world is made of the various states of the condensation of air. As a result, we are not surprised when he tells Strepsiades that clouds are the most powerful supernatural forces in our lives. When Strepsiades protests that he thought clouds were mere vapour, the master becomes abusive and the clouds, in the shape of the chorus, burst into song denouncing the brazen applicant as too stupid to have been allowed into the school, at all.

By this early stage, it is clear to us that the depiction of Socrates violates the facts of his life as we have come to know them. We know that Socrates went about on the streets barefoot and was oblivious of the clothes he wore. Furthermore, he criticised the Sophists for charging fees for their teaching, let alone those who set up whole institutions for the purpose of earning money on a large scale. The Socrates we know even denied that he ever taught. He said that he had no wisdom of his own to bestow on others. He was a mere 'midwife' of the wisdom of others. He helped them to realise what they already knew.

But let us suspend our sense of justice for the time being. This is a comedy, after all. It must exaggerate and even tell harmless lies to make us laugh. Unfortunately, far worse is to come. The master says that he can teach any average man to acquit himself well in the courts. Far more seriously for the temple audience, he ridicules Zeus and the other gods of the Athenian state. Eventually, he dismisses Strepsiades as too poorly of memory to learn rhetoric, but agrees first to cure his son of his profligacy and then to teach him to become a master lawyer to rescue his father from his quandary. This, Socrates does, after receiving at least a large sack of flour from Strepsiades, but the result, when it emerges, is not what the unfortunate supplicant needed. The first proof of his son's new, sophisticated self is that he beats him up after a disagreement about the merits of the old poets, such as Sophocles, versus the new, such as Euripides. The boy then resorts to the advocacy he has just learnt to justify his behaviour. He asks his father whether he had not struck him as a child. So justice is now done, and he will next beat up his mother. Strepsiades, no mean scoundrel himself, is so disgusted by the evil of the new teaching that he summons his slaves and brings down 'the logic factory' in flames.

These first public charges laid at the door of Socrates are, of course, malicious and grave. He is clearly corrupting the young and worse: as someone who undermines the official religion of the state, he is a most dangerous enemy of democracy, the sovereignty of the multitude over their own affairs. The accusations are, in other words, the first stones thrown at Socrates on his road to ruin. He will never forget the damage done to him by this young ruffian and the greybeards of the temple who stand behind him. He will mention it at his trial and he will be right. It is remarkable how faithfully the charges hurled at him eventually by his formal prosecution will reflect the accusations levelled at him here by Aristophanes. In part, they will be that Socrates 'is an evil-doer and a curious man, searching into things under the earth and above the heaven, and making the worse appear the better cause, and teaching all this to others.'

But why did it take another 24 years for him to be brought to trial for these perversions? The answer is not hard to find. We are told by Plato that no-one regarded Aristophanes' play seriously at the time. Such comedies were inserted between the more serious plays, the tragedies, as a breather, as comic relief. But this is typical of the liberties that Plato sometimes takes with his reporting. He also tells us that Socrates bore no malice against the playwright and that the two were friends several years before the trial. If true, this is likely to have been in gest only, prudence born out of fear. It would have been in Socrates' interest to belittle the impact of the play, for as long as possible, by avoiding a feud that would keep its memory alive. Aristophanes was certainly not among the 15 friends who were present by his side on the day of his execution.

A greater reason why the play's first performance in 423, as well as its second showing some years later – did not set in motion an immediate official reaction against Socrates was, to my mind, a reflection of the state of the political class in those years. Within that class, Socrates enjoyed the friendship of many powerful men, and many more lesser men regarded him as a national treasure. He was a good man, and a wise man. Previous to the first staging of The Clouds, Chaerephon, his friend in the play who was bitten by the flea, had asked the holy oracle of Delphi whether there was, anywhere on earth, a man who was wiser than Socrates. The answer had been that of all mortals, Socrates was the wisest. This verdict of Heaven, no less, had reverberated throughout Athens and among her vassals, even beyond among the Spartans.

Socrates' most devoted disciples and students came mainly from among the wealthy, with himself frequenting the dinner parties of their fathers in the aristocratic faction of Athens. Yet again, Athenian society was at that time a chaotically free polity, a haven for libertines, in fact, which enabled the free-born, at least, to level disgraceful charges of criminality and impiety against their foes without fear of libel. The individual citizen's right to free expression was seen as the foundation of the state and guarded jealously against the encroachments of politicians. Less than a generation earlier, the great Pericles himself and his mistress had been caused much grief by private plaintiffs.

It may be worth mentioning here that Plato, on whom we rely most for the character and beliefs of Socrates, was a toddler at the time of the first performance of the play – the earlier date of his birth, 427 BC, now being discarded by the latest scholarship. He may have seen the second, revised performance some years later and, as a young boy, he may have seen Socrates at the home of his uncle Charmides, but it would take around another fifteen years before his father, Ariston, would ask Socrates to accept him as one of his students.

Let us return to the question why Socrates was not prosecuted for blasphemy and subversion in those early years of his infamy, as claimed by the temples. As we have seen, he had powerful friends and he was popular in the city. Athens was a compact city where anyone with the distinct appearance and reputation of Socrates would have been known almost to everyone else. The city was so compact, in fact, that a fit man could walk from one side of it to the other in an hour, and if you exclude women, children, slaves and foreigners from the population of only 125, 000 people, the number of supporters you needed to make you influential was even smaller.

But who really was Socrates? Where did he really come from. What did he believe in or say? What explanation did he offer for his eccentricities of dress and behaviour? Was, for example, his practice of not wearing shoes a brave face he put on his poverty, or did he seek to set an example for an ethical life, a life of disregard for wealth and personal comfort? More important still, when circumstances changed to allow him to be prosecuted, as we shall see later, why did he seem to welcome it? The authorities tried to persuade him to pay a moderate fine or even escape, but he would not cooperate with them. Why? Why?

For over two millennia now, even the illiterate in much of the world have wondered at the man who could remain as calm and composed as he did when he drank of that bowl of hemlock. I have just hinted at the enormous legacy he has left us, for such is now the awe in which the whole of the world holds the achievements of ancient Greece and Rome that, whatever branch of Mankind we hail from, we regard Socrates as one of our founding fathers.

Bertrand Russell says in his History of Western Philosophy that Socrates is a curious case among historical figures. There are some about whom we know much, while about others we know little. But about Socrates we are not certain whether we know much or little. As a result, one may write a book of several volumes about him and not raise an eyebrow. On the other hand, some say that it is pointless to write about him, at all, for Plato, Xenophon and Aristophanes, the three important sources we have on him, even Aristotle a generation later, paint varying portraits of their subject.

This latter thought is usually dismissed as an exaggeration, for many of the seemingly contradictory images with which we are presented need not really be so. They can apply to the man at different stages of his long life, and they can be a matter of emphasis, or examination from a different angle. We need to work hard to penetrate through the fog of either the adulation, on one side, or the scorn, on the other, that our principle sources heap on their man.

Let us start with Xenophon, who was a historian and student of Socrates and whose reminiscences have, on that account, been regarded by some commentators as reliable. Others have viewed him much less kindly. Russell dismissed him as a source on Socrates' philosophy, but not regarding his memories of Socrates the man:

There has been a tendency to think that everything Xenophon says must be true, because he had not the wits to think of anything untrue. This is a very invalid line of argument. A stupid man's report of what a clever man says is never accurate, because he unconsciously translates what he hears into something that he can understand. I would rather be reported by my bitterest enemy among philosophers than by a friend innocent of philosophy.

Xenophon was certainly no philosopher, but Russell is unkind to him. He was not stupid. He was the successful and famous – some would say infamous – commander of the retreat of the 10,000 mercenaries who attempted their luck at king-making in Persia, but failed, through no fault of their own. By the time he began to write about Socrates, his former teacher was long dead and he, Xenophon, had retired to an estate in the country to be a gentleman farmer, nostalgic about his eventful past and longing to propel himself to the centre of the world once more. He has left us several purported memoirs of Socrates, including, curiously, one about the great man's pronouncements on household economics. Nor was he in Greece during the three years that preceded Socrates' trial and execution. Most seriously, he worshiped Socrates even more than did Plato, with his reminiscences reading as if he were conducting Socrates' defence at the trial. He is, above all, obsessed to prove that the philosopher had not turned his back on the official gods of Athens and that, far from corrupting the morals of the young, he had guided them in the right, ethical direction. If we decide to rely on him, therefore, it ought to be about Socrates the man, rather than the thinker. As such, he can be enlightening, as well as transport us for a moment to the Athens of the fifth century BC. Here is an example:

In the second book of his Memorabilia of Socrates, Xenophon tells us that a sophist called Antiphon who charged fees for his own teaching, set out to lure away some of Socrates' students. To this end, he went to one of Socrates' classes and told him, in front of his students, that by not charging fees, he indeed proved that he had little to offer, as he himself often admitted. Why did he trouble himself and others by pretending to teach, and was not the proof of his misery the poor state of his clothes and his practice of going about barefoot.

You live in such poverty that no servant would tolerate from his master. You eat and drink poorly and you wear the same suit summer and winter; you go barefoot. Why do you devalue your knowledge and why do you go without the pleasures of earning some money for your pains. ... And if your apprentices go on to imitate you, surely they will be miserable, too.

To this Socrates answered thus. Obviously, Antiphon, you would rather die than live as I do. But what is it that you really find unpleasant in my way of living? Those who take money, have to deliver what they promise, while I, who make no promises, entertain myself with the company I choose. And why do you despise my food and drink? Is that because my food is not as nourishing as yours, or is it because my diet is plain and less varied? Surely he who likes his own type of food and drink, does not wish for any other. ... As for what I wear, know that we wear clothes to suit the weather. But have you ever seen me not leaving my house because it is too cold outside or because it is too hot. ... We wear shoes to walk easier. But has that stopped me going anywhere I wish? ... If I have no passion for delicacies, if I sleep little, if I do not get into sordid love affairs, it may be because I spend my time pursuing longer term pleasures. ... What could please a man more than watching himself improving every day, or having the friendship of the best of men?[4]

Elsewhere in this dialogue, Antiphon refers to Socrates's house, and Xenophon tells us that though Socrates possessed little, 'he always had enough', which suggests that he may have had some regular income to sustain him and his family, that is, his wife Xanthippe and their three young sons.

Similarly, Aristophanes' farce has its uses in our quest. As we have seen, his Socrates is an immoral teacher of legal fakery, knowingly willing to help criminals escape justice in return for a substantial fee. This is far beyond the bounds of decency, even if we allow the artist a wide license to exaggerate in order to raise the laughter that is the essential purpose of his trade. But surely any comic play has to contain an element, if not a chunk, of truth if it is to be successful. It will not be staged at all. In that case, what might that element, or chunk, of truth be in Aristophanes' famous work that has survived over 23 centuries? It may be Socrates' religion. Though he was accused by some of atheism, he often talked of God, rather than of the gods, as the pious demanded, and he spoke of the immortality of the soul, if Plato is to be believed. In his case, the soul did not come into being with the newly-born child. It was not 'an attunement' of the body, as some others speculated.

These ideas were disturbing to many Athenians. If any had heard of them, it had been in the stories of barbarians, such as the wicked Magi, the clerical class of the Medes and Persians who had, not long ago, burnt Athens to the ground and come close to turning the Greeks into slaves.

On yet another point, young Aristophanes, who had almost certainly met Socrates many times, sounds well informed. His play depicts the middle-aged

16

Socrates as a man who has studied the practical sciences and who still dabbles in trying to discover the secrets of nature. The later Socrates protested that he was not concerned with natural science, which was the bulk of 'philosophy' at the time, but did not deny that he held the scientists, despite their disagreements, in great respect. He himself by then had come to switch his attention entirely to the needs of the human soul and society.

We can guess at what Aristophanes was nodding. Socrates had spent years as a disciple of Archelaus, the most prominent natural scientist of his day in Athens. He may even have succeeded Archelaus as the head of the latter's teaching institution. This is the great commentator John Burnet's firm view. If so, he might have well been an affluent man at the time of the first performance of the comedy, or at least until a few years earlier, unlike the aged philosopher of Plato who pleads poverty and says that he does not receive any money from his students.

Our main source, Plato, spent at least ten years by the side of Socrates as student, disciple and friend. Just as importantly, he did not delay the publishing of his memories and thoughts about Socrates for too many years. We can assume that he went to work on what would be the great project of his life immediately, during the ten years or so when he seems to have disappeared from view in Athens and travelled to Sicily and other parts of the Greek diaspora.

His voluminous writings about Socrates are in the form of dialogues – purport to tell what Socrates tried to convey to anyone who would listen. He nowhere claims that the dialogues were recorded verbatim by secretaries on the scene but, despite many wooden or long-winded passages, they contain little that appears outlandish or unexpected. We suspect that he would have recorded some of his observations of the trial at the time, and we may be confident that some of the other students and friends of Socrates, too, almost all of whom were highly educated for their time, had done similarly. These notes would have been available to Plato in later years when he published the dialogues and it would have been difficult for him to distort the image of Socrates seriously when many people in his own circle retained fond memories of the great sage.

This is at least true of the earlier dialogues, though they are numerous enough. In his middle and especially later writings, his Socrates becomes deeper and more philosophical – in a technical sense. Whereas the historic Socrates, the man we know from other sources and Plato's own early dialogues, seems to us focused almost exclusively on the ethics of achieving a better life for the individual and constructing a better society for him, Plato's later Socrates is a man who has much wider interests, such as geometry. He also becomes more religious, more of a mystic, particularly after Plato travels once more to Sicily to visit the Pythagorean philosophers there.

Thus the mature Plato is suspected of using his revered old teacher to give greater authority to his own, evolving views. We can be charitable to him by saying that he believed he had heard Socrates hinting at such doctrines or that the doctrines could be arrived at by employing Socrates' dialectical method. It is no justification, of course, and it was clearly not good enough for Aristotle, Plato's own greatest student who spent many years in his company. Aristotle went as far as accusing Plato of reducing almost all of philosophy to mathematics. While the remark may have been made in gest, perhaps to cause a little hilarity, it nevertheless hints at his disapproval. It is said that the Academy, Plato's famous teaching school, had carved over its entrance porch the sentence 'Let no-one enter here who is ignorant of geometry'. If true, it would suggest how deeply Plato had fallen under the influence of the school of Pythagoras and the Italian Greeks. Socrates would not have been happy.

But while all our sources present us with difficulties, our quest for the real Socrates need not appear completely hopeless. Putting all our knowledge together, including the tumult in Athenian society after the death of Pericles, and by taking account of the changes that overcame Plato's thinking towards the end of his eighty years, we might be able to climb to the canopy of the trees to see a little more of the wood. If we could do so, a number of basic facts about Socrates might come into view.

He was born in Athens into what appears – at least to this writer – to have been a middle class or even affluent family of long establishment. His father, Sophroniscus, was a sculptor and master stonemason who cut stones for the Parthenon. As such, he might have been in constant demand as Athens underwent a frenzy of re-building and development under Pericles. His mother, Phaenarete, was a midwife and matchmaker who appears to have had social pretensions. She traced her descent to Solon, the great lawmaker. The fact itself that the names of Socrates' parents and even grandparents have survived suggests that the family was well respected in the community and that it laid claims to having played a part in the civic history of the proud city. These were surely important factors in the making of him.

The year of his birth is reported to have been 469 BC, and he is said to have worked, as a young man, at first, at his father's trade, stonemasonry. Diogenes Laertius says that before studying under Archelaus, Socrates studied under Anaxagoras, the man who brought Ionian philosophy to Athens and became a close friend and mentor to Pericles. If this is true, Socrates would not have switched to Archelaus until 434 BC. In that year, Anaxagoras left Athens to deflect criticism from Pericles. A little later, Pericles' opponents gained the upper hand in the popular assembly and deposed him for a year. They also prosecuted Aspasia, Pericles' talented, wealthy and influential companion, 'for corrupting the women of Athens', though they failed to convict her. Another close friend of Pericles died in prison awaiting trial.

Around that time, Socrates seems to have had a social entry to the ruler's home. It is said that he claimed to have learnt rhetoric from Aspasia. If this was not in the form of watching the great lady making speeches in public arena, but social access to her, it remains a puzzle why some commentators still describe Socrates as having been born into modest means.

The next time Laertius makes a reference to Socrates seems to be of the years after 429BC, the year of Pericles' death. He quotes Mnesimachus as saying that Socrates was a close associate of Euripides and had 'laid the foundation' for at least one of the playwright's tragedies.

Philosophy under Anaxagoras and Archelaus primarily meant natural science, though ethics were also included. The two men taught that the sun was a fiery mass bigger than the whole of the Peloponnese, and that the moon merely reflected the light of the sun. They believed that stars were also fiery masses, but too far to affect us. Of more immediate interest to the populace was their ability to predict the eclipses of the moon accurately. They also explained rainbows. We are told that Socrates travelled to Samos with Archelaus.

In his middle years, Socrates fought in at least three battles against Sparta and her allies and showed great valour and unusual physical strength and endurance. He served as a hoplite soldier, which required him – as a citizen soldier – to buy his own body armour and weapons, another indication that the poverty of which he complained in his late life had not as yet afflicted him. It appears that he never ceased to have regular students and assistants from among the aristocratic and wealthy faction of Athens. Rich men sent their sons to him for their higher education and this would have required a fixed place and regular sessions. None would have reasonably expected him to render them this as a favour, without any remuneration. In Plato's Apology, we read that he did not charge for his instruction of the young; but payments might not have, necessarily, been in the form of money. They could have been in the shape of animals, parcels of food, services or other gifts. In one dialogue he himself says that he accepted the gift of a crown from Alcibiades, the student and friend who later committed treason by going over to the Spartans.

Socrates was famously 'ugly'. He had a snub nose, which he praised in gist for not depriving the eyes of a wider view, and he was bald. He also had over-large and bulging eyes. Nor did he wear shoes or care for new clothes, except on special events, for example, a banquet at Plato's home. His appearance was generally shambolic and unkempt.

It seems that he was married twice, with his second wife, Xanthippe, being much younger than he was. At the time of his execution, the youngest of their three sons was still a toddler, suggesting that she would have been, at most, in her late 30s, over 30 years younger than her husband. Xanthippe was criticised by his friends for her fiery temper and occasional physical assaults on him, including an attack at a market place. No account survives to explain her frustrations, but we may well guess: the constant dearth of money, many long evenings of loneliness with squealing children as he left to eat and drink with the rich 'in pursuit of philosophy'. Speaking of wine, he in fact drank little, but on occasion proved a great capacity for it without succumbing to drunkenness.

Let us now return to the question why it took 24 years after Aristophanes' accusatory play before Socrates was brought to trial to face its serious charges. For this, we must tell a little of the history of Athens in those decades.

Two years before Pericles died in 429, he took Athens to war against Sparta and her allies, probably convinced that if he did not do so, Sparta would soon wage war on him. Previously, during his long years of dominance over the small city state, Pericles had wreaked smaller wars against insubordinate allies to reduce them to resentful vassals. He had subsequently taxed them heavily 'for their protection', but spent much of the money on subsidising the lives of the poor and unemployed in Athens and initiating extravagant building projects, such as the Parthenon. Humanity has great reason to be grateful to him for doing so, for he created that environment in which science, philosophy and the arts flowered so spectacularly, but his vassals did not share the sentiment and their resentment grew even deeper, forcing some of them to turn to Sparta.

A major problem was that while the might of Athens was unmatched at sea, her power on land did not equal that of the superb, almost professional, Spartan army. Even so, in the first few years of the Peloponnesian war, including after Pericles' death, there was no cause to panic. It was thought likely that the two sides would arrive at a peace settlement sooner or later. But this did not happen and, for years, virtually every summer the Spartans laid waste to the countryside around Athens, with the Athenian navy only able to raid some of Sparta's sea ports. Large numbers of refugees poured into Athens to shelter in the safety of its walls and trade and agriculture suffered from a deep depression. To make matters worse, official positions in the government were mostly drawn by lot from among the populace and the resulting incompetence brought more disappointment in its wake. An opportunistic aristocratic faction eyed the chance to seize power from the democrats.

That chance arrived in 404 BC, when the Spartans eventually triumphed over the Athenians and imposed a junta from among the aristocrats to rule over them. The new government, who came to be known as the Thirty Tyrants, proved especially cruel and murdered scores of people. As a result, Athenians revolted in sufficiently large numbers to force Sparta to agree to the return of democracy, provided that an amnesty was given to her collaborators.

Socrates was not among the latter. In fact, he had demonstrated outstanding courage in not carrying out an specific order that the junta had issued to him.

In order to turn him into a collaborator and benefit from the appearance, they had told him to arrest and bring to them one of their critics, which would have meant the man's swift execution. Socrates had gone home, instead, and it was said that he would have been punished for his disobedience if the new regime had itself not been overthrown soon afterwards. The Tyrants had also publicly ridiculed his ideas and told him to stop talking to the young.

But Socrates was no friend of the democrats, either. Previous to the defeat of Athens, when it had been the turn of his clan to hold the presidency of the ruling council, he had blocked the execution of a number of naval commanders who had been accused of dereliction of duty in abandoning their own wounded sailors to chase the defeated Spartan navy. Furthermore, he had been a noisy critic of some aspects of the constitution under the democrats, particularly its practice of appointing people to important positions in the government by lottery.

Still, while his traditional enemies among the democrats could not bring any political charges against him with a good hope of securing his conviction by a jury, he was now more vulnerable than he had been before the defeat. The democrats felt insecure and they could not forgive him the fact that some of the Thirty Tyrants, particularly Charmides – Plato's uncle – had been among his friends and students. Fearful of an uprising led by the same aristocratic faction, they looked everywhere for enemies to destroy or neutralise.

Beside these political leaders, Socrates's older enemies, the shadowy men behind the temples, also simmered. They came together in 399 and resurrected Aristophanes' charges of 24 years earlier, blasphemy and corruption of the minds of the young . All that they needed now was to prepare the formalities. They found three private citizens from among their supporters willing to launch the ostensibly private prosecution, and they agreed next that the charges were serious enough for the state to justify the employment of 500 men to serve on the jury – for jury men were all paid in ancient Athens. Socrates would have been forgiven to describe it as the rule of the mob, a paid mob, and one baited to root out the enemies of the state that paid it.

It is perhaps worthwhile to quote Plato on the occupations of the three dutiful citizens who launched the prosecution, for their descriptions sound very modern. They were Anytus, a democratic politician, Lykon, a lawyer, and Meletus, 'a young and unknown poet with long straight hair, scanty beard and a hooked nose'. The last would, during the trial, be forced by Socrates to contradict himself. Whereas the charges said that Socrates had undermined the official religion of the state by preaching the existence of new gods, Meletus called Socrates an atheist who believed in no deities at all. How could he be an atheist if, at the same time, he preached the existence of new gods, Socrates said in one of his three speeches to the court. He was found guilty, nevertheless, though not by a large majority.

Even though no account has survived of the speeches of his prosecutors at the trial, there is no reason to distrust the accuracy of the case for the defence as recorded in Plato's early dialogue, The Apology. A large number of people had been present, some of whom were as jealous as Plato was of their memories of the great man, and their accounts are likely to have been in circulation at the time of Plato's publication. Socrates comes across as a defendant who is not trying whole-heartedly to acquit himself. He did not confront the charges directly, he seemed haughty and he did not flatter the jury: He had been a gadfly to the horse of the state. 'If you get rid of me, you will need to find someone else to replace me', he claimed.

He also resorted to a conspiracy theory, though in his case it was, at least partially, true. He said that beside those who had brought the prosecution against him, there were 'a multitude of invisible accusers' who had been influenced by Aristophanes' play, The Clouds. In the last speech, after his conviction, he was offered the chance to escape execution by proposing a reasonable fine. He suggested that the state feed him at its canteens for the rest of his life. When Plato and his others pleaded with him to be serious and suggest a fine, which they would pay on his behalf, he proposed such a derisory amount that the jury convicted him to death by a larger majority than it had found him guilty of the charges in the first place.

Some commentators have said that he did not want to live any longer. He was a man of 70 years, after all, and in those times of 'three scores and ten', a man would be grateful to have reached his greatest expected span. But a closer examination of his life – as far as we can claim to know it – refutes the theses. He loved life, he loved people, he was a most curious man who was eager to know what happened next, he took intense pleasure in the mystery of things. Furthermore, he had a wife of at least thirty years younger than himself, plus three young sons. One would have to be unusually cynical – to use that word before his future admirers brought it into use – to attribute no parental sentiment to him. He had called one of his sons Sophroniscus, after his own father, and as we have seen in the case of Plato, some of his contemporaries did live to be much older than 70. Just another ten years of parental supervision would have given the children an important boost in their lives.

The explanation for his preference of death over life may be sought in his strong sense of duty to family, friends and society at large, as proved in the conduct of his earlier years. In one battle he had stood behind, at imminent risk to his own life, to defend his friend and student, Alcibiades. How was he to know at the time that Alcibiades would one day embarrass him by joining Sparta against Athens. At another battle, he had carried a wounded Xenophon on his back for miles to save him from captivity or death.

In one of the earlier dialogues about the period after his conviction, one of his friends, Crito, tells him in his prison cell that he has prepared for him to escape. Socrates rebukes him. By living in the state of Athens, he says, he has promised to obey its laws. How could he justify saving his life when the state has ordered him to forfeit that life? His friend accuses him of betraying his young children for the sake of his principles. Socrates stands firm, and his sincerity has to be believed totally. He just could not return to the street of his home to take his children for a walk, knowing that he had lowered his head in front of a mob to beg forgiveness for a crime he had not committed. He told the jurors that he could have produced before them as was usual practice, his weeping wife and children to arouse their pity. But he would not do so. He would not divert their attention from the vital principles at stake.

That sincerity is reinforced by his never betraying any sign of doubt about the wisdom of his chosen path, by his constant cheerfulness in prison after his conviction, by his inspiring reception of his visitors there when awaiting the implementation of the sentence, and by his ability to focus his mind completely on obscure philosophical questions on the morning of his death. He even turns some of the fables of Aesop into verse when the prison door has closed behind his visitors.

A word is perhaps called for on 'the voice' that Socrates often claimed to hear. He sometimes called it a divine sign and sometimes a 'guiding daimon' or little deity. It was, he said, always a prohibitory voice that only dissuaded him from taking a particular course of action he was contemplating. It never urged him on to a new course, nor encouraged him in his present plans. While it may not be a legend attached to his name only after his death, it is not particularly convincing. It would be highly unusual. People who hear voices invariably remember them as exhortatory, always ordering the person into action, never preventing them doing what they wish to do. On the whole, Socrates was not dogmatic about his deities or his tendency to believe in life after death. As we have seen, he sometimes referred to a single God, sometimes to a plurality of deities. For example, he said at his trial that executing him would send him to a better place, but he admitted he was not sure what he meant by that. 'Either it is a long sleep which will be welcome as a rest', he said, 'or else, it will be where I shall meet the heroes of Homer'.

One of Socrates's core beliefs, which the twentieth century in particular proved utterly mistaken, was that knowledge and virtue were inescapably related, that the attainment of knowledge always and automatically made us better people. The converse of the statement was that vice arose always and only out of ignorance. Thus none of us committed any wrongdoing intentionally. We only committed crimes because we did not know what we were doing. Furthermore, virtue was enough to guarantee a person's happiness, for the virtuous man, the wise man, could not be harmed from the outside. He would have little that others could take away from him. All he had to do, therefore, was not to harm himself on the inside, not to harm his own inner 'soul', which came from committing wrongs against others, itself the result of ignorance. These of his beliefs are described as paradoxes because they seem to be contrary to common sense. They are known as the Socratic Paradoxes.

Despite his not leaving us – probably never writing – any account of his thoughts, Socrates is often described by today's philosophers as one of the greatest of their class. Why is that? The immediate answer must be that he championed the pursuit of knowledge at supreme cost to himself. By doing so, he inspired generations of subsequent thinkers to enquire into abstract questions in the hope of advancing the ethics of living happier lives and establishing better societies. He also left us what we call the Socratic Method. It was not started by him. According to Plato, he learnt it from Zeno, a disciple of Parmenides, but he developed it. It is the method of trying to reach a clearer understanding of issues through questioning and answering in order to eliminate contradictions in our assumptions or in their consequences. It has proved very useful in logic, not so in ethics. It is totally unsuitable to the pursuit of scientific knowledge, but then we think we know that Socrates largely confined his enquiries to those issues where one might make a useful contribution.

Plato in his later writings attributes to Socrates the theories of universals and definitions. But Aristotle contradicts him and later analysts doubt him.

If Socrates could be with us today and spoke to an average child in the first years of a primary school, he would have been humbled by how little he and his era knew. The ubiquitous mobile telephone in the child's pocket with its ability to consult encyclopaedias instantly would have brought him to his knees. But he would have no reason to feel humiliated. As a genuine seeker after truth, he would have been elated to witness our progress. His 'faith' in the greatness of Man would have been confirmed. This is because the achievements of the ensuing centuries have been – as Newton described it – the result of standing on the shoulders of the giants who came previously, pioneers of whom Socrates was one of the greatest. By putting Man – fragile, vulnerable Man who is nevertheless capable of showing selfless love and creating the most uplifting works of art and peer into the most distant corners of the Universe – at the centre of his thoughts, Socrates may also be described as a founding father of Humanism.

Alternatively, we could describe him as a traditional holy man, a seer who heard voices from his invisible daimon, as he sometimes called it, but a holy man who was clearly no dogmatist, ready always to change his mind on seeing greater evidence for the contrary claim. But whether as a holy man or saintly humanist thinker, his eccentricities of poor dress, modest food and going about barefoot seem to me to have been a means to an end, to set an example to others. Could it not be, for example, that every time he walked out onto the streets barefoot, he wanted to bring a little relief to those of his neighbours who could not afford to put shoes on the feet of their children even in the frost of winter? Could it not be that he wanted to speak as near equal to those men and women who went about in tattered clothes? Should we therefore not lower our heads to him in humility? Should we not derive inspiration from the joyful face he always presented to the world, and from his eagerness to be at the centre of events, to watch his fellow human beings with love and amazement? He will, nevertheless, remain an enigma for many more millennia.

*

**Socrates, father.**

You were my first sight of a great mountain:
Solid, eternal, indomitable, swarms of people revolved around you.
But some of the time, you were mine alone,
To hug, to climb, to perch on your peak for the long view.

One day, suddenly, you were no-longer.
The house fell silent, the men ceased to call.
Mother sobbed all night.
I heard someone say: He will soon forget.

Days, weeks, months, years.
I caressed your books,
I sniffed your coat.
The scent of your sweat brought you back a while.

Then, ... revelation: You could have returned,
But chose not to.
You nodded towards that bowl of hemlock
'For the greater good'.

I wish I knew you.
Your legend goes on:
The man who put God
Before his young son.[5]

# Epicurus

*The hedonist who lived an austere life*

6

Empty is the word of the philosopher who heals not the heart of the
tormented man

History has been unkind to Epicurus. Was he not the man who told us to seek
pleasure all day, and all night too, oblivious of the pain of others? It is untrue
by the throw of a moon rocket, and it was designed to be so.

How could such injustice be inflicted on a good man? That fate has befallen
many a sage due to the popularity of their teachings, of course, and by their
being championed by lesser men after their deaths. But Epicurus suffered
additionally, and severely, at the hands of rivals. I shall report at greater length
later in this book on a combination of forces that came into being between the

pagan temples and Christian churches in both Roman and medieval Europe to besmirch his name. For the moment, I shall confine myself to saying that Epicurus really was the opposite of the egotistic. He taught that while happiness was the right and natural aim of every person, it required a clear conscience and that it was impossible to achieve happiness in an unjust society. He was acutely aware of the fragility of our wellbeing, for he had himself suffered in his youth when he had had to abandon Athens to go to the aid of his parents who had become refugees.

Epicurus rose above that calamity through learning and observation. More importantly, he enabled and inspired large numbers of people, from slaves he allowed into his classes to Roman senators centuries later, to live happier and more useful lives. He made no distinction between men and women, noble born and those in bondage, and his example of living frugally in harmony with nature might prove the saving of our overcrowded and fouled planet in the twenty-first century, if it informed the minds of sufficient numbers of us, a most unlikely outcome.

Epicurus was clearly inspired by the example of Socrates living a simple, ethical life, but differed from the colossal sage of the previous century in important ways, particularly from the mystical Socrates we find in the later writings of Plato. Unlike Socrates, he heard no divine voices directing him at crucial moments, and he went to great lengths to be at the forefront of the thinking of his age regarding the natural world. In that respect, he adhered to the atomist theory of Leucippus and Democritus, but concluded that human beings were free agents living in society and that 'the gods' were mere combinations of atoms in a world of their own, far apart from any concern for our lives. This latter speculation, as with the real, historical Socrates, laid him open to the charge of atheism.

Epicurus was also much less of a public figure than Socrates had been. He urged his disciples and followers not to become involved directly in the daily organisation of their communities, even though their need to live in a just society implied such an involvement if the need arose. How could, otherwise, those communities survive for long if disorder afflicted their streets. Justice, peace, economic prosperity and an evidence-based education based on the study of the natural world mattered to him deeply.

The Athens in which he found himself was a much more disheartened place than it had been a century-and-a-half earlier. Alexander 'the Great' – whom modern psychologists might well diagnose as a psychopath – and his Macedonian military successors, had reduced the proud ancient city to the status of a semi-autonomous provincial town like many others in their empire. Athens was now a far cry from the outgoing, vibrant city of Pericles. It was much less free, it was poorer, and it was in cultural decline.

Unlike many other ancient thinkers, however, Epicurus may yet recover fully from the distortions inflicted on him by Christians, in particular. There has been some such recovery already, for scholars have worked hard since the Renaissance to wipe off the dust from his much-abused face. But only about 80 pages has been available from his voluminous writings, and these are often fragmentary, some even quotations from the writings of his detractors.

Uniquely in the case of classical writers, it is hoped that the shortcomings in our knowledge of the true Epicurus will lighten soon, and we think we know exactly where our hopes lie: in a ruin called the Villa of the Papyri in Herculaneum, still partly buried under some 25 metres of ash from the volcanic eruption of Vesuvius in 79 AD. More on this exciting prospect later in this chapter.

Though both his parents were Athenians, Epicurus was born in February 341 BC in Samos among the Greeks of Ionia. The family had moved to that island off the coast of Asia Minor as part of an Athenian settlement some ten years earlier and thus young Epicurus risked losing his Athenian citizenship if he stayed there permanently. The law further required him that, as a citizen, he undergo a military cadetship of two years in the service of Athens. So after first studying for a number of years on Samos under a Platonic teacher, he went to Athens at the age of eighteen.

While still in Athens after the completion of his cadetship, events took a drastic turn for the worse for his parents on Samos. After Alexander's death in 323 BC, the local tyrant expelled the Athenian settlers from the island and Epicurus' family became refugees in nearby Colophon on the coast. Epicurus left Athens to be with them and there, in Colophon, he continued his education under a follower of the atomist philosopher Democritus. The teacher, Nausiphanes, was to nauseate him for the rest of his life, but the atomist theory he taught made a deep impression on the young man and saved his later thinking from any inclination towards the mystical teachings of Pythagoras through Plato. Ironically, Pythagoras, who had eventually settled among the Greeks of southern Italy, had also been born on Samos, some 230 years earlier. Also born there was Epicurus' full contemporary, Aristarchus, who is the first known proposer of the revolution of the earth around the sun. These facts are relevant to his story, for they formed the mental environment in which young Epicurus would mature as a philosopher.

He next became a school master in Mytilene on the island of Lesbos and remained there for a few years until, as far as we know, he could no longer resist the lure of Athens. In about 306 BC, almost a century after the death of Socrates, he moved back to the renowned city and set up a school of his own near Plato's Academy. By then, the Academy had at least two rivals, Aristotle's Lyceum, and the Stoa[7] of the Stoics. Epicurus bought a house with a garden or orchard near the Academy and began to attract students of his own. Soon his fame spread and The Garden, as the school came to be called, prospered.

'Prosperity' is perhaps the wrong word here. Epicurus' disciples were not required to throw in their personal properties or incomes into a common lot, as was the practice of some cults, and they were expected to live frugally. They brought in their own food and contributed to the upkeep of poorer students if they could. What distinguished the Garden radically from its rivals, though, was that it threw its door open to everyone, men and women, free born and slave. In the wider society, only free males could be citizens and respectable women, let alone servants and slaves, played no part in public affairs.

The success of the new school caused the ire of the men of the Stoa, in particular. The scandalmongers among them pounced on the admittance of women to the Garden to spread rumours that Epicurus was an insatiable womaniser and even a glutton who vomited twice a day due to over-indulgence. Some of his women students were given spicy nicknames, such as Big Boobs. Poor Epicurus. He taught that sex probably caused more trouble than fun, for as an acute observer of human behaviour, he knew how often emotional entanglement and jealousy followed sexual intimacy. At any rate, while Epicurus may well have had relationships, there is no mention of a wife or children of his own in his will and, surely, any serious deviation from his core principles of austerity and simplicity would have exposed him to his students as a hypocrite and caused the disintegration of his school.

Instead, Epicurus' fame as a sage spread farther afield and more students flocked to him. To his discredit, he seems to have enjoyed the adulation that some of his more ardent followers heaped on him. They raised him almost to the level of a holy man. He also became a little too dogmatic about his beliefs towards the end of his 71 years. The latter weakness was perhaps a practical necessity. Any leader of an institution such as his would have wanted to guard against its disintegration from the inside by headstrong or over-ambitious students who thought themselves as accomplished as their master. One such student did break away to join his rivals with lurid allegations of misconduct by him.

In his final will and testament, Epicurus made provisions for the upkeep of the children of close disciples who had pre-deceased him. It implies that the orchard attached to the house was extensive enough to bring in a substantial annual income, perhaps from both the sale of fruit and timber. As can be seen in an excerpt from the will at the end of this chapter, he seems, in fact, to have been a wealthy man with a large household and able to subsidise the study and upkeep of some of his poorer students.

But to understand fully the appeal of the Garden school, it is important to cast an eye on what had happened to philosophy in Athens since the death of

Socrates, for philosophers had, over that time, withdrawn from the world to confine themselves to the pursuit of personal salvation.

After the execution of Socrates in 399 BC for undermining the official gods of the Athenian state – but really for being an irritant to the insecure democratic politicians who ruled the city at the time – his prolific disciple Plato had established a philosophical school, the Academy, and gradually attributed ideas and leanings to Socrates which had not been at the forefront of the master's mind. Socrates, as we saw in the previous chapter, was preoccupied with improving society, government and the life of the citizen. But as Plato grew closer in his later decades to the Pythagoreans of Italy, his philosophy became more mystical. He began to see divine significance in mathematical perfection and used Socrates as his mouthpiece and original elaborator of his new beliefs.

By contrast, after Plato's death in 347 BC, his most prominent student, Aristotle, broke away from the Academy and spent more time studying natural phenomena. On at least one occasion, he said of his late master – no doubt partly in hilarity – that he had reduced all philosophy to geometry, a clear reference to the Pythagoreans. Aristotle then joined the court of Philip II of Macedon to be tutor to the young crown prince Alexander.

A dozen years later, with Alexander by then the tyrannical Hegemon of the whole of Greece and pushing eastwards into the Persian empire, Aristotle set up his own school, the Lyceum, in Athens, and directed it for some 12 years until he, too, faced accusations of blasphemy and had to flee to his mother's estate where he died shortly afterwards. But although his philosophy was very different from the Academy's, the two most prestigious schools of thought remained too intellectual to appeal beyond a small number of affluent families. Others, if they did not seek solace in the dark rites of Dyonisus, looked for a philosophy of life that approved of turning one's back on politics to be part of a small community of one's own, a self-selected clan. Epicurus's people became one of these new communities. The two such other schools of thought were the Stoics and the Sceptics, whose names have come down into most modern languages as adjectives.

Sharp divisions between these new, inward-looking schools made them quite distinct from, or even at times violently antagonistic towards, one another. On the whole, whatever the Epicureans said, the Stoics opposed it, while the Sceptics concluded that no-one really knew what the answers were because our ability to arrive at true knowledge was miniscule. While the Epicureans tried to be as much minded by the evidence that could be gathered from the contemplation of the physical world, the Stoics indulged in divination, providence and fatalism, and sought solace in soothsayers and fortune-tellers. The Sceptics ridiculed the Stoics in particular, but even they sought credit for their claims in logic. One of their better known resorts to logic gained circulation among intellectual magpies down the centuries:

> If God is willing to prevent evil, but not able to,
> Then he is not omnipotent.
> If he is able, but not willing,
> He is malevolent.
> If he is both able and willing,
> Why is there evil?
> And if he is neither able, nor willing,
> Why call him God?

The argument used to be attributed to Epicurus, but modern scholarship inclines towards its having been coined, about150 years later, by the Sceptic Carneades. The latter had become head of Plato's Academy, but come to doubt the ability of both our senses and our reason to arrive at the truth of things and was uncertain of the attainability of justice. However, one feels that Epicurus would have been familiar with the argument, given his materialism and practical atheism, his gods being mere conglomerations of moving atoms in a separate, dreamlike universe of their own, oblivious of our affairs.

What has especially made the Epicureans distinct down the ages – and whose misinterpretation has caused them infamy – is their analysis of pleasure and pain, which in turn shaped their philosophy of life and community. Epicurus believed that the natural state of Man was a general sense of satisfaction with being alive, which he defined as not being in pain, and pain he defined as discomfort, whether in the form of an aching body or an anxious mind. It followed, then, that we must avoid, as much as we could, the stresses and anxieties of a conventional life style if we wanted to be happy and feel comfortable in our existence. In practical terms, this meant a reducing, to the bare minimum, the materials that went into keeping us alive. Thus a minimal amount of work to satisfy the material needs of ourselves and our dependants was to be recommended. If, somehow, a greater material wealth came our way without our asserting ourselves to obtain it, all the better. But we should share it with our friends, because giving was more pleasurable than receiving.

By the same token, we must avoid becoming accustomed to luxuries, for we would become anxious if we suddenly lost access to them. In his own case, he would occasionally allow himself a piece of cheese with his bread and water or glass of diluted wine. He called such occasions 'feast days', on which he would also permit himself a glass of undiluted wine.

A good life, however, was far from a mere answering of the body's material needs. Humans were social animals who needed the company of family and friends to make their short lives as pleasant as possible, and they were intelligent beings who needed to exercise their minds and to enhance their welfare by striving to be at the forefront of the thinking of their peers. To these ends, Epicurus valued loyal and intelligent friends as one of our highest achievements, and he urged people to pursue philosophy, as far, of course, as it did not cause them any anxiety. As 'philosophy' in his time was an all-embracing term that included virtually the whole field of learning, no-one needed to fear that they would ever become bored in the process. If you could not conclude why crabs were so different from fish, you could turn to the theory of music, and if you could not decide how far away the sun was from the earth, you could discuss what distinguished the great poets from lesser ones.

Unlike the centrality of numbers in the universe of Pythagoras or the five basic elements – earth, air, water, fire and aether, the divine substance – of Aristotle, Epicurus taught that the world was ultimately made of 'atoms', exceedingly small particles that were indivisible and constantly in motion, but came together in different combinations to form different entities. He was not, as we have seen, the initiator of the atomic theory. That went back to Leucippus and his student Democritus – the latter incidentally being so hated by Plato that he, Plato, wished all his books burned – but Epicurus further developed it. A logical consequence of the theory was that when we died, our souls or consciousness died with us, for the soul, too, was made of atoms and dispersed. 'Death means nothing to us', Epicurus would drill into his students, and it was pointless to be afraid of it. 'When we are alive, there is no death, and when there is death, we are not alive to know it', he loved to quip. Socrates also hinted at the mortality of the soul, though hesitantly, when he said at his trial that death meant nothing to him. It was either a long sleep, complete oblivion, he said, or else, an awakening of the consciousness in another, better world where he would be with the heroes of Homer. Socrates and Democritus had been contemporaries in Athens.

As a complete materialist, Epicurus had to struggle with the old question whether humans were free agents or not. The atoms of Leucippus and Democritus were purely mechanistic and moved in space in straight lines according to rigid natural laws, until they collided with other atoms. It followed that the course of every event in the universe was predictable. Even human decisions that were taken after long deliberation were, in the end, dictated by the atoms that had gone into us. But this was unacceptable to Epicurus. He had observed for himself that it was possible to change the seemingly predetermined direction of one's life. To solve the puzzle, he came up with the idea that atoms did not always move in straight lines. They sometimes changed course for no apparent reason and swerved as free agents. This element in our make-up gave us the freedom of action that we witnessed in our daily lives.

Curiously for his materialism, Epicurus did not deny the existence of 'the gods', as the Athenian government – now only a municipal government – said they existed. But his definition of them was such that it made them completely irrelevant to humans. His gods were bunches of atoms that entered our minds, as did dreams and thoughts and concepts. This still made them real. They were also perfect and wise beings far above any temptation to sully their hands with our affairs, either for good or bad. Some commentators have thought that his gods were designed to enable Epicurus and his school to deny accusations of atheism, which had cost Socrates his life and caused Aristotle to go into exile. But this interpretation is probably uncharitable. Epicurus may well have believed in the existence of other worlds inhabited by spirits, for there were still many mysteries that he could not resolve. At the core of such mysteries was our very existence. Why were we here in the first place. He merely saw no evidence that any external forces intervened on earth. Nevertheless, the position was still a daring one and it is a mystery why he and his school were tolerated.

A core belief of the Epicureans was the primacy of the senses. We could rely on what we saw or touched at face value to enable us to function within our physical environment, and we could use the knowledge we gained from our senses to speculate on the nature of the things that were less accessible, such as the sun, which must obviously be a very large and hot rock, not a god, as some said, or the soul that was made of atoms, physical particles. The moon was cold, but bright. It must, therefore, be reflecting the light of the sun. The stars were extremely far away, yet their light travelled vast distances to reach us. They must be extremely hot, like the sun. As guessing was free, none of these ideas was particular to Epicurus. But he was an eloquent propagator of them and he selected for himself and his followers the ones thought most logical.

Judging by some of his jibes at nearly all his famous predecessors, Epicurus must have been an uplifting companion. He called the great Democritus 'that gossip-monger', and Plato's Academy 'those appeasers of Dyonisus'. To him, Aristotle was 'that reckless spender who, after devouring his inheritance, turned to soldiering and drug selling'.

He must have also been, at least in his youth, irritatingly argumentative, as was also Socrates. He referred to his Ionian teacher Nausiphanes as 'that jellyfish who bragged like a sophist, … He became so angry with me that he cursed me and called me a school master'.

Epicurus' attitude to death and his ability to remain cheerful in the intense pain of his last weeks, coupled with the frugality of his lifestyle and his enjoyment of the conversation of friends, have inspired countless later thinkers. In the chapters on Seneca and Khayyām, I shall discuss some of the most prominent among them, and we shall also see how some Roman statesmen and artists sought to give their hedonism intellectual justification – and thus bring

Epicurus into disrepute – by championing him in fashionable society. For the moment, let us return to the exciting prospect of finding our hands on more of his lost writings.

It began in 1750 (the year of Bach's death.) on a slope overlooking the Bay of Naples in southern Italy. Some locals in the hamlet of Ercolano, near the site of ancient Herculaneum, were digging a well when they found a piece of sculpture. The frenzy of a treasure hunt that followed alerted the authorities and led to experts digging tunnels into the slope on behalf of the Bourbon royal family. Numerous statues of superb artistic merit were uncovered, including a breath-taking seated Hermes reputedly by Lysippus, Aristotle's friend, and it became clear that the remains of a once-magnificent Roman palace or mansion – owned apparently by Julius Caesar's father-in-law Julius Caesar's father-in-law Lucius Calpurnius Piso – had been located. It had laid buried under some 25 metres of volcanic ash, needless to say from that eruption of August 24, 79 AD, which killed Pliny the Elder and was so vividly described by his nephew, Pliny the Younger.

In the earliest stage of the excavation, the workers found sticks of what they believed to be charcoal. They burned an unknown number to keep warm in the tunnels, until someone noticed glints of ancient lettering on some of them and realised that they had been, in fact, scrolls made from papyrus. Some were found in a basket at a doorway, others strewn on the floor of a hall, while many more were on shelves in the centre or on the walls of a particular room, the only library from the ancient world to have survived the rigours of time and climate intact. It appeared as if a desperate last-minute attempt had been made to rescue the scrolls before super-heated radiation and a typhoon of toxic gases killed the 16,000 or so people who still remained in the two towns of Herculaneum and Pompeii.

The new discovery caused even more excitement among scholars than the bronze and marble statues had among antique dealers, but early, clumsy attempts to unroll them, including by the great chemist Sir Humphrey Davy in 1818, turned many of them into heaps of dust. Eventually, more delicate techniques were found and now, multi-spectral imaging techniques and computed X-ray 'virtual slicing' are being used to read some of the still un-wrapped scrolls to produce digital images of their contents without opening them. Problems remain, however. In some cases, the blackened papyrus is virtually unrecognisable from the carbon-based black inks used by the ancient scribes and even more sophisticated methods are needed. These are being developed by scientists.

To this end, the Italian government has rightly stopped further excavation of the building and urged the experts to concentrate instead on improving the preservation of what has already been unearthed and on deciphering those of the scrolls that remain unread. The official total number of scrolls or fragments stands at 1814, with 340 complete or almost so. By 2011, using the latest techniques, some 1200 rolls or fragments had been deciphered to reveal large chunks of Epicurus' books 14, 15, 25 and 28 on nature. The author of 44 of the rolls was found to be the 'Epicurean' philosopher and decadent poet Philodemus of Gadara, apparently a friend of the mansion's owner. Other scrolls are by some of the earlier followers of Epicurus and more faithful to the spirit of the sage.

What is most exciting, however, is the suspicion of libraries elsewhere in the 'the Villa of the Papyri'. The experts estimate that over 2500 square metres of rooms and halls have yet to be un-earthed. Furthermore, they think that there may well be other buried mansions in the vicinity with even larger libraries. Some of Piso's neighbours before the eruption were known to possess many more scrolls that have – so far – been found in the Villa. If so, we can be hopeful that, in addition to more of the lost writings of Epicurus, more information may come to light to reveal more about the inspiring life and ethics of the great man. His writings on the natural world are, for obvious reasons, mostly unfounded, primitive guesses.

Epicurus died at the age of 71 in 270 BC, but despite acute pain for a fortnight, apparently from kidney stones blocking his urinary passage, he remained cheerful. According to his biographer Diogenes Laertius[8], he celebrated being alive till the very last moment and did not stop either working or cherishing his friends. On the morning of his death, he wrote a letter to one of them that bears quoting in part:

> On this blissful day, which is also the last of my life, I write this to you. My continued sufferings from strangury and dysentery are so great that nothing could augment them. But the cheerfulness of my mind, which arises from the remembrance of our past conversations, counterbalances all these sufferings. I am asking you to care for the children of Metrodorus (from the revenue from Epicurus' own properties) in a manner befitting the devotion you have given to me and to philosophy since you were a youth. ...[9]

Incidentally, the recipient, one Idomeneus, was a court official. It implies strongly that, contrary to the often repeated claim that Epicurus forbade his followers any involvement in politics or public affairs, his strictures on the subject were not as absolute as it might appear. It must have been only a strong recommendation.

Epicurus' will and testament deserves quoting at greater length. He left all his properties and possessions to the school to enable it to continue its work, and he made provisions especially for his servants and the children of faculty members who had pre-deceased him:

> And should anything happen to Hermarchus (his successor as head of the school) before the children of Metrodorus grow up, Amynomarchus and Timocrates shall provide, as much as possible from the revenues bestowed by me, for their needs, as long as they are well-behaved. And let them take care of my other arrangements, also, to the best of their abilities. ...
>
> All my books are to be given to Hermarchus. ...
>
> Of my slaves, I hereby emancipate Mys, Nicias and Lycon. I also give Phaedrium her freedom. ...
>
> Amynomarchus and Timocrates shall be the guardians of Epicurus, the son of Metrodorus, as well as of the son of Polyanus, as long as they live and study philosophy under Hermarchus. Likewise, they shall be the guardians of the daughter of Metrodorus. When she is grown of marriageable age, they shall give her to whomsoever Hermarchus shall select from his companions in philosophy, provided she is well-behaved and obeys Hermarchus. Amynomarchus and Timocrates shall also, out of the income of my estate, give them sufficient support each year, after due consideration with Hermarchus. And they shall make Hermarchus co-trustee of the revenues, so that everything may be done with the approval of that man who has grown old with me in the study of philosophy, and who is now left as the head of the school. And when the girl comes of age, let Amynomarchus and Timocrates pay her dowry, taking from the property a sum deemed by Hermarchus to be reasonable. ...
>
> They shall also provide for Nicanor, as I have done hitherto, so that all those members of the school who have helped me in private life and have shown me kindness in every way and chosen to grown old with me in philosophy should, so far as my means can go, never lack the necessities of life. ...[10]

This excerpt alone might explain why Epicurus' legacy has proved so enduring. The love that he showered on those around him till the very last moments of his life would have ensured their subsequent devotion to keeping his memory alive for as long as they lived.

Finally, some excerpts from Epicurus' surviving works may server to further disabuse the face of this wise and compassionate man from the distortions inflicted on him by lesser men in the following centuries:

> It is not the young man who should be thought happy, but the old man

who has lived a good life. For the young man at the height of his powers is unstable, carried this way and that by fortune, like a swift stream. The old man has come to anchor, as though in a harbour, and the good things, for which he previously dared not hope, he has now brought to safety in his grateful recollections.[11]

When we argue that pleasure is our aim, we do not mean the pleasure of profligacy or sensuality ..., but the freedom from physical pain and mental anxiety. We do not aim at continuous drinking or the satisfaction of lusts, but sober reasoning, analysing our motives in the choices we make or in what we avoid. ...

Let no one hesitate to study philosophy when young, and let no one tire of it when old, for it is never too soon, nor too late, to devote oneself to the well-being of the world. Whoever says that the time for philosophy has not yet come or that it has already passed is saying that it is too soon or too late for happiness. Both the young and the old should study philosophy so that, while old, one may still be young with all the joy he has gathered in the past, and while young, one may at the same time be old through fearlessness of the future.[12]

# Seneca

*'A breast stocked with good thoughts'*
*The great man of the world whose Stoic humanism was tried severely*

13

Philosophers, it is said, do not practice what they preach. But they practice some of what they preach. ... and we ought to respect the climbers, even if they slip. ... I am not a wise man, nor shall I ever be one. ... but it is enough for me to make a little progress each day and detect and renounce my failings. ... I should like to meet my death as calmly as I contemplate its name. ... I behold all land as if it were mine and all my own land as if it belonged to all. ... Good words and a breast stocked with good thoughts are not to be despised.[14]

*

Seneca was, without any doubt, one of the grandest men who ever lived. For five years or more, and at some of the most crucial moments of his era, he directed the central government of the world's most civilised empire that stretched from Britain to Mesopotamia, he owned beautiful mansions, seaside villas, gardens, vineyard and farms, and he presided over one of the most prestigious families in Rome. He also died one of the proudest deaths in all history.

But was he a great man deserving of our admiration some 2000 years later? Here we should wade in some controversy, for he was a politician at the hub of unrestrained power. Inevitably, he made enemies and we cannot disregard their criticisms of him out of hand. According to them, he accumulated wealth unbecoming of a philosopher of frugality. We know, too, that he did not admit of any shame regarding that wealth. He would say that, as a statesman, he had to make daily compromises. He could not refuse gifts bestowed on him by his suspicious imperial patron, even if it had been seized from its original owner without good cause. Nor could he, for long, ensure the cooperation of thousands of generals, senators, lesser officials, priests and merchants if he did not indulge in the bountiful patronage they expected of a man in his position. Thus he entertained them regularly with the most delicate meats and oldest wines his estates could produce. This, he said, though somewhat defensively, was not in dissonance with his personal belief that regarded giving as one of the principle aims of any man's life, that it even enriched the giver more than it did the receiver. As for himself, he did not drink wine and lived for long periods on bread and dried figs alone. Nor would he waste fuel to warm the water of his bath. While he built 'vapour baths' lined with marble tiles for his family and visitors, he would himself bathe only in cold water, his luxury being, whenever possible, a tub of water warmed by the rays of the golden god in the sky.

If triumph over adversity is to be valued for the effect it has on others, Seneca's turbulent life would be sufficient by itself to win our admiration. But more relevant to posterity has been the enduring moral legacy that compensates for the apparent shortcomings of character that he displayed regarding material wealth, at least in the earlier part of his life. In the millennium that followed his death, his writings became so influential that the Christian church could not resist forging documents to claim him as a secret convert. In a society and political system rife with barbaric practices, he propagated the idea that all men and women were of equal worth. He would have abolished slavery two millennia ago if it had been possible politically and economically, and he would have overthrown his cruel, tyrannical, emperor Nero if he had been able to do so. In the end, he lost his life because he could no longer serve that newly emancipated monster of a sovereign.

How would have Seneca lived the remainder of his life if it had been allowed him, given that the world he had known – and to whose improvement he had devoted his considerable energies – had vanished without the possibility of repair?

It has been said that Seneca's philosophy is better depicted in his actions than in his copious writings. This is arguable, with the most recent scholarship suggesting that there is little contradiction between what he advocated and what he practiced.[15] But an account of his sickly childhood, his rigorous education, his traumatic middle period and, particularly, the demands of his office as he administered the empire amidst grasping princes and potentially rebellious armies, might help us to understand both his actions and his writings.

What emerges, I hope, will be, not the cardboard profile of a saint, but the fuller figure of a man in whom beat a troubled heart, a realist who had seen too much to harbour illusions about the world, but one who, nevertheless, felt he had to project the carefree exterior of the man of the street to achieve what little he could, for as many as he could. 1800 years later, Jeremy Bentham and his godson John Stuart Mill would be moved.

*

Lucius Annaeus Seneca and his two famous brothers were born clearly fortunate in their genetic inheritance. The sons of a successful lawyer and an equally gifted, aristocratic mother, each became distinguished in their separate ways. The older son, who later changed his given name from Novatus to Gallio, became the governor of the large province of Achaea in Greece and, as such, is honoured by Christians for dismissing a complaint by the Jews of Corinth against St Paul the Apostle. The youngest son, Mela, did not seek senatorial or high governmental office. Instead, he continued his philosophical studies longer than usual, concentrated his time on administering the family's estates and, as a member of the equestrian class, accumulated a large fortune of his own by managing some of the emperor's wealth. The genes continued to outcrop in later generations, too. Mela's son, Lucan, became one of the most celebrated poets of the Latin language and, as such, so enraged the jealousy of his young friend Nero that, at the age of 25 years, he was banned by the emperor to publish any more of his poems.

The family had moved to Rome from their native Corduba, in the far-flung western province of Hispania. The epic migration, though softened with the aid of carts and litters, had been undertaken between1 and 3 BC, when young Lucius had been small enough to be carried in the arms of an aunt.

They are believed not to have been ethnic Spaniards, but to have hailed originally from the Italian province of Etruria, to the north-west of Rome. In Spain they had become wealthy knights and landowners, able to send Marcus – Seneca the Elder – for lengthy periods to Rome to study rhetoric and attend the law courts where distinguished advocates drew ecstatic applause from spectators. Marcus would regret for the rest of his life that he had not been sent to Rome earlier to hear 'the living, vibrant voice of the great Cicero' at the Forum or in the Senate, in person. By then, of course, the courts could no-longer prosecute the emperor or his cronies for corruption or misuse of power. It gave Marcus a low opinion of many of his colleagues. They were little more than mouths for rent, he said.

Marcus was a stern and traditional figure, and evidently an inspiring father. Towards the end of his career, he wrote a book of legal cases, the Controversiae, for his sons. He would have previously recalled the stories at many a family dinner table and they clearly had a formative effect on Lucius in particular. By the time of his death in 39 CE at the rare age of 93, the elder Seneca was still only a middle-ranking figure himself in society, but he had reason to hope that at least one of his three sons might rise to the highest circles of influence in the empire. At the same time, he had reason to be apprehensive. Never neglectful of warning his sons of the dangers of sailing too close to the wind in an age of callous emperors and equally murderous empresses, he would not have been reassured to hear that Lucius, by then a successful lawyer, poet and writer of tragedies, was having an affair with the emperor's youngest sister, the wild and beautiful Julia Levilla, and the emperor was no other than Caligula.

The latest scholarship revises the date of the younger Seneca's birth to about the start of the Christian era, between 1 and 4 BCE. We are on firmer ground on the future philosopher's early youth and education, for he writes at length on both subjects. A traditional schooling gave him a grounding in Latin, Greek, arithmetic and, from around the age of fifteen, rhetoric and philosophy, the latter stretching from zoology to theology. His teachers included some of the ablest philosophers in the city and of these, he has left us vivid portrayals of three. He appears not to have fallen for the Pythagorean inclinations of Sotion, who told him of the theory of the transmigration of souls, including from humans into beasts, though Sotion did make him a vegetarian for a year until 'such Jewish practices' were banned by Tiberius. Another, Attalus, made a more lasting impression on him:

> Something of [Attalus's] high enterprise has remained with me. Thus I have abstained all these years from such delicacies as oysters and mushrooms. They are not food, but stimulants to appetite and gluttony ... Never touched wine, and always avoided hot-air baths. ... From other denunciations I desisted, but in that case I returned to what I had abandoned with a moderation that came much nearer to abstinence than indulgence, a moderation perhaps even more difficult than abstention, for certainly it is often easier to abandon a habit altogether than to keep it within modest bounds.[16]

From around 25 CE, for some six years, Seneca lived in Egypt with his aunt, apparently the same maternal aunt who had carried him in her arms on the long migration from Spain. He went there in the hope of a cure for his asthma and consumption, for the more consistently warm climate of Egypt was thought medicinal in itself. No doubt, however, the ancient land of pyramids and pharaohs, including the tragic Cleopatra – who had been brought to Rome in chains during his father's youth – not to mention the fabled, Greek library of Alexandria, exercised an extra educational pull on the studious young man. The enterprise was made easier by the exalted position of his aunt's husband in Egypt. He was the province's prefect.

Speaking of his illness, Seneca tells us that it made him so depressed at times that on many an occasion he contemplated ending his life. But each time, he wrote, he was prevented from doing so by the thought of how it would affect his father. 'Love of philosophy also saved me', he wrote.

A quick glimpse at what we know of Lucius's youth and early manhood confirms what we would expect, a brilliant intellect. But it suggests also a young man of extraordinary courage. A measure of his courtship of excitement, perhaps even his disregard for life, is provided by his rapid rise in professional and social circles when this was certain to cause envy in some powerful circles. By around his 40th birthday, he had attracted the ire of no less a figure than the emperor himself, the infamous Caligula. The emperor spent long hours each day judging legal cases at the Forum because he loved his own voice and admired his talent as a speaker. But on more than one occasion, he had felt humiliated by Seneca's eloquence. He had been reduced even to denouncing Seneca's style as 'mere sand without time', a reference to the ennobling purpose that humble sand could acquire, but only if used in an hour glass.

Whether it was due to this professional slight, or else, the rumours of Seneca having won the heart of his 'wild' sister Julia, Caligula came close to ordering Seneca's execution. But he was dissuaded from doing so by Seneca's serious illness. One of his wives or mistresses interceded with him, saying that Seneca had only a little time left of his natural life.

Fortunately for Seneca, Caligula was soon assassinated by a group of senators and others who wished to revive the republic. However, their hopes were thwarted by the Praetorian Guards who immediately promoted their own choice to the purple. They found Caligula's timorous and simple-minded uncle, Claudius, hiding behind a curtain and hauled him to their headquarters to be declared the new ruler. This was unwelcome news to Seneca on another level. Claudius's wife of the time, Messalina, a particularly manipulative and ruthless woman, set out to use her influence over her impressionable husband to root out any of his relatives who might harbour claims of their own to the throne, and these included Claudius's two nieces, the princesses Julia and her elder sister

Agrippina. Thus both were quickly, in 41 CE, accused of plotting to overthrow the new incumbent and exiled to small islands near the western coast of Italy in the Mediterranean. Seneca was charged with adultery with Julia and exiled to the much larger island of Corsica which he still found a cultural backwater. Nor were the unhappy lovers, if that is what they were, allowed to communicate with one another. We can assume the effect on Seneca's mental health in his island prison when he heard, later that year or early in the next, that Julia had died, apparently through being starved on the orders of Messalina. His exile was to last a full eight years, though it went into the further making of him. He used the thousands upon thousands of hours of enforced idleness to read, and read again, until he had learnt almost by heart, as many philosophical texts in Greek and Latin as he could obtain.

Messalina has a reputation for extreme promiscuity in Western literature. It is said, for example, that she would hire herself out to brothels some nights each week for the thrill of it. But whether or not this is largely the work of her enemies after her fall, enemies she made on a considerable scale, until, seven years into her reign in 48 CE, Claudius was informed that she planned to poison him and replace him with her current lover . Claudius was away from Rome with the army. He returned swiftly and ordered her execution. There then followed a race between rival factions at court to find him a new empress, with the result that his surviving niece, Agrippina, won. But as marrying nieces was illegal, the senate was leant on to make the practice lawful and, furthermore, to beg of the emperor to marry Agrippina in the interest of the state. Agrippina was over 25 years her uncle's junior, but ruthless by nature and wounded by her exile and the murder of her sister, she would succeed where Messalina had failed. She brought Seneca, Julia's reputed lover, back from exile, persuaded the emperor to adopt her twelve-year-old son Nero as his own and give him preference as heir apparent over his own, slightly younger, son Britannicus. She also persuaded him to let her appoint the new commander of the Praetorian guard. Finally, five years later in 54 CE, when she was ready, she poisoned her uncle and bribed the Praetorians to declare Nero the new emperor. In the spirit of the Greek tragedies that were popular at court, she did not know that she, too, was promoting her own murderer.

It is said that Seneca begged of Agrippina to let him go to Athens to continue his philosophical studies, but that Agrippina refused. She wanted him to be tutor to Nero and be her advisor and assistant in administering the empire. Whatever the truth, Seneca believed that, in a system of arbitrary rule, tutoring princes to grow up to be wise and just was a most noble task. He set about the job earnestly for the remaining years of Nero's minority and probably a little beyond, when Agrippina, as co-ruler with her son, appointed him, unofficially, as the chief minister of the state. He would function alongside the new Praetorian commander, Sextus Afranius Burrus, who would concentrate on military matters.

The historians are agreed that Seneca was fortunate in his partner Burrus. For as long as the two men, together with Agrippina, the queen mother, had influence over Nero, they cooperated as if they were brothers, wisely, smoothly and discreetly. Not a single public argument is reported between them. The result was the Quinquilium Neroneanis, the historians' nostalgic term for the first five years of the new emperor's reign, when the law courts delivered justice without interference from the state, the Senate was treated with respect, grain flowed in from the provinces and the treasury was full. But the two ministers' self-respect and moral principles would also be tested severely. The young emperor did not only spend his time whoring, drinking and engaging in street fights. Those felonies were easy to bear. But when he poisoned his brother Britannicus, the stench of shame would have overwhelmed Seneca's high office by association. By the time in 59 CE, when Nero eventually succeeded in murdering his mother, too, Seneca and Burrus were clearly in office in name only. Yet they could not resign without seeming to be critical of the emperor. When Burrus died in 62, Seneca asked Nero to be allowed to retire. But his request was turned down, though he was permitted to spend most of his time away from the palace on his estates.

The end came for Seneca in 65 CE, a year after a great fire had destroyed most of Rome. This was believed by many, perhaps unjustly, to have been started by Nero himself to clear the ground for a new palatial complex. More relevantly, perhaps, the treasury had been exhausted by the new emperor's profligacy, the populace could no-longer be indulged with barbarous games, Nero had debased the majesty of his office by performing in theatres, and the Senate, formerly mollified by Seneca, had come to feel humiliated. Thus an aristocrat by the name of Gaius Calpurnius Piso conspired with a group of senators and Praetorian commanders to murder Nero and proclaim himself emperor. The conspiracy was, however, discovered in the spring of that year and the names of the ringleaders obtained under torture. Seneca's nephew, the poet Lucan, was among them. He and many others were ordered to commit suicide and so was, a little later, Seneca.

Tacitus tells us that when the emperor's men arrived at his mansion to inform him of the order, Seneca protested his innocence. It was true, he had received a request from the chief plotter Piso to meet him, but he had declined to do so. However, if the emperor's decision was final, he was honour-bound to obey. He asked for time to revise his will. When this was refused, his wife Pompeia Paulina insisted on sharing his fate. On yielding to her wish – perhaps they imagined the worst that might happen to her once he was dead – the two severed several veins in their arms. The soldiers would not allow Pompeia to die. They bound up her wounds and saved her, after which 'she never attempted suicide again'. As for Seneca himself, 'his age and his frugal diet' were blamed for his not bleeding sufficiently. Poison was tried. That, too, failed. Then while he dictated his last thoughts to a scribe regarding his family and household, he severed more of his veins and ordered his servants to carry him to a hot vapour bath to assist the bleeding. Eventually, we are told, he died from pain and from asphyxiation in the thick vapour. He was cremated shortly afterwards without any ceremony, as he had stipulated in his will 'at the height of his wealth and power'.

There is no direct evidence to suggest that Seneca was implicated in the Pisonian conspiracy. But so high was his moral standing in society at large that he might well have been the conspirators' first choice to succeed Nero. It was probably only after he had declined to meet Piso that the latter became the plotters' foremost candidate for the purple. What we know for certain is the opprobrium in which the Senate, the equestrian class and the army held Nero. In such an atmosphere, Seneca would have had a good idea of the nature of Piso's request for the secret meeting. He chose not to inform Nero of the request and, to the suspicious, rattled tyrant, that would have been proof enough of his guilt.

Seneca once said that it was Socrates' death by drinking that bowl of hemlock voluntarily that made him the great man he became in the subsequent centuries. The sincerity of this belief is reflected in the manner of his own death. He embraced his end calmly, with an open face, not only to safeguard the spirit of those around him in those traumatic hours, but also because he believed, as did his hero Socrates, that we should not fear death. It was merely one of those 'externals' over which we had little control. We ought, instead, fear only our own actions. Only a lack of virtue could harm us. The man who had harmed no-one had a clear conscience, and if he was not overly dependent on material comfort and possessions, he could devote his time to the true goods, the pursuit of knowledge, the contemplation of art, the pleasures of companionship, the enjoyment of whatever good fortune came his way.

A little digression may cast light on what Seneca might have suspected, at the time, to be the true motivation of his monstrous former pupil. While his own execution and that of his nephew Lucan were to be expected, would Nero go on to punish the rest of the extended family also? Seneca must have wondered at that, and Nero did go on to murder some of them. He ordered both of Seneca's brothers similarly to end their lives, but not for a whole year after his immediate passion against the plotters had subsided. This would suggest that neither Gallio nor Mela had been mentioned in the interrogations. The death of Gallio falls outside the extant writings of Tacitus, but he implies that the two brothers' demise was due only to Nero's greed for their fortunes.[17]

*

Schools of philosophy, or lines of thought, evolve, merge, diverge and split with the passage of time, and in doing so, they are directed often by interpreters and reformers acting out of a variety of motives. These may be, at best, due to a genuine conviction on the part of the reformer that the original founders had been mistaken in some of their conclusions. At worst, the changes may owe their origin to careerism. Attention-seeking, but charismatic, personalities have frequently found personal fulfilment in breaking away from rivals within their movement to set up cults of their own. But more usually, a need arises to adjust the core beliefs of a community to new political or economic circumstances or, especially, to regain intellectual credibility in the light of new scientific discoveries, to ensure the movement's survival.

A crucial influence on Seneca's philosophical innovations were the extensive writings of Posidonius of Apameia (135-51 BC), a Greek polymath and traveller who had been born in Syria, but died either in Rhodes or Rome. In his youth, he had studied at the Stoa in Athens, but had broken away from his colleagues there to incline towards the mysticism of Plato. Whereas Panaetius, his revered teacher at the Stoa, had doubted the truth of divination, Posidonius adopted it fully and gave it fresh authority with his own mastery of nearly all the sciences of his time, from astronomy to anthropology. After a period as the president of the ruling political council in Rhodes, he travelled to Rome and thenceforth into western Europe, where he calculated the precise relationship between the daily tides of the Atlantic and the revolution of the Moon around the earth. His measurement of the distance between the Earth and the Sun was remarkably accurate for the mathematics of his time.

Indeed, such was Posidonius' regard for what could be measured that he might well have agreed, while in a flippant mood, with the observation of a much later physicist, Lord Rutherford. Speaking within the context of science or knowledge in general, the 'father of nuclear physics' once said: 'There is only physics. The rest is stamp collecting'. For Posidonius, as indeed for many of the other Greek and Roman philosophers, philosophy was largely the study of nature. The Stoics divided philosophy into three branches: physics, which included theology, ethics and logic, with logic important only as a device to perfect their arguments in defence of their system. Seneca on at least one occasion made fun of extreme logicians by saying: 'Mouse is a word, and mouse easts cheese. Therefore word eats cheese. Soon I shall be catching words in mouse traps'.

Here, the reader who read the previous essay on Epicurus may ask whether the personal ethics of a Stoic differed much from those of the Epicureans. There was, indeed, much that overlapped between them, and this should not surprise us. All the branches of 'the philosophies of security', idolised Socrates and regarded themselves as but his true followers. They all believed in the simple life, a life lived according to the needs of nature and free from as much material possessions as possible. They also regarded 'virtue' – true knowledge or wisdom – as the shield that protected the individual from being harmed by all that was external to his mind. Where they differed resulted from their various interpretations of the life and teachings of Socrates as related by the sources. The Stoics laid weight by Socrates' loose talk of 'God' and the possibility of life after death – though in a purely spiritual form – when the sage had defended himself at his trial in Athens in 399BC. The Epicureans, on the other hand, opted for the other possibility raised by Socrates during that same defence, that death might turn out to be no more than 'a permanent sleep'. Thus the Epicureans claimed that the soul was merely an orderly combination of atoms that dispersed for ever when a person died. This earned them the ire of the Stoics, as well as the Christians. The Stoics later fell further under the spell of Plato's intense religiosity and thus helped pave the way for the success of Christianity in Europe.

Seneca's motives in his own philosophical ponderings were as pure as those of any great master in the past. Philosophy was not his career, nor was appearing to be at its cutting edge a required qualification for his job as a statesman. By the time of his later, and definitive writings, in particular, he had already succeeded in the world beyond all expectations, for he was, by background, only a second-rank aristocrat, a member of the equestrian class, a mere knight, not a patrician. He had become immensely rich, a senator and, at times, the most powerful man in the empire. His reforms of Stoicism emanated from his personal temperament, as well as from both his continuous reading of past masters and his own perceived need to habituate Stoicism – with its superior ethics, as he saw it – to the social, political and economic circumstances of his own era and place for the good of all.

The Stoics of the first century are known as 'the later Stoics' and their leading thinkers included the masters yet to come, Epictetus and Marcus Aurelius, a freed slave and an emperor, respectively. They had become even more deterministic than they had been earlier, believing that every minute event in the world was the result of previous events. Individual believers among them could be childishly fatalistic, indulging in soothsaying and divination. All this clashed with their claim regarding free will. Russell uses this latter belief of theirs to evoke their whole universe:

> I think that a Stoic, if we could make him submit to a Socratic interrogation, would defend his view [regarding free will] more or less as follows: The universe is a single animate being, having a soul

which may also be called God or Reason. As a whole, this Being is free. God decided, from the first, that He would act according to fixed general laws, but He chose such laws as would have the best results. Sometimes, in particular cases, the results are not wholly desirable, but this inconvenience is worth enduring, as in human codes of law, for the sake of the advantage of legislative fixity. A human being is partly fire, partly of lower clay; in so far as he is fire (at any rate when it is of the best quality), he is part of God. When the divine part of a man exercises will virtuously, this will is part of God's, which is free; therefore in these circumstances, the human will is also free.[18]

Russell goes on to say that the defence breaks down when we consider the causes of our volitions. 'The Stoic, when he is engaged in urging a tolerant attitude to sinners, will himself urge that the sinful will is a result of previous causes; it is only the virtuous will that seems to him free. This, however, is inconsistent.' He might have added that it was also human.

And so why has Seneca's name and moral legacy continued to inspire many into the present day, when some of his core beliefs we can dismiss out of hand as unscientific or, indeed, childish? One answer is that he was a good man who left a clear mark on the ethics of the educated in the centuries after his death. He was, in his own words, 'a breast stocked with good thoughts'. He was also generous to all around him, with himself subsisting on bread and fruit. But another, perhaps the more important explanation, is the heroic manner of his death. Given his connections and the shambolic nature of government in first century Rome, he could have easily fled to a far-flung corner of the empire – to his beloved Greece, for example – and Nero might have even found it politic not to pursue him. But he stayed behind in the style of his hero Socrates to emphasise that, as the former chief statesman of the empire, he abided by its laws, and that he was not afraid of death, but regarded it merely as a stepping stone to union with 'the soul of Nature', Reason or God. The shrewd politician within him might have also hoped to soften the attitude of the tyrant towards his family and household after his death by not resisting the command he had received.

Finally, as for his quaint theological views and vision of the universe, who among us does not have an elderly relative or friend who clings to equally irrational opinions and is yet beloved immensely by many? Lucius Annaeus Seneca, 3 BC-65 CE, was such a man, and one of the greatest of our forefathers.

## Looking Back: 9th January 2014

Nero's men will soon knock on the gate:
'Cut your veins, or else …'.
So, this is how it ended.
You always sailed close to the wind.

For five decades or more,
You tried to envisage this day.
How prepared would you be when it came?
Would you prove equal to your greatest test?

Death was a farce, you said.
It did not frighten the wise man.
Our souls of fire would be free at last
To fly heavenwards to their place of birth.

That day has now come.
You have expected it for weeks.
In the hot sun of middle morning outside,
Not a ripple moves across the pool.

The birds in the garden, too,
Have fallen silent, as if stunned.
The orange trees bend over from thirst;
The servants, the gardeners, the librarians have
become stone statues.

You will savour the splendour of this mansion no longer.
How much would you pay for just one more year?
Nero has robbed you of the daily sounds of your house,
The laughter of your grandchildren.

You tremble inside,
You issue commands.
All must be brave.
None must see you're human.

Nothing must reveal that you find it sad.
God has decreed it.
What must pass, must pass.
Do you believe that?

Yes, you believe it.
You just wish that God
Had better logic:
Why you, not Nero?

# Boethius

*The man who invented the mother of all consolations*

19

Love, that of erth and se hath governaunce.
Love, that his hestes hath in hevene hye.
Love, that with an holsom alliaunce
Halt peples joyned, as hym liste hem gye.
Love, that knetteth law and compaignye,
And couples doth in vertu for to dwelle.[20]

Can we look up to Ancius Manlius Severinus Boethius for inspiration? If he is remembered at all, nowadays, he is known as a second-rate philosopher from a distant Germanic kingdom in the 'Dark Ages' who was not even allowed to

51

mature enough to see his 45th birthday.

I think that we can, even though I shall make ready to be beaten down into the dirt with the nearest broom stick.

I contend that he was 'the last of the Romans', a phrase previously used often in his case, and a brilliant thinker who improved on the philosophy of the ancients which he then transmitted in chunks to Western Europe in the Middle Ages. He shone out of the darkness that was descending on Europe rapidly in the wake of the disintegration of the Roman empire. In a new fear-ridden, superstitious epoch, he honoured the mind of Man by saying that we ought not to abandon our reason, and tried to be as rational as he could, in line with the greatest of old Greeks, and his great work of literature, De Consolatione Philosophiae, gave comfort to myriad readers in the following epochs and inspired such giants of letters as Dante and Chaucer. He may even be a cause of my writing this essay in English.

In an age hungry for saints, The Vatican resisted sanctifying him for thirteen centuries.

*

Much water had passed under the bridges of the Tiber in the time that separated Boethius from his hero Seneca. He was born some 200 years after Seneca's execution, but in those two short centuries, the formerly insignificant Jewish cult of the Christians had become the official religion of the empire, with a painfully convoluted, largely Platonic theology, and given rise to a new intolerance. The empire itself might be said not to exist in practice. Its former heart, Rome, was now the capital of a Germanic tribe, the Ostrogoths, while the great regions to its west were divided among Visigoths, Franks and Vandals. The imperial highways were returning to the forest, mail was delivered no-longer, large-scale commerce had stopped and literacy was rare. News was local only.

As for the eastern half the empire, based on Constantinople, it existed and would do so for another thousand years, but it was becoming less Roman every day and more Byzantine. Soon, it would produce its last emperor who spoke Latin for his first language.[21]

Boethius was born in the early 480s into one of the wealthiest and most noble families of Rome, the Anicii, a family which had produced two emperors and numerous consuls and senators going back to the celebrated days of the republic. But his father, who was consul in 487, died early and the boy was brought up in the household of another aristocrat, Quintus Aurelius Memmius Symmarchus, a close family friend and man of letters. Symmarchus ensured the best possible education for the bright youth, with some sources speculating that he sent him to Athens or even Alexandria for his higher studies. Later, he even gave him his daughter, Rusticiana, in marriage.

Under the Ostrogoths, the proud old families of Italy could only aspire to the level of high civil servants. They were still designated senators or consuls, but political and military power rested in the hands of the king, Theodoric, and his fellow Goths. Fortunately, though, Theodoric[22], the battle-hardened old warrior that he remained, was not a typical ruler of his tribe. He had been a hostage in Constantinople in his youth and given a thorough Latin education there. Later, he had seized Italy – from another Goth – on behalf of Constantinople. He knew that his people, of whom there were only about 100-200,000 tribesmen, were few in number and incapable of administering an ancient land with the collective memory of Italy and a Catholic allegiance. So he wooed the great and the good of the natives, though he would not allow intermarriage between the races. The old Roman families might belong to a separate church, but they would help him ensure quietude in his new realm. As a result, he gave Italy its longest period of peace and prosperity since Valerian, two-and-a-half centuries earlier and was later remembered as Theodoric the Great.

Under such circumstances, and helped additionally by the sponsorship of his father-in-law, as well as his own personal brilliance, Boethius rose exceptionally rapidly in the administration. He was a senator by the age of 25 and a consul a few years later. In 522, when he was – at most – 42 years old, he was given the grand honour of seeing his two sons nominated to act as partner consuls with him – 'one for the east, one for the west', he crowed. The boys were too young for practical responsibility and so the declaration only indicated the king's full confidence in the father. This was further proclaimed in 523, when the king promoted him to the highest office in the administration, Master of the Offices, in effect, chief minister at Ravenna, the imperial capital in north-east Italy.

It was not to last. Only a year later, Boethius found himself in prison awaiting his sovereign's decision whether or not to execute him for treason. The king's spies claimed to have evidence that he had conspired with Constantinople to overthrow Theodoric.

It seems highly unlikely. The most that can be laid at the Chief Minister's door is that, in the extensive correspondence that his office conducted with Constantinople daily, he had been a little too keen to patch up differences between the two capitals. Despite a pretence of subordination, Theodoric regarded himself the equal of the emperor. He was the king of Italy and the ruler of Rome, the seat of St Peter. He was also the king of a mighty people, the Ostrogoths, and demanded the respect that his people expected. So when the pope, John I, returned from a visit to Constantinople, Theodoric imprisoned him together with the other members of his delegation. John had made too many concessions to the eastern wing of the church in their doctrinal deals and, what was even more serious, he had crowned the new emperor, Justin, in person. He had done so while Justin was persecuting Theodoric's fellow Arian Christians in the east and, at the same time, promoting the militant imperialist, Justinian, to be his apparent heir.

Boethius had a personal interest in preserving the status quo in Italy. He was already his king's highest official and he knew that any war with Constantinople would be long, ruinous and unpredictable, as it indeed proved later. The only plausible explanation for his condemnation is that he sought to appease the drums of war he thought he heard in the east without seeking the approval of his master. This he did, apparently, by encouraging the pope, to whom he was close, to be flexible in his negotiations in the east with the patriarch there. As John the Deacon, the pope had been his teacher a couple of decades earlier, and both were, of course, Catholics, not Arians.

The sources agree on how the drama unfolded. At a meeting of the executive in the presence of Theodoric, a former consul was accused of secret contacts with Constantinople. Boethius jumped to his feet and belittled the charge. 'The charge is false, my lord King', he shouted. 'If Albinus is guilty, so am I, and so is the entire Senate'. As if this were not sufficient to incense the old warrior further, witnesses were produced to implicate Boethius himself in the plot. He denounced them as enemies whom he had demoted for fraud, but Theodoric was not convinced. He was analysing the scene more ominously than was his chief minister, for he had sources of information of his own. They included spies at the imperial court itself.

Everyone, most of all the statesman who was Boethius, could see that Theodoric's enemies were on the rise, in the west and south, as well as in the east. Recently in North Africa, the Germanic kingdom of the Vandals, fellow Arians, had converted to Catholicism and their new king had gone to extremes to show how thoroughly he had burnt his bridges with Theodoric. He had executed Theodoric's sister who had married into the Vandal court. At the same time, the eastern and western churches, including that of the Gauls who were Catholics, were settling their doctrinal differences with the east and exacerbating their differences with Theodoric's Arians. Theodoric must have analysed that war was inevitable and appeasement made you appear weak.

Whether it was a king's paranoia, as I have hinted here, or else, Theodoric had good reasons to ask whether Boethius was involved in a plot. He dismissed his chief minister without a formal trial. This was a new precedent for him, and it was out of character. He pondered in such matters. He then ordered a meeting of the senate in Rome and threatened the senators with disbandment if they did not condemn their colleague to death. His anger was clearly not subsiding and the senators quailed. And yet, Theodoric did not command that Boethius be killed immediately. He banished him to Pavia in the north-west and waited for at least another year to make up his mind. This came in late 524 or early 525. A short while later, he ordered the killing of Boethius' father-in-law, the saintly Symmarchus, also.

In his youth, Boethius had wished to give over his life to philosophy alone, but not for the purpose of his own, selfish enchantment. In the words of the commentator Hans von Campenhausen, he wanted to become 'the schoolmaster of the West'. Beside Seneca, he wanted to emulate another of his great heroes, Cicero, in transmitting as much of the wisdom of ancient Greece to the Latin west as a human lifespan would allow. His New Year's resolution in this regard is worth quoting for its charm, as well as its youthful precocity:

> I wish to translate the whole work of Aristotle, for as far as it is accessible to me, into the Roman idiom and consciously offer his complete utterances in the Latin tongue. Everything Aristotle ever wrote on the difficult art of logic, on the important realm of moral experience, and on the exact comprehension of natural objects, I shall translate in the correct order. Moreover, I shall make all this comprehensible by interpretative explanations. I should also like to translate all Plato's Dialogues, and likewise explain them, and thus present them in a Latin version. When this is accomplished, I will furthermore not shrink from proving that the Aristotelian and Platonic conceptions in every way harmonise and do not, as is widely supposed, completely contradict each other. I will show that they are in agreement at all the philosophically decisive points. This is the task to which I will dedicate myself, so far as life and leisure for work are vouchsafed to me. I know that this is as useful as it is laborious, and that it needs the assistance of those powers which are ever alien to envy and jealousy.[23]

Alas, his life was cut short for him to realise his great ambition, but he was nevertheless able, amidst numerous public undertakings, to translate quite a number of books and essays from Greek into Latin and make his own contributions, too, in the form of commentaries. A detailed description of these falls well outside the scope of this short essay, but two of his commentaries on the writings of an earlier, militantly anti-Christian philosopher has surprised many down the centuries. The offender was Porphyry, or Porphyrios of Tyre, who had died in Rome over 200 years earlier, but not before completing a collection of 15 tracts, Adversus Christianos, against the new sect of Christianity. Such was his vehemence against the doctrines and behaviour of the Christians, and in calling for harsh punishments upon them, that the emperor Constantine had ordered his works to be burned.[24] Yet, here was Boethius, a responsible state official and ostensibly devout Catholic brought up in an orthodox Catholic household, venerating the thought of an excommunicated thinker. The commentaries are explanations on Porphyry's Isagoge, an introduction to logic and philosophy.

I shall re-examine the puzzle a little later, but by far the most influential work by Boethius has been his Consolation of Philosophy. It is a five-book dialogue in the tradition of Plato, but resorts to the playful, satirical juxtaposition of verse and prose to discuss some of the most basic problems of philosophy and theology. It has been described as 'by far the most interesting example of prison literature the wold has even seen'[25].

Boethius wrote it in the last year of his life, he says, and in his prison in the backwater of far-flung Pavia, cut off from friends and elementary comforts. But although we do not know the exact circumstances of his confinement, it would appear that Theodoric was still treating him with some respect, if not affection. Boethius was allowed pen and parchment. That is obvious. But what else? Was he allowed at least a servant to ensure he did not go deprived of a decent diet? Was he allowed regular visits by his loving and loyal wife, the lady Rusticiana, if not others in his family? He seems to have had his books around him, also, or at least some of them, for he invokes many books in the pages of the Consolation. Does this imply that he was held under house arrest, rather than in a prison cell? It is similarly clear that whatever he wrote, he was allowed to send away for safe keeping or even publication. Dangerous, high-ranking political prisoners are not normally accorded such liberties.

Whatever the circumstances, Boethius was understandably distraught about his sudden fall from grace and the seizure of his assets that would have affected the well-being of his family. He was only about 44 years old and at the height of his manhood. He would have, until very recently, looked forward to decades more of vigorous life. Thus, he starts the Consolation with a verse that laments the ill fortune that has befallen him:

Blessed is death that intervenes not
In the sweet, sweet years of peace,
But onto the broken-hearted,
When they call him, brings release.

Yet, death passes by the wretched,
Shuts his ear and slumbers deep;
Will not heed the cry of anguish,
Will not close the eyes that weep.[26]

After a while in such dark mood, he suddenly sees a most beautiful lady appear before him. She is of ancient age, but seemingly not of this world. She is vigorous with a lively complexion. She wears a dress of distinction, though threadbare, in places, from long use, and torn away in others by violence. She is noble, well-spoken and wise. She is, of course, the spirit of philosophy, Philosophia. He addresses her through his tears and asks if she, too, has been incarcerated under false accusations. She is free, she says, but has complaints of her own about her treatment at the hands of those who ought to know better, her own brood. The passage is worth quoting at length here, for apart from revealing how much Boethius venerates Plato and lampoons those who came after Aristotle, it also shows the literary style of the Consolation:

'Could I desert thee, child,' said she, 'and not lighten the burden which thou hast taken upon thee through the hatred of my name, by sharing this trouble? Even forgetting that it were not lawful for Philosophy to leave companionless the way of the innocent, should I, thinkest thou, fear to incur reproach, or shrink from it, as though some strange new thing had befallen? Thinkest thou that now, for the first time in an evil age, Wisdom hath been assailed by peril? Did I not often in days of old, before my servant Plato lived, wage stern warfare with the rashness of folly? In his lifetime, too, Socrates, his master, won with my aid the victory of an unjust death. And when, one after the other, the Epicurean herd, the Stoic, and the rest, each of them as far as in them lay, went about to seize the heritage he left, and were dragging me off protesting and resisting, as their booty, they tore in pieces the garment which I had woven with my own hands, and, clutching the torn pieces, went off, believing that the whole of me had passed into their possession. And some of them, because some traces of my vesture were seen upon them, were destroyed through the mistake of the lewd multitude, who falsely deemed them to be my disciples. It may be thou knowest not of the banishment of Anaxagoras, of the poison draught of Socrates, nor of Zeno's torturing, because these things happened in a distant country; yet mightest thou have learnt the fate of Arrius, of Seneca, of Soranus, whose stories are neither old nor unknown to fame. These men were brought to destruction for no other reason than that, settled as they were in my principles, their lives were a manifest contrast to the ways of the wicked. So there is nothing thou shouldst wonder at, if on the seas of this life we are tossed by storm-blasts, seeing that we have made it our chiefest aim to refuse compliance with evil-doers. And though, maybe, the host of the wicked is many in number, yet is it contemptible, since it is under no leadership, but is hurried hither and thither at the blind driving of mad error. And if at times and seasons they set in array against us, and fall on in overwhelming strength, our leader draws off her forces into the citadel while they are busy plundering the useless baggage. But we from our vantage ground, safe from all this wild work, laugh to see them making prize of the most valueless of things, protected by a bulwark which aggressive folly may not aspire to reach.'[27]

The full text of the Consolation is available 'on-line' or can be downloaded onto 'e-readers' for little money. It ought to be enough for me here to take an overview of the book and recall the immense impact that it has had down the centuries.

Altogether the length of a slim paperback in modern translations[28], the Consolation is divided into five 'books' – what we would call tracts or pamphlets. They contain long passages, in the interrogatory style of Plato, on such topics as the covetousness of Man, the fickleness of fortune, true nobility, the bondage of passion, predestination and the seeming impossibility of free will when God knows, from tens of thousands of years earlier, every turn and twist of every hour of our lives. On this, the prisoner is told that he is wrong. 'God is like a spectator at a chariot race'. He watches sees the decisions the charioteers take, but this does not cause their decisions. Furthermore, for God, there is no past, present and future. For Him, all is in the present.

At first, Lady Philosophy treats Boethius gently, given the fragile state of his mind. Then, gradually, she prescribes 'stronger medicines', until, eventually, he is a happy man once more, or at least he says he is. We are not quite convinced. Is he being merely polite to his visitor, especially one who is supposed to be the embodiment of all wisdom and virtue? For the Lady is really a theologian, rather than a philosopher in the modern sense of the word. Her views on the hierarchy of Heaven are dictated dogma, while she also exudes much that is reasonable, wise and compassionate.

One moment, she tells Boethius of the futility of hatred, or of how criminals ought to be treated as patients, rather than be punished. The next, she may expand on the innate wickedness of some souls in true Neo-Platonic fashion:

On this I said: 'I see how there is a happiness and misery founded on the actual deserts of the righteous and the wicked. Nevertheless, I wonder in myself whether there is not some good and evil in fortune as the vulgar understand it. Surely, no sensible man would rather be exiled, poor and disgraced, than dwell prosperously in his own country, powerful, wealthy, and high in honour. Indeed, the work of wisdom is more clear and manifest in its operation when the happiness of rulers is somehow passed on to the people around them, especially considering that the prison, the law, and the other pains of legal punishment are properly due only to mischievous citizens on whose account they were originally instituted. Accordingly, I do exceedingly marvel why all this is completely reversed — why the good are harassed with the penalties due to crime, and the bad carry off the rewards of virtue; and I long to hear from thee what reason may be found for so unjust a state of disorder. For assuredly I should wonder less if I could believe that all things are the confused result of chance. But now my belief in God's governance doth add amazement to amazement. For, seeing that He sometimes assigns fair fortune to the good and harsh fortune to the bad, and then again deals harshly with the good, and grants to the bad their hearts' desire, how does this differ from chance, unless some reason is discovered for it all?'

'Nay', she said, 'it is not wonderful if all should be thought random and confused when the principle of order is not known. And though thou knowest not the causes on which this great system depends, yet forasmuch as a good ruler governs the world, doubt not for thy part that all is rightly done.'

Who knoweth not how near the pole
Boötes' course doth go,
Must marvel by what heavenly law
He moves his Wain so slow;
Why late he plunges 'neath the main,
And swiftly lights his beams again.
When the full-orbèd moon grows pale
In the mid course of night,
And suddenly the stars shine forth
That languished in her light,
Th' astonied nations stand at gaze,
And beat the air in wild amaze.
None marvels why upon the shore
The storm-lashed breakers beat,
Nor why the frost-bound glaciers melt
At summer's fervent heat;
For here the cause seems plain and clear,
Only what's dark and hid we fear.
Weak-minded folly magnifies
All that is rare and strange,
And the dull herd's o'erwhelmed with awe
At unexpected change.
But wonder leaves enlightened minds,

When ignorance no longer blinds.[29]

Historians of philosophy all seemingly agree that the Consolation is not a Christian book, though they also seemingly agree that where it lifts its hat towards Plato and his followers, rather than towards Christ, it is on 'minor' matters, such as the return of the soul to its source, God, rather than eternal bliss in a physical heaven. In other words, its Neo-Platonic hierarchy of being is what matters. Its three pillars – the One, the Intellect and the Soul – are seen as virtually the same as the Christians' trinity. But what did Boethius aim to convey to his readers – in between the lines – by designing his book so that it did not contain a single reference to either Christ or Christianity? After all, he lived in an age when it was expected of every writer to wear his orthodoxy on his sleeve. Furthermore, earlier in his own life, he had written several tracts on Christian theology where he took care not to insert a single idea that was at odds with the teaching of the Catholic church in Rome. Conversely, could he really have been so innocent of the possible interpretations that his readers – or future readers – might put on his last and crowning work?

Before I express an opinion on this old question here – for whatever little it is worth compared to that of the real experts – let us take a glance at what past and present scholars have written upon it.

The late professor Sir Arnaldo Dante Momigliano[30] of London University, probably the world's most prominent scholar of Roman history in the twentieth century, had no doubt reading Boethius' mind in those last months of his life in Pavian confinement: 'many people' he wrote, 'have turned to Christianity for consolation. Boethius turned to paganism. His Christianity collapsed—it collapsed so thoroughly that perhaps he did not even notice its disappearance'.

In 1980, David C. Lindberg of Chicago University wrote that Boethius' fate at the hands of historians had alternated for a hundred years. In his Science in the Middle Ages[31], he wrote: 'the classicists have assimilated him to an earlier period, the medievalists have projected him into a much later one, neither side entirely willing to accept the enigma of a sincerely Christian who was also a serious Hellenist'.

More recently, the late professor P. G. Walsh of Glasgow University, who was himself a devout Catholic, detected no dilemma on Boethius' part. In his introduction to his translation of the Consolation in 1999 he wrote that we 'did not need to assume that Boethius subscribed to every doctrine propounded by Philosophy'. He continued: 'probably, Boethius plays the role of a latter-day Origen in speculatively advancing the arguments of the philosophers, even at the risk of departing from Christian orthodoxy.'[32] But this leaves the reader with the unanswered question 'why'. Was it not more prudent for a political prisoner accused of treason to mention, just in passing, that while he wanted to

60

preserve the thinking of the ancients for posterity, he himself was a convinced believer in the official religion of the state?

By contrast, for Victor Watts, a former Master of the renowned theological institute of Grey College in the university of Durham, the long-existing doubts about the Christianity of Boethius cannot be dismissed easily. In his Penguin Classics translation of the Consolation in 1999, he writes: 'It seems, nevertheless, strange that writing in the presence of death Boethius still prefers reason to faith, and makes no mention of what must be the only fully meaningful consolation for a Christian, the Incarnation of Christ and the doctrine of Grace. ... the Boethian doctrine of salvation ... , is essentially pagan in inspiration. This is why in his Dialogue of Cumfort Sir Thomas More rejects the philosophers of old'.

Watts may well be wrong in assuming that, in his confinement in Pavia, Boethius knew that he was 'in the presence of death, that Theodoric would go ahead with the expected punishment of traitors and execute him. But his explanation for Boethius' strange behaviour is nonetheless shared by many of commentators of a religious inclination. He believes that where the Consolation differs from Christian doctrine – for example 'in the implicit denial of creation ex nihil in the Timaeu poem – is not of fundamental significance in the Consolation.

One may beg to differ here. Christianity without the doctrine of the creation out of nothing would be a very heretical Christianity indeed.

As for me, having read all these views and, also, having spent years researching the life of another medieval heretic – see chapter 5 – the most probably explanation lies elsewhere. Boethius, largely cut off from the world for a whole year or longer, in either a prison cell or under arrest in a modest house in a poor district of Pavia, had time to give vent to his Stoic temperament, if not explicit creed. He decided, for once, not to be a hypocrite. He opted for writing something which might survive because it was honest about doubt, the doubt of an intelligent man's uncertainly regarding the truth of received doctrine, the doubt that has been with us since the first homo sapient emerged from his cave. Furthermore, the manuscript of the Consolation would have been given to the safe keeping of his family only. He would not have to publish it in the remainder of his life if the king pardoned him. But if Theodoric did go ahead with the injustice and executed him, then what did Boethius or his destitute family have to lose? Furthermore still, anyone could see that some of Boethius' arguments in the book were superior to those of 'the Lady'. He was not insisting on the truth of any doctrine. It was the tale of a discussion, amusingly told, to make a reader think for himself. At the most selfish level, it would perpetuate him name. It would be a fit monument for a philosopher to leave behind him.

And a very great monument it proved. It has been described as the most important philosophical text in Latin in the subsequent 'Dark' and Medieval ages, and it was translated by numerous hands into numerous other languages. For me, the most significant of the latter has to be the translation into Old English by King Alfred in the ninth century, the only English king ever to have been given the title of 'Great'. By doing so, Alfred helped to give enough prestige and substance to English to enable its speakers resist the long onslaught of French under the Normans later. Without Alfred, this essay might well have been written – if at all – in a modern descendant of Norman French.

And so, yes, we can admire Ancius Manlius Severinus Boethius. Aware that he had brought disaster upon himself in midlife, he would also have been broken-hearted about the suffering of his family which he had caused, by being at least not vigilant enough about the plots of his enemies at Theodoric's court. He had been too complacent about the king's confidence in him. Now, here he was in utter disgrace, with his wealth confiscated and his family plunged into penury. He decided that he must not allow the calamity to destroy him as a rational being. He determined to concentrate his mind on writing a work of literature and philosophy that might entertain and enlighten those yet to be born. Little did he know just how phenomenally he would succeed.

\*

Why did God afflict little children with leprosy?
What free will did the Holy Spirit allow the cripple?
You wished to understand.
But could not.

The Fathers told you to be humble.
You were too human to understand.
God was kind and merciful.
Kneel in prayer and you would be spared.

It was a paradox.
They appealed to your reason
To judge itself unreasonable.
Was that no homage to reason, after all?

Then the king's executioner arrived.
You were barely past two scores of years.
Was God good or evil?
What did the pagans think?

# Omar Khayyām

## *A 'Greek' stranded among aliens*

33

Lost to the wine of the Magus? I am.
Pagan? Zarathustrian? Haereticus? I am.
Every nation has its notion of me,
I am my own man, whatever I am.[34]

Every year on May 18, my wife and I, hopefully with a few friends, raise a glass to 'Our lord Omar'. It is fun and it has almost become a ritual ever since 1996, when I became serious about writing a 'life-and-times' biography of him in English. So, on the anniversary of his birth, I design a meal of classic ingredients that he would have recognised and the wine will be a red Shiraz, not the most complex of wines to be worthy of him, that is true, but one, I fancy, whose ancestral vine was alive in one of the vineyards of the city of that name in southern Persia when Khayyām visited in the summer of 1080.[35]

Who really was Khayyām? Did I find anything about him that we didn't know before I embarked on my six years of research into his life and his world? Do I like him any more today than I did when I first found his little book of subversive and humorous, yet also sad, verses among my father's otherwise pompous books in our little town of Sahneh in the Kurdish highlands of western Iran some six decades ago?

Three things had immediately endeared him to the child in me: His simple Persian shone through the gloom of a millennium of borrowing of Arabic words into the language. This use of basic words enabled him to retain his freshness and to reveal something of his inner torment as an Iranian. He was contemptuous of all those holy men who had ready answers to every question, and he confessed to his ordinary human needs of love and fun, colour and warmth, all of which were publicly frowned on by the men of God.

At the time, of course, I could not have any notion of the phenomenon that Edward FitzGerald in the latter part of the nineteenth century had made of Khayyām all over the globe. I had to wait for that until years later in England, where my earnest father had sent me to become civilised, because only the upright English were good enough for the further education of his eldest son. Unfortunately for him, the English at once unleashed on me the miniskirt and Bertrand Russell. Goodbye son, in whom he had invested so much hope. But Britain gave me the English language and that meant falling in love with Khayyām once more, even though his English emanation was only a partial reflection of him.

It is said that FitzGerald's Rubāiyāt of Omar Khayyām has, weight by weight, contributed more phrases to the English language than have the Bible and Shakespeare together. I doubt if anyone has actually counted, but FitzGerald is always in print in a hundred languages and continues as bedtime companion to millions of people. Some years ago at my club in London, I found myself at lunch with three strangers, two Englishmen and an American. When they heard that I was writing a biography of Khayyām, the two Englishmen immediately burst into FitzGerald and the American said that he longed to see the expression on the face of a friend of his back home when he, the American here, would give him, the American there, a copy of my biography for Christmas. His friend had been giving him a new edition of FitzGerald for the past dozen years, each one with only slightly varying illustrations or some other minor embellishment.

Even so, I was surprised when the Chinese National Radio sent their man in London to interview me about the project. The Chinese, though, seemed to have got the wrong end of the stick. They were more interested in Khayyām's mathematics than in his quatrains.

So, who was he? He was born in Iran's north-eastern city of Nishāpūr on May 18, 1048, to Ebrahīm Khayyāmi[36], a herbal physician whose family or clan name, Khayyāmi, may be roughly translated to mean 'Of the Tentmakers'. He later took the singular form of the description, 'Khayyām' or 'tentmaker' as his pen name. Perhaps it had been a nickname his friends had given him early in life. We do not know, but in all the contemporary sources, he is referred to by his surname of 'Khayyāmi'.

Anyhow, from the earliest childhood, the boy showed an unusual head for figures and, for this reason, Ebrahīm employed for him, among others, a famous teacher of mathematics by the name of Bahmanyār who still clung to the old Iranian faith of Zoroastrianism some five centuries after Arab invaders had ended its domination of the region. Consequently, the boy wrote three pamphlets on mathematics and a short commentary on Euclid's treatise on music while still at school. (In this respect, he reminds one of Bertrand Russell – and is it not also a neat coincidence that both were born on May 18th?)

In his later writings, Khayyām says that he did not find in his home city of Nishāpūr a rich sponsor to publish his work and to enable him to continue his studies. So, after his father's death when he was 18, he migrated to the city of Samarkand, in today's Uzbekistan in central Asia. There, amid high tension between the mosque and the state, Omar found his sponsor in the person of his late father's friend, the chief judge and the city's governor. But he somehow also managed to win friends at the royal court while publishing a ground-breaking book on algebra that provided solutions to three classes of cubic equations. In his preface to the book, he comes across as a precocious, even rather obnoxious, young man who denounces nearly all other scientists of the region as impostors. A typical mathematical prodigy, one might say, with powerful connections to make him untouchable.

Towards the end of his stay in Samarkand, in 1072, the king, who had only three years earlier executed the city's chief imam for daring to tell him to be a more observant Muslim, chose Khayyām to be one of his drinking companions and took him to Bukhara, the capital, a few hundred miles to the west, apparently to build an astronomical observatory for him there. A contemporary writer surely exaggerates when he says that the king sat Khayyām on 'the throne' beside him. This would not have been the formal throne, but a raised platform for social and family occasions. It suggests that the young man's wit and good looks were extraordinary, a suggestion supported by other circumstantial evidence, including one of his own early stanzas, and these, combined with his brilliance as a mathematician and musician, appear to have helped open other doors to him throughout his life.

Bliss in Bukhara was not to last long, for the Saljuq emperor in Isfahan had designs on his neighbouring kingdom and invaded it a year later for its wealth, and for its artists and scientists. So Khayyām went to Isfahan. Whether or not he did so freely, or not, I could not discover, but it is my feeling that he went gladly. Much would have been promised him, the emperor was even younger than he was and, besides, he was going to be accompanied there by a number of friends and acquaintances from the Bokhara court. Among these, was the king's young daughter, the Princess Terken, who had been betrothed to the 15-year-old emperor, Malik Shah, since they had both been small children.

Khayyām's main task was to help build a much bigger observatory in Isfahan, and this he did with great enthusiasm. There, he also led an active and fulfilled life as one of the highest-paid officials of the state and a confidant of both the emperor and his powerful chancellor, the Persian Nizām al-Mulk. The Saljuqs were recent Turkish invaders from central Asia, but were by then being assimilated into the more advanced culture of the Persians and relied thoroughly on Persian experts and administrators to run their new, extensive empire.

Some 20 years later, however, in 1092, Khayyām's world crashed around him when he lost the protection of his close friend, Malik Shah. First, the chancellor was assassinated – coincidentally in this writer's little birthplace of Sahneh in Kurdistan – by a member of the so-called Assassins sect, the Islmailis of Iran. Then, a few weeks later in Baghdad, the emperor was poisoned, allegedly by the supporters of the late chancellor who suspected him of complicity in the great man's murder. I myself think it more likely that the poisoning was carried out by the agents of the caliph, the hereditary spiritual leader of Sunni Islam at the time, who was the emperor's estranged son-in-law and who feared – rightly – that Malik Shah had come to exile him from Baghdad in order to turn the city into his summer capital. In any case, the result was that the empire fell into civil war between the emperor's two leading wives. Terken was perhaps largely to blame. She first hid Malik Shah's death from general knowledge for quite a few days, until she had seized the treasury back in Isfahan and forced the army's commanders to proclaim her young son as the new sovereign, even though an older son by Malik Shah's other wife had a greater claim to the throne. Predictably, the emperor's brothers also joined the fray and the empire fell into a ruinous dynastic war that was to last several years and, coincidentally, pave the way for the success of the first Crusade against Jerusalem seven years later, in 1096.

In the chaos, the mullahs of Isfahan who had, for years, seethed with rage at Khayyām's arrogant flaunting of his unbelief, seized their chance and passed a fatwa of apostasy against him, one of their explanations being that he loved 'the Greeks, not Islam'. This was a clear, and justified, reference to Khayyām's adherence to the teachings of the great classical philosophers of Greece and Rome, the influence of whom can clearly be seen in his poems, the rubāiyāt.

Terken, now beset by rebels and rivals on every side, had no choice but to abandon her old friend to the wolves.

Khayyām was now advised by friends that the mullahs would forgive him if he announced that he had at last seen the light of Islam. As in the case of the novelist Salman Rushdie in our time, it only made the mullahs smell blood. He set out for Baghdad, probably in disguise, saying that he would go on from there to Mecca on the hajj pilgrimage. But as he arrived in the city of the caliphate, every blasphemer and prostitute flocked to him to confirm his reputation as a heretic. I found no evidence that he completed the pretence pilgrimage, only that he sneaked back into Iran, bypassed Isfahan and retired to his home city in the far north-east which had not been touched by the civil war. There, he enjoyed the friendship of the governor, a powerful Saljuq prince, and retired to his private estate until the excitement subsided some years later. The contemporary sources tell us that he made a public exhibition of himself by exaggerating his devotion to Islam. This he did by attending congregations in mosques more than was expected. It seems to have worked, for some time later, in the opening decade of the twelfth century, he regained his freedom of movement and even felt confident again to reflect on life and love and the universe in yet more rebellious stanzas. His fame spread as a revered sage and philosopher in the whole region and kings and emperors befriended him once more before he died on December 4, 1131, at the age of 83.

That Khayyām should have found it hard to identify with Islam should not surprise us. He was brought up in a city which had until the Arab conquest of the seventh century been a sacred centre of Zoroastrianism, and he had in his childhood fallen under the spell of Firdowsi, the Persian epic poet whose great tales of heroism and glory in pre-Islamic Iran had recently swept the Iranian world from Tajikistan in the Himalayas to Kurdistan in northern Mesopotamia. Khayyām's rubāiyāt are sprinkled with the names of Firdowsi's heroes, the mythical and real Iranian emperors such as Jamshīd, Bahrām and Parvīz, showing that Khayyām addressed his poems exclusively to the world he himself inhabited, the world of wounded Iranian pride mourning its ancient civilisation fallen under the feet of uncouth swordsmen from the Arabian desert and the Turkic steppe.

There were still also daily happenings on the streets of Nishāpūr that had revolted his sense of humanity when a schoolchild. He had seen how his beloved Zoroastrian mathematics teacher, Bahmanyār, had had to dismount and stand aside for Turkish soldiers or Muslim preachers to pass, how the city's Jews had to wear patches of yellow cloth on their coats to warn Muslims to avoid physical contact with them, how non-Muslim houses had to be lower than their neighbours', and how the jizyeh tax levied against non-Muslims was sometimes used to drive them bankrupt so their properties could be seized and their children auctioned as slaves.

In addition, Khayyām was a scholar of 'the Greek sciences'. He was steeped in the works of the classical writers and, though I have not found any evidence to this end, he must have read them in the original. This would not have been unusual, but expected. Some of his professional heroes of the past, for example the openly atheistic physician Rāzi (or Rhazes, 865-923), were so proficient in Greek that they wrote poetry in it and, in Isfahan, he himself had at least one student of Greek upbringing. Also one of his closest friends, who was one of the younger sons of the chancellor Nizām al-Mulk, had an Armenian princess for a mother. The lady had been taken to Greek-speaking Constantinople as a hostage when very young and had spent some years there. We have to assume that Khayyām frequented her mansion in Isfahan and that, there, he came into contact with many other speakers of Greek. Similarly, there would have been dozens of scholars of Latin in Isfahan whose job was to deal with official correspondence with the Byzantine court in Constantinople. That correspondence was all in Latin, but the officials would likely have been ethnic Greeks.

Thus all the indications are that while he pretended to adhere to the harsh Ash'ari school of Islamic jurisprudence to please the chancellor Nizām al-Mulk and the new converts, the Saljuq Turks – though not Malik Shah himself who was a sceptic – Khayyām regarded the religion of the Arabs as inferior to the other major creeds that had adherents in the region: Zoroastrianism, Christianity, Judaism and Buddhism. Sooner or later, he was bound to come to grief and it is perhaps surprising that he did not do so until he was 44.

In my opinion, Khayyām had three great achievements. A mathematician friend of mine, Philip Bond, places him among his top ten intellects in all history, and it might be argued that without his work on algebra in 1072 in Samarkand, later great mathematicians such as Leibniz and Newton would have been delayed. We cannot know. A second achievement came in 1079 in Isfahan when the shah inaugurated Khayyām's new solar calendar. To devise it, he and a handful of colleagues calculated the average length of the year to within 5 seconds of the figure an atomic clock would have given him at the time, and he achieved that degree of accuracy without telescopes or any of today's precise instruments.[37] His calendar is, to this day, more accurate than the Gregorian system currently in use in most of the world and which was inaugurated in Rome five centuries later. According to the Institute of Physics, Khayyām's calendar needs a correction of only one day every 3,770 years.

Khayyām's third achievement, which has given much more pleasure and inspiration to people, is, of course, the Rubáiyát. These he must have written for himself and his friends, probably to be sung at private concerts. Inevitably, some leaked out to the hostile world outside and they were used against him.

One mullah is on record as describing them as 'serpents on the body of the holy law'. As I said earlier, they nearly cost him his life. They certainly cost him his liberty for many years.

As no contemporary manuscript of the rubāiyāt, let alone one in his own hand, survived the subsequent Mongolian and later Turkic invasions of Iran to reach our time, scholars of Persian literature attribute no more than about 120 stanzas to him on the basis of historical quotations, internal hints and style. Of these, I chose only 50 quatrains to translate to accompany the biography. I wanted to be virtually certain that they were really his, and I chose so few because I found it difficult to translate them if I wanted to imitate the rhyme and rhythm of the originals, as well as remain close to their literary meaning. In any case, some of them repeated the others' themes and some were not perfect gems of form and content, which is true of the work of almost all poets. They all have their less inspired or difficult moments.

An interesting fact revealed itself when I arranged my chosen quatrains in order of youthfulness and age. It proved an easy task. For example, one stanza in which he mentions his luxuriant hair and pink cheeks to enquire into God's purpose in designing him so, was obviously written by him when he was a young man:

> What a handsome face, what beautiful hair.
> My height a cypress, my skin so fair.
> And yet, my Maker, what purpose did He
> Assign to my life, when he painted me?

Others in which he mentions the fatwa clearly belong to his mid-forties, when he, as the former untouchable close friend of the shah, became vulnerable with the sudden removal of the sovereign.

> Lord of the fatwa, what a rogue you are.
> Drinker though I am, I prefer by far
> From the juice of grapes to secure a thrill
> Than to cheat orphans of their fathers' will.

Others, in which he seemingly declares his last will and testament, naturally fell to the bottom of the list:

> And when you gather at the old tavern,
> Each other's latest trivia to learn,
> Drink the best of wines, drink to absent friends,
> Leave a glass empty when it is my turn.

69

Previously, all Khayyām anthologies had been arranged alphabetically according to the last letters of their last rhyming words. This is usual in the Middle East and makes it easy for the reader to find a particular poem if he remembers how it ends. But when I arranged mine in the new order, in the order of ageing, it suddenly became apparent that Khayyām had left us a short, though vague, autobiography, after all. It fits the pattern of his life, for as much as we know of it, and it provided an insight into the progression of his mind and moods as he matured as a thinker. Written probably over four or five decades, the little poems in my arrangement begin as the utterances of a precocious youth who is only tangentially concerned with the mysteries of the universe. They proceed onto harder ground when the professionally successful and well-connected middle aged man has come to reject the received wisdom of his age and is not afraid to say it because he has the emperor himself for a friend and fellow sceptic. Then, suddenly, the tone darkens with the fatwa and the fear of tomorrow. Finally, the last quatrains mourn the passage of precious time and the loss of loved friends before Khayyām says farewell to the world.

Was he a convinced atheist or a vague theist? Was he a secret Zoroastrian, at least emotionally, thinking it no worse than any other religion, but at least one that was the creation of his own ancestors? Was he merely a philosophical agnostic? There are indications to lead us in all those directions. I have not made up my mind, despite the fact that when, in 1961, his remains were recovered from his grave for a new grand mausoleum that the last of the Pahlavi shahs was building for him, he was found to have been buried in a walled chamber in the style of the Zoroastrians of his time. But probably he was all of those, and none, as his mood took him.

> Lost to the wine of the Magus? I am.
> Pagan? Zarathustrian? Haereticus? I am.
> Every nation has its notion of me.
> I am my own man, whatever I am.

In some of his quatrains I detect strongly reflected the materialism of the Epicureans, the belief that there is no metaphysical realm outside what surrounds us, while some of the others are imbued with the longing of the Stoic for a simple life. Of one thing, though, I am certain. He suffered from severe depression at times in his life, which ought not surprise us. Apart from abhorring the widespread injustices of the age, most persons of genius suffer from wide swings of mood, and this alone might have made him dependent on alcohol, giving an extra excuse to the pious to denounce him as an ungodly heretic:

> Without strong wine, I cannot endure,

I cannot pull forth this tired carcass;
I long for that breath when the maid offers
One more cup to me, but it has to pass.

Then, at 72, perhaps on his birthday, his mood swings to the other extreme:

Today I will shed my robe of restraint,
Let trails of red wine my white beard taint.
No more Piety. I am SEVENTY.
If not dance now, when might it then be?

Do we know what he looked like? Not precisely, though we can have a good idea. When they moved his remains to the new mausoleum in 1961, they found that he had been a big man, 'in the mould of a heavy-weight wrestler', with a large head, 61-62 centimetres in circumference[38]. Unfortunately, the photographs and the measurements – if they still exist – are now being guarded in Iran as if they were state secrets. The new Islamic regime is not keen to draw attention to this most famous black sheep of the family and the gardens of his mausoleum, were at one time allowed to wither for lack of money to water them. But we do know that the Arab conquerors of Iran gave the nickname of 'Yellow Moustaches' to the people they had overcome, and that by Khayyām's time, the Iranians had still not mixed thoroughly with the Arabs and the Turks. A century or so later, an Arab critic who had read contemporary accounts of his physical appearance – sources that are now lost – says that when Khayyām spoke – or recited his poems? – excitedly, his long hair rose and fell to enable one to see through to his skull at his temples.

So it is probably safe to say that he was a big man with fair hair similar in appearance to some inhabitants in the northern Caucasus today. Perhaps, one day, scientists will be allowed to build a semblance of his head on the basis of his skull. Until then, we will have to be content with the knowledge that he harboured a strong conceit about his own beauty when young and that, probably, women loved him as much as he seems to have loved them.

We know less about his private life than we do about his career. While we know, for example, the precise details of his salary – 10,000 gold dinars, which at least one treasury minister to resent it – we do not know the name of his wife. A few years ago, I read Richard West's biography of Chaucer. I have also read several biographies of Shakespeare. I would say that we know more about the private life of Khayyām than we known about those other two great poets much closer to our own time.

Anyhow, unearthing what we know of him, studying the lives and writings of a number of his acquaintances, colleagues, teachers, mentors and patrons, and the events that directly or indirectly affected him, enabled me to conjure a reasonably clear portrait out of the shadows. I am surprised that Iranian and other scholars had not previously attempted such a work, given the huge extent of his fame in the world thanks to FitzGerald since 1859. The several books that have been published on him in Iran in recent years are more literary criticism or refutations of his unbelief than what would be described as biography here in the West.

Even in the freer atmosphere under the monarchy in Iran before the Islamic revolution of 1979, one famous writer, the late senator Ali Dashti, dismissed a history of the Iranian calendar attributed to Khayyām by merely deeming it as too sympathetic to Zoroastrianism. By contrast, when I read that same text, I thought it likely to be by Khayyām for precisely those sentiments, though I must add that the work struck me as the writing of a very young man, not yet mature in his judgements .

To sum up, researching Khayyām's life and writings for nearly a decade gave me the feeling that we might, metaphorically, describe him as a Stoic philosopher of the breed of Seneca who found himself surrounded by an alien people. In his youth, he had been egotistic and ambitious enough to seek personal advancement by endearing himself to men of power, and these were either the high clergy of Islam or, else, the newly arrived war lords of the Turkic, Saljuq tribe of central Asia. I found that as early as the summer of 1080, when he was only thirty-two years old and his friend and protector Malik Shah was still alive and at the height of his power, Khayyām felt forced to write an utterly orthodox and bland monograph on the truth of Islam in order to deflect criticism of him – and by extension Malik Shah – as an apostate. The monograph is as far removed from the spirit of the rubāiyāt as any piece of writing can be, and it is so un-original, and so flat in tone, that it would have been seen as wholly pointless.

But Khayyām's world collapsed clearly after the assassination of Malik Shah in 1092. How precisely he managed protect himself from mobs and Islamic judges for decades, we do not know. Did he go about in disguise in the initial stages of his anathema, when he was outside the relatively safe haven of far-flung Khorāsān province in the north-east? Did he have to employ a strong bodyguard even there? He was certainly wealthy enough to afford that. Not a single mention of his activities or whereabouts has survived from the first decade or so of the twelfth century. He had to keep a very 'low profile', as we say nowadays.

Nor were his circumstances ideal afterwards. While he was wealthy and while he was safe, he still had to pretend attachment to a theology and a legal system that he disliked deeply, and he had to refuse repeated pleas from bright students who were eager to learn 'the Greek sciences' at his feet. Those who did not know him well, denounced him as haughty, too selfish to stoop to teaching.

But he did not want to teach what he did not believe to be true, and what he believed to be true was forbidden. Nor could he even, for the risk of being found out, comment in private on the writings of the classical thinkers or on the natural world in which he was passionately interested.

But he enjoyed the support of like-minded friends, combined with the joys of beholding nature at its best, as we see in the following rubāii:

> This garden, this park, these broad skies,
> Hillocks, waterfalls, meadows, butterflies.
> Do send for my friends, those tingling wits
> Who lighten my heart, who brighten my eyes.

It is perhaps the joy of such moments in Khayyām's surviving poems that dominates the mood of Edward FitzGerald's free translation of him. The combination of the two men's works continues to bring light to millions of lives long after them. Not bad.

> Drunk again, Khayyām? Doctor will be mad.
> A girl in your arms? Love her, make her glad.
> All will end in doom. No. Do not be sad.
> We are still here. That cannot be bad.

Altogether, I conclude that, despite the fear and dislocation of his middle years after that infamous fatwa was levelled against him, Khayyām probably looked back on his life at the very end and feel pleased. His son-in-law has left us an account of his last day, at the age of eighty-three. After lunch on December 4, 1131, we are told, 'my lord' began to read a book of philosophy by Avicenna. Then – provided we can believe the whole of this – for it may part be designed to pass a notorious heretic as a holy man – 'he slid his gold tooth pick into the book, set it aside, and called the household. He bade them farewell, for he knew his end was near. Then he lay down to sleep and never rose again'.

That reading the works of his predecessors was one of the joys of Khayyām's life cannot be disputed. But there were other consolations too. He had had a life that had been full of tingling conversation, mathematical discovery, music and merrymaking, travel, the private conversation of kings and emperors. This is best told us by a scribe called Nizāmi Arūzi Samarqandi, Khayyām's one-time secretary. In a short book which he called The Four Discourses and which he devoted to the lives of eminent persons, including Khayyām, he writes that in 1112, probably in the autumn, when the air was cool and the grapes were ripe, he joined his former master for dinner at the home of the prince governor of the region:

In the midst of the merriness (the man is too wise to say that by then the wine had begun to speak), my lord Omar said that he had chosen a spot for his grave where each spring sprinkled him with flowers twice. I was puzzled, but I knew that he never boasted falsely. When later, several years after his death, I was visiting Nishāpūr once more, I employed a guide one Friday to take me to his grave, for I owed much to my late master.

As we entered the cemetery and turned left, [my guide took me to] the foot of a wall [and pointed out the spot to me]. Pear and apricot trees had spread their branches [over the grave] from a neighbouring orchard, and sprinkled so much petal over the ground that the grave could not be seen. I could not help crying, for far and wide in the inhabited world, I could not imagine anyone of his stature.[39]

# Spinoza

## *The lonely and loving man who sought an unloving God*

I do not know how to teach philosophy without disturbing the peace.

I have striven not to ridicule, neither to bewail, nor to scorn human actions, but to understand them.

If you want the present to be better than the past, study the past.

The wise man thinks of nothing less than he does of death.

\*

Dreaming is free, and day-dreaming comes just as readily to us. So, on this fine day in late September 1676, we have come to the ancient city of The Hague in the United Provinces of the Netherlands to experience the thrill of meeting probably the most loveable of all the great philosophers. Baruch (Benedictus) Spinoza has found refuge here for the past six years. Do you see that larger house over there? That's where he lodges.

But I think that before we knock on his door, we should briefly review his life so far and remind ourselves of why he is so loved – and cursed – in equal measure by one or other faction. There is a nice coffee house around the corner. I suggest we go there for about half an hour. Is that agreeable to you?

All right. But one thing we must do first. Or rather several things. Please make sure your mobile phones are switched off. If we give the slightest hin t to the locals that we've come from the future, there will be riots, and who can blame them? Even in this relatively enlightened republic. After all, we could be their descendants coming to visit them. And if Spinoza himself finds out that we're a million times more knowledgeable about the natural world than he is, he'll feel so humiliated as not to say a word for fear of ruining himself in our eyes.

You may tell him, if you wish, that dipping his pieces of glass in water as he grinds them into lenses would protect his lungs. But it's too late, I fear. He'll be dead in the spring, from both tuberculosis and from years of inhaling that glass dust. He's been grinding lenses since boyhood and, I'm told, we'll find a layer of silica dust everywhere in his room, even on his clothes.

Now, in case my nightmare still comes true and your mobiles are somehow discovered, let's all stick to one story. They're a new kind of English snuff box with an alarm clock built in to remind you it's time. If anyone insists that we open up the boxes and share the snuff with them, we'll have to flee. So do your absolute best. All right?

I suggest we tell people we're here to buy lenses for microscopes and telescopes from Doctor Spinoza. Don't drop any hint we're interested in his philosophy or science. He's rumoured to be an unbeliever, even an atheist, though he denies it vehemently. Worse still. Some are certain he's a spy for the French who've occupied part of the country. His being a Jew doesn't help. Tell everyone we're merchants from London and tell the café owner we're likely to come again. Ask him if he has rooms for us to stay in, on our next visit. I'll give him a large tip, as well, enough to make sure a big smile gets fixed on his face for a week.

Let's begin, then. Spinoza's only forty-three years old and was born and brought up in the Jewish quarter of Amsterdam. His Hebrew name is Baruch, and his Portuguese name is Benedito. I say Portuguese because his parents were refugees from Portugal, refugees from the Catholic Inquisition there and in Spain. So he speaks Portuguese, and also Spanish, because that's the main language of the Jews of Amsterdam. He has studied Hebrew and speaks Dutch.

He's had a strong sense of Dutch patriotism since childhood and is very fond of the Dutch. He has also learnt Latin and French, but writes philosophy in Latin only.

He writes in Latin partly because that's the language that his peers have in common in Europe, and partly because he would otherwise draw too much attention to himself among the locals. He's experienced what an enraged mob can do. They lynched the famous De Wits brothers, liberal politicians and his friends who were denounced for their realism towards France.

As a child, 'Bento' – that was his nickname – was the bright hope of the central synagogue in Amsterdam. People saw in him all the aibutes of a fine future rabbi. But he began to ask awkward questions early, perhaps under the influence of his father, Michael, who ran an import business and mixed with gentiles and knew such artists as Rembrandt. His mother died when he was six, and his father when he was 21. So he inherited responsibility for his younger brother and sister when he was barely a young man. To make matters worse, his father had got into heavy debt after the first Anglo-Dutch war and Bento had to go to court to escape his creditors. He was rather reckless. He made the elders angry by going to a civil, Dutch, court, instead of the usual rabbinical one. Then, he gave his share of his mother's estate to his sister and started work as a teacher in a Dutch school.

There the real trouble started. The school was owned by a dare-devil freethinker who would one day be hanged in France for plotting to assassinate Louis XIV. The man taught him Latin and what they call here 'the new science', Copernicus, Harvey, etc, and the philosophy of Descartes. Bento boarded at the headmaster's home and fell in love with his daughter Clara, but Clara married a richer student and Bento went off women. At least that's what we're told.

Curiously, while Bento began to parrot some of the ideas of his new mentor, he went on being a loyal member of the synagogue. He read the traditional prayers to commemorate his late father over eleven months and he protested that he had no intention of disturbing the faith of others. But he would not hide the result of his researches that showed, he said, that the five books of Moses could not have all been written by him. Nor that the bible justified any form of violence being inflicted on anyone. Nor would he stop there. He said that the established religions were all false and no scripture had divine authority. All had been written by ignorant men.

So when he was 23 and wouldn't repent, the elders offered him a salary for life if he would merely stay quiet. He refused. They excommunicated him. Not only that. They used the harshest words they could find in the Torah. They called on the she-bears to tear him apart, and they shouted it from every rooftop – particularly from the rooftops so that their Calvinist neighbours could hear it – that Benedito de Espinosa was no-longer one of them, that none of them was allowed, any longer, to spend even a single minute under the same roof as him.

We have to sympathise with them. There they were, the Jews, refugees from torture and forced conversion at the hands of Catholic priests and roaming pike men in Spain and Portugal who especially enjoyed killing children, and they had been given safety by this idealistic new republic of rebels. But it didn't mean they could relax. They couldn't take their safety for granted. In fact, early this same century, the Dutch state had ordered them to enforce Jewish law more ardently among their followers to make sure the odd atheist among them could not infect the Dutch. You may think that the southern Jews' alien dark looks, strange ways and foreign accents were bad enough. The last thing they needed was to become known as a haven of heretics who questioned God himself.

It is said that one day a knife-wielding fanatic attacked Bento in front of the synagogue and reached close enough to make a large gash in his jacket. He was shaken and fled to a suburb where some of his Christian friends lived. It was then that he Latinised his name to Benedictus Spinoza, and it was there that his skill in grinding and polishing glass into lenses proved a saviour. Oh, good. We seem to have the place to ourselves.

– Good morning.

– Good Morning Sir.

– I see you've got some excellent cakes here. Can we have a pot of coffee for four, please, and a tray of your cakes?

– Certainly, Sir.

Let's go to that far corner. Yes, I was saying. The Jews have, as you know, this tradition of learning a craft or trade which has almost become a religious duty with them. They've experienced so many sudden upheavals, being uprooted without notice, having to leave their homes and country because Christian zealots have lusted after their properties, that they've had to be prepared all the time. They know they can take away their skills with them, not their property. Bento chose to be skilled in the new craft of grinding and polishing glass into lenses for spectacles, microscopes and telescopes. He was excellent at it from the start and so he began to earn a modest living from it.

At the same time, the bug of the new learning had bitten. Are we surprised? Of course, not. The three of you know this better than I do. This is a most exciting age to do philosophy. Rene Descartes – who, by the way, spent the bulk of his adult life in this same little country and wrote all his major works here – had only a generation earlier revolutionised philosophy, geometry and physics, provoking the pope to put his works on the Catholic Index of banned books. Thomas Hobbes, too, had turned political theory on its head. You probably know his famous condemnation of the Scholastic thinking of the previous thousand years by heart. Let me see if I can recite some of it:

> It hath no otherwise place than as a handmaiden of the Roman religion; and since the authority of Aristotle is only current there, that study is not properly philosophy (the nature whereof dependeth not on authors) but Aristotelity.[41]

And before Hobbes, Francis Bacon had also, in effect, turned his back on the Christian centuries. It was a kind of degenerate learning, he said, which

> 'did chiefly reign amongst the schoolmen who, having sharp and strong wits and abundance of leisure, and small variety of reading, but their wits being shut up in the cells of a few authors (chiefly Aristotle their dictator), as their persons were shut up in the cells of monasteries and colleges, and knowing little history, either of nature or time, ... spin out onto us ... cobwebs of learning, admirable for the fineness of thread and work, but of no substance or profit.[42]

As with Descartes when he lived in Holland, Spinoza has also been something of a nomad, though much poorer than Descartes. Only one of his books, on the innocuous subject of Descartes' geometry, has been published under his name. His major work, the Ethics, remains locked in his desk and his Tractatus Theologico-Politicus, which is a curious mixture of biblical criticism and politics, has been printed very surreptitiously. It was hoped no-one would find out its authorship, but that leaked out quickly and raised the ire of all authority, Calvinist and Jew alike, and including the up-and-coming new dictator, Prince William of Orange, the future king of England. He's banned it.

Earlier I said that Spinoza was suspected by some of being a traitor. This is because his influence has been largely among the French émigré community here and this caused him to make a mistake. He accepted the hospitality of a French general for a few weeks. The man wanted him to write a new work and dedicate it to Louis, Louis XIV. Spinoza refused and so nothing came of it, but he had to hide for three months when he returned here for having had anything to do with the French at all.

Are we ready now to go and knock on his door? The poor man must be anxious. Very few people visit him. I hear he doesn't leave his room for days at a time and lives on only a few pieces of copper a day.

– Excuse me, please. Can we have the bill?

– Yes, Sir. ... It's a nice day for late autumn, isn't it?

– It's lovely. Probably better than in London. The sea was especially choppy yesterday, when we left Harwich.

– What brings you to us, Sir?

– Ah, Doctor Spinoza. Someone's hoping to build a 40-foot telescope with lenses made by him. His fame has spread all over Europe, as you probably know.

– Ah.

– I hear he's not very well.

– I shouldn't worry, Sir. The old gentleman's been like that for years. I reckon he'll outlive us all. He lives on nothing, you see. He's as thin as a needle.

– Old? He's not that old, you know, not even quite forty-four.

– Is that so? Poor man. Personally, I have nothing against him. He harms no-one, I say, despite the tongues.

– We know nothing of that. We've only heard of his lenses. Here you are. Please keep the change.

– Oh, most generous Sir. Please come again, even if your government does join the French against us, as people say they will. And next time, if you'd want to stay for a few nights, we have excellent rooms upstairs.

– Thank you. We'll remember that. Goodbye. ...

*

**HT:** Doctor Spinoza. Good afternoon, Sir. I hope you're expecting us.

**BS:** I am, indeed. Welcome. Your letters have been most interesting.

**HT:** May I introduce my friends? They are two philosophers and a scientist who'll be writing about you. This is his lordship Bertrand Russell.

**BS:** Pleased to meet you, my lord. I can't say I've heard of you, but no-doubt the whole world will hear of you one day.

**BR:** Not in Latin, I'm sure. Please call me Bertie.

**HT:** And this is professor Roger Scruton, who's also a great fan of yours.

**BS:** Meester Scruton. Welcome.

**HT:** And this is professor Peter Atkins, a world-famous professor of physical chemistry at the university of Oxford.

**BS:** Most welcome, Sir. Please follow me. My kind landlady's put her drawing room at our service and I've prepared a pot of coffee, my own special blend for you. This way, please. Ground floor. ...

**HT:** Ah, coffee. That reminds me. We've brought you some from London. I got it from a famous shop in a village called Soho, to the west of the city. I guess you've not been to London. The shop's called the Algerian Coffee Shop.

**BS:** Algerian. Mm. Berbers. The Barbary coast. Coffee experts now. Thank you.

**HT:** And some pipe tobacco, though I suspect it's nothing like some Dutch blends, such as Holland House and Clan.

**BS:** What are they? I haven't heard of them. ... But then, I don't know everything about my own country, as small as it is. ... Thank you. Most generous. ...

**BR:** Doctor Spinoza. I'd like to say that you can relax with us. Your reputation will survive this little meeting.

**BS:** You're trying to make me complacent. Go on.

**BR:** Not at all. I've been under your spell ever since I read a book about you by Sir Frederick Pollock.

**BS:** Oh, really? I'm amazed. A book about me in London and I haven't heard of it. When was it published?

**BR:** Oh, ... Ah... I'm afraid I can't tell you, now. But your reputation's well established in London, chiefly through your correspondence with Mr Oldenburg of the Royal Society, where I'm a member myself. Personally I think you're the noblest and most lovable of the great philosophers. Ethically, you're supreme and, as a natural consequence, you are, and likely to be for a hundred years, regarded as a man of appalling wickedness.[43]

**HT:** Hold on a moment, your lordship. You're only predicting. You don't know.

**BS:** This is getting exciting. You obviously think my metaphysics is rubbish, my lord. What other appalling things are you predicting for me?

**BR:** Oh, I shouldn't worry about your metaphysics. That's the fate of nearly all metaphysics. As soon as the scientists invent precise enough instruments and methods to investigate an aspect of it, that branch either becomes rubbish, or else it becomes a new science, even a new trade. For example, you yourself have already demolished a lot of Descartes' metaphysics. Only thirty years ago, the whole world went along with him that the pineal gland was the base of the soul, just because it was at the centre of the brain and rather round and cute. It's nothing of the sort, of course. He should have first tried to prove that the soul existed at all, before trying to locate where it lived. Descartes also thought there were only three substances in the world. God, Mind and Matter. You follow Parmenides, instead, that there is only one substance, God or Nature. You say that all other things, you, me, hyenas, are mere attributes of God.

**HT:** Forgive me for intervening, here, Sir, for I'm no philosopher. But I can't resist telling you that one of Lord Russell's most brilliant students – by the name of Ludwig Wittgenstein – devastates some people with his mocking of metaphysics. He says that the best thing for any philosopher to do is to wait till someone says something metaphysical and then show that it's nonsense.

**BS:** Oh, dear. Oh, dear. I can't say I'm surprised. Teachers like my lord Bertie here ought to set better examples to their pupils. My lord, I suppose you don't believe even in God?

**BR:** In the same way as you don't believe in the soul. You believe, as I do, that our mind and consciousness are of the body and die with it. That's the deepest heresy to followers of the Abrahamic religions, isn't it.

**BS:** What other predictions do you make for me?

**BR:** The rest of it all looks good. I think that you, Descartes and young Leibniz will be remembered as the three great rationalists of this age, those who believe that mental reasoning alone can lead us to the truth of things. Opposing you will be Mr Hobbes, whom you've been reading on politics, I hear. He and his successors in England, Ireland and Scotland are likely to become known as the British school, as opposed to your Continental school of rationalists. They'll be in the direct line of succession from Democritus, empiricists, people who demand evidence for our beliefs.

**BS:** Mm. That's even more damning, but then again, I don't expect everyone to understand me immediately. Give them some time, I say.

**BR:** That's only a rough division . There will be overlaps, as always. And then, after a hundred years or so, the world will re-discover you, your ethics, I mean, and in a big way, particularly as exemplified in your way of living.

**BS:** I'm surprised you've heard of Leibniz. He came to see me only recently and spent many hours with me. He's keen and bright. But he hasn't published anything. You think he has a future, do you?

**BR:** I'm not impressed by him or his character. He's a grasper and social-climber. But he's extremely bright and knows it, and he's full of energy. He's veering towards disagreeing with you radically. I think he'll say the world has an infinite number of substances, almost like the atomists among the ancients. And he's so keen on worldly success that he'll disown all personal recollection of you, or almost all.

**HT:** May I bring in Roger Scruton here, Sir? Roger, you think very highly of Doctor Spinoza's metaphysics, don't you, as well as of his ethics?

**RS:** Yes, I do, even though I don't think it a good idea to try to prove metaphysical and ethical beliefs by resorting to Euclidian geometry. The Doctor's critics will go on ceaselessly to emphasise that weak point. But even then, I see them, the proofs, and the method, as bearing witness to his great elasticity and vigour of mind, and to his unparalleled gift for seeing far-reaching connections.[44] But first, I'd like to step back from his ethics a little and examine his metaphysics. With the bare minimum of concepts, he's concluded that the physical world is all that there is. Lord Russell here is in full agreement with that. He's also concluded that the whole system is bound by laws that relate every part of it to all other parts. But these laws can explain what we observe only if the system as a whole has an explanation, only if there's an answer to the question: why is there anything at all?

**BR:** I can see the drift of your argument, Roger. Be careful or you'll soon make him sound like a mystic. He's not a mystic. What he's really after is science. He just doesn't have the tools.

**RS:** Wait a moment, my lord, because you're not going to disagree with the gist of what I want to say. Doctor Spinoza's concluded that the cause of the world cannot exist outside it, nor can it be part of it. The world must be 'cause of itself'. In other words, its existence follows from its nature; it has to exist because there cannot exist anything that negates it. This means we can no-longer engage with ordinary science. Science, your kind of science and my kind of science, the only kind of science we all care about here, deals with one event following another. It needs the existence of Time. It cannot deduce the coming into existence of the Universe from when there was no Time. Pardon the awkwardness of my language when I say 'when there was no time'. That's clearly a contradiction in terms. What I want to say is that science comes unstuck when there is no event previous in time to the one that needs explaining. Only if we see the world 'under a certain aspect of eternity' – I'm using Doctor Spinoza's phrase here – only if we see the world under that 'certain aspect of eternity', can we hope to solve the mystery of its origins.

**BR:** But that phrase is too vague. 'Under a certain aspect of eternity'. I wish I could see it meant something real. But I can't. I do have some hope for science, though. I shouldn't be surprised if, one day, physicists and mathematicians determined the precise age of the world and even came up with an explanation of how it came to be, and why it had to be, as Benedict believes, along with some of the ancients, rather than the deepest nothingness only. I'm not sure we can dismiss science that easily.

**RS:** May I say, Doctor Spinoza, that you're superb when you say that the highest aim of Mankind ought to be to attain an intellectual love of God. I can understand you fully. This God of ours has, of course, to be, not the deity of the tribes, not the dispenser of miracles who would intervene to change the course of events that He himself has initiated, but the God who is the world, who is us all. And to attain that love, we must not only shed the superstitions of the established religions, such as God loving us back or punishing us, but our modern superstitions, too, such as putting ourselves on God's throne, worshipping ourselves. Only after we go through another disenchantment, only after we discard our present love of ourselves, can we find a new enchantment, hope to understand God, to see that we are with God and in God.

**HT:** Isn't it amazing, Roger, how widely two well-informed philosophers can differ in their analysis of the views of another? Lord Russell admires doctor Spinoza because he, his lordship, is an atheist. You, a man of faith who sometimes even calls himself a Christian, admire him just as much precisely because you're a man of faith. Yet again, another man of faith, Leibniz, who was interviewing Dr Spinoza only recently and who has even read his forthcoming, unpublished Ethics, is convinced that Doctor Spinoza is bent on nothing less than the wholesale destruction of all faith and working towards the universal revolution that Leibniz thinks threatens Europe.[45] I must say: the combination of you all makes me feel a little depressed. How can anyone be sure they know their Spinoza? The doctor himself says he's no atheist. Leibniz accuses him of precisely that. Another contradicts himself by calling him 'that God-intoxicated atheist'. The churches and synagogues who ought to love him have banned his works. What does he actually say?

**BR:** You might say 'God only knows what he says'. Ha, ha, ha, ha. But let me bring us down to earth for a moment. Benedict, you follow Mr Hobbes in believing in an authoritarian state, to the extent that we must never rebel against the worst of sovereigns. But you also say that the citizen must not give up all his rights. You say that freedom of speech is particularly important. There are some contradictions here which you need to reconcile. Another recommendation of yours is that the state be the responsible authority for determining religious doctrine, not the churches. Nor are you quite convincing that we human beings have an appreciate amount of free will when all our decisions and all events in the world, down to the flight of an insect, have previously been dictated by God or Nature. …

**HT:** Talking about Nature, we've got a modern scientist here among us and I've not brought him in yet. Peter, what do you think? You're much more up-beat about what lies in store for the scientists than for the philosophers, aren't you?

**PA:** Yes I am, or at least optimistic. Science – or rather, the scientific method – is the only way we have for achieving reliable knowledge and its range of applications is without bounds. Just think how much we have achieved over the past 30 years. Indeed, science has achieved more in the past 300 years that humanity did over the previous 3000 years. The technological advances that spring from science are extraordinary and seemingly unstoppable. It sometimes looks as if the world changes overnight. Who would have thought 30 years ago that today, most people would have a small box of tricks that enable them to speak to – and see – people on the other side of the world at the touch of a button? But the intellectual advance that has been driven by the scientific method is even more extraordinary on the scale of the very small, the very large, the very short and the very long. What other mode of endeavour can claim so much success? And we optimists – all scientists should be optimists, driven by the expectation of elucidation – are hopeful of answering all those questions that continue to stump philosophers. Yes, it's optimism that distinguishes scientists from philosophers, who in the main take a pessimistic view of the possibility of achieving an understanding of the deep questions of existence. Theologians, of course, are even worse: they pile obscurity on to pessimism and consider that we should stand in awe at the prospect of the unknowable, rather than beaver away to reach comprehension, or they naively claim that comprehension will come only when we are dead and our brains cease to be a barrier to understanding. Confidence in the scientific method is growing all the time. Just last year, 2013, for instance, the prediction of the existence of the Higgs boson was confirmed. It's quite extraordinary, in my view, how scribblings on a piece of paper are found to match the real world.

**BS:** Did I hear you well, Professor Atkins? Among other strange things you just said, I heard you say: 'last year, 2013'.

**PA:** Oh, oh, … I'm sorry, Sir. You must have misheard me. … Or, or, or was it a slip of the tongue on my part? …

**HT:** Peter, another friend of ours, the philosopher Raymond Tallis, who's also a scientist, disagrees with you rather vehemently, doesn't he? He thinks scientists still need philosophers to show them the limitations of the scientific method. He's argued with you that science has not made any progress – nor can it ever make progress – in understanding either human consciousness or the nature of Time. But you sound confident it can.

**PA:** Yes, I am confident, or at least optimistic: We're already simulating little bits of conscious activity and time itself isn't much of a problem, once you disregard out perception of it. I think Raymond, whom Doctor Spinoza has probably not yet met, has his proposition inverted: it is philosophers who need scientists to show them the limitless power of the scientific method. By all means, let philosophers, with their clarity of thought and often witty exposition, examine moral and ethical problems, but they have no role to play in the discovery of the fabric of reality. Even the greatest waste their time when they sit in an armchair and consider that they can discover the nature of the universe just by thinking about it. That's what the Greeks did millennia ago – we have come a long way since then. It is also what doctor Spinoza has done here. Simply by thinking, without appealing to deeply probing experiment, he has come to the conclusion that the universe is made up of just one substance, which he calls God/Nature but just as well might have called it anything. His conclusion if well-meaning, but meaningless. He's trying to be a scientist, but doesn't know how. He simply hasn't got the right tools and his conclusions are merely engaging musings, like most pre-modern philosophy and certainly all theology. The right tools are observation, experiment, measurement, tests, and public sharing of interpretations, all set in a mutually supportive reticulation of concepts. When he says that the universe is made of one substance, he's making a scientific statement, but the remark is meaningless, unless he means by that one substance, not God/Nature, but mathematics. Then he might be right. Oh dear, I must confess I'm beginning to shock myself.[46]

**BS:** ... ...

**HT:** Doctor Spinoza. Are you all right? ... Doctor Spinoza? ... Sir? ...

**BS:** ... I ... I'm afraid I'm not well. Could you ... Could you perhaps come back another day. I'm very sorry about this. ...

**HT:** No, no, Sir. We understand. We understand completely. It's us who ought to apologise. I'm terribly, terribly sorry that we seem to have unsettled you. Goodbye, Sir. It's been a real honour. We'll be in touch. We'll be at the inn, round the corner, in case you'd like to see us again. Goodbye.

\*

Understandably, Spinoza never called for us back. His lungs were deteriorating rapidly. He died a few months later, on February 21, 1677, at the age of forty-four years and four months. He died from tuberculosis made worse by years of inhaling microscopic filaments of glass. But until his last moments, he remained composed and tried to appear cheerful to those around him.

On the morning of his death, a doctor recommended that his landlady prepare a broth of chicken for him. He ate of the broth and enjoyed it. So the landlady and her family relaxed and went out. When they returned in the afternoon, they found he had died. His possessions, including his books and his manuscripts, locked inside his desk, barely paid for his rent and doctor's fees.

His passing was mourned deeply by all those who knew him, even those who disagreed with his rejection of traditional religion, for they could not fault his frugal lifestyle, his kindly manners, his avoidance of sensual pleasures and lack of malice towards those who had denounced him. Thus a throng of admirers risked their respectability in a Calvinist society by turning up for his funeral. The procession included six carriages belonging to eminent figures in the city and beyond. He was buried in the grounds of a church.

His philosophical admirers worked intensely over many months to publish his remaining works before the year was out, at considerable risk to their reputations and careers, if not their safety. They would continue to champion the thoughts of the man who had preferred to live in obscure penury rather than be a rich and honoured professor of philosophy at the university of Heidelberg. He had declined the honour – and the comfortable living that the position offered – because it had required him to avoid teaching philosophy of a controversial nature. But he had placed integrity on a higher level and preferred to leave posterity a legacy of a different kind.

The posthumous publications set in motion an even more vociferous campaign of vilification against Spinoza. Descartes had been bad enough, even though he had said that the existence of God could be proved through mathematics. This 'little Jew', as Voltaire would call him a century later, took liberties with everything:

> Then a little Jew, with a long nose and wan complexion,
> Poor, but satisfied, thoughtful and solitary,
> Spirit subtle and hollow, less read than celebrated,
> Hidden beneath the mantle of Descartes, his master,
> Walking with measured tread, approached the great Being.
> Excuse me, he said, speaking very low.
> But I think, between ourselves, that you don't exist.

Voltaire was right in one respect. He, like many others, had not read Spinoza first-hand, or at least not much, but learned of him through his denigrators. This is partly because Spinoza's preference for resorting to the methods of Euclid to prove the truth of his beliefs made him hard to follow. Furthermore, his central claim that God and Nature were one and the same, that there was only one substance in existence, stood the opposite of our daily observation of enormous and radical diversity in the world. As my friend Peter Cave describes it with his characteristic wit, Spinoza's doctrine rules out pigeons, pebbles and people as substances – as indeed, it rules out the universe itself as a substance distinct from, yet created by, God. Thus, Descartes and many others are rejected.[47]

I love Spinoza for wholly different reasons. As a fellow human being, I share his longing for a greater purpose to my existence than those I fashion for myself, and I cannot but admire enormously his courage in demanding the dignity of being allowed to be true to himself. I share his pain, while I sympathise with him in his loneliness, his ill health, his poverty, the generosity he displayed towards others despite owning so little. His nobility of spirit is difficult to match, but a model to admire and emulate.

Quite clearly, Spinoza's God is not the God of the Judaic religions, nor even the more obtuse Mazda of Zoroastrians, the deities of the baggage of eras, the ancestral godfathers of tribes, grumpy grandfathers grown too old and too grand to appear any longer among us children. In my moments of weakness, and reluctant to invent new words a la Heidegger and others, I choose to identify Spinoza's God with that mystery of mysteries that is going probably never to be solved by the scientists, despite my friend Peter Atkins's strong hopes. That mystery is, to me, why things exist at all, why there is no oblivion instead, an oblivion so utter that even the rule of oblivion itself could not exist. Every atom in my body cries out that nothing ought to exist. Yet there is existence everywhere around us, and there is, lately in us humans, love and altruism, language and insight, the ecstasy of the art and the rapture in virtually every moment of consciousness, of the red glow of dawn and of the smell of mint. Then there is the reverence I feel for the Spinozas of my species, no matter how misled they were by the limited evidence of their senses and the shortcomings of their blunt tools.

I choose to interpret Spinoza's exhortation that we love God intellectually with equal indulgence. He meant to say, I tell myself, that we should try to follow the latest findings of the science of our time, from the minutest scale of a quark called Charm to the grandest of the multi-verses, if indeed their existence be proved right. We are told by the mathematicians that all came out of nothing, Absolute Nothing, as Peter Atkins spells it in higher cases. But how can that be? Surely there was something before that primordial explosion that had the potential of giving rise to the explosion? How naïve, someone will shout. There was no 'before' prior to the Bang, because there was no Time before then. Time only came into being afterwards. I do not believe it, because I would go mad if I did.

The mere posing of such questions, the thrill of their contemplation, may not be as overpowering as 'religious experience' in the superstitious Middle Ages, but it is breath-taking, nevertheless, and so I come close to understanding why Spinoza compared the pursuit of knowledge, the quest after a truer understanding of the world, to coming face to face with 'God' as reported by prophets, visionaries, mystics, and mad men.

I do not wish to resort to quoting mystics in connexion with Spinoza or any other of the great ones among our ancestors. I grew out of mystics – including my own revered and much-loved father – a long time ago. I do not wish to provide free fodder for their cults. But a line from the preamble of Rumi's

Masnavi comes to my mind (it was my late father's favourite):

Har kasi az zanne khod shod yāre mann:
Az darūne mann najost asrāre mann.

All saw in me their own likenesses.
None heard the cry supressed in my heart.[48]

This seems to me to apply to many of the writers who have pronounced on Spinoza over the years. My favourite among them is one of the most recent, Margaret Gullan-Whur of University College, London. So let me end this short essay with the last paragraph of her book, Within Reason: A Life of Spinoza:

> Coleridge, who rejected much of Spinoza's doctrine, underscored, as I do, the value of this concept: 'How can common truths be made permanently interesting, but by being bottomed on our common nature?' Spinoza, denying anthropocentric understanding any epistemic merit if this consisted merely in a convergence of unreasoned human agreement, proposed instead an heuristic based on the belief that we learn most surely from what is common to all bodies, and that this interrelatedness extends beyond the commonality of merely human nature. This immense and entirely non-parochial philosophical bequest, generated by a physically fragile individual struggling to cope with alienation, grief, sickness and obsession in a small corner of seventeenth-century Europe, remains neglected by our – only partially differently – fragmented society.[49]

# Beethoven

*The philosopher god of the arts, but also the greatest man who ever lived?*

50

Music is a higher revelation than all wisdom and philosophy. Music is the electrical soil in which the spirit lives, thinks and invents.

Recommend to your children virtues that, alone, can make them happy, not money.

My misfortune is doubly painful because it causes me to be misunderstood.

For me, there can be no enjoyment in company, no intelligent conversation, no exchange of information with peers; only the most pressing needs can make me venture into society. I have to live as an outcast.

I will take fate by the throat; it will not bend me to its will.

\*

Over the years, I have had to ration myself to Beethoven's music for fear of its becoming too familiar. I listen to him only several times a year. I need to see him with fresh eyes each time. In the absence of God, in some bleak moments, only Beethoven can fill my eyes with tears, give meaning to my life, make me wish to embrace every man or woman I encounter on the streets. I must not become accustomed to his voice. That would leave me far too poor.

But he is not everyone's favourite composer. Some, who identify him only with the most rousing passages in his 'heroic' symphonies and concertos, denounce him as bombastic. While this may in part be due to their personal temperaments, most of this group of listeners have, I believe, not given themselves time to know his music better. They prefer the consistently elegant compositions of Mozart and Haydn who invoke only pure beauty. But there is much in Beethoven that is also elegant, quiet, subtle, lovely. As with a great continent, his output is too vast and too varied for generalisations – his works are often stylistically disparate from one instance to the next – and, in invoking beauty, the man who wrote the most loved piano sonata in the world, the 'Moonlight', is surely unsurpassed. It could not be otherwise. Beethoven was one of the most colossal talents of all history, certainly the greatest in music, and he was a thinker. He also wrote from the heart and was of a fragile, supersensitive nature. Apart from those compositions he wrote to commission, those of his works that have survived into the modern repertory reflect his mood of the day, as well as the humanistic dreams of his class of intellectuals at the dawn of a new, optimistic industrial and scientific age. Being human and, moreover, a man whose life was a long defiance of physical pain and loneliness, lived amidst poverty, disease, discrimination and war, his moods swung from one extreme to another, to the extent that some have suggested – mistakenly, I think – that he suffered from bipolar disorder, or madness at times.

To go as far as describing Beethoven – who did have his feet of clay – as the greatest man who ever walked on the planet is to invite ridicule, of course. It is a meaningless, theatrical hyperbole. There is no general agreement on how to define greatness. But I shall persist, and there are probably millions of others who, on reflection, might be tempted to share that soft-headed, arguable opinion with me.

Furthermore, Beethoven's grip on the daily life of the planet continues to strengthen. His language is the universal language of music. Unlike the words of a Homer or Shakespeare, our other gods, it does not date and does not need translating. He breaks new barriers every day. For over two centuries, with the growth of the middle classes in the nineteenth century and the spread of the gramophone and broadcasting in the twentieth, the sea of his devotees in the West has spread steadily, while elsewhere in the world – possibly with Mozart and Bach trailing behind him – he is the only Western artist that has made such culturally far-flung lands as China and Japan his own. For many among that vast crowd of billions, he is the chief god we have, despite his feet of clay.

*

Beethoven's life is too well known – and too easily accessible elsewhere – for me to recount here in detail. I shall, instead, focus on those aspects of it that made him what he was, and which make clear what a heroic will he had to assert often to overcome the many hardships and injustices that plagued his way. I shall rely on the latest scholarship, which is still developing after two centuries, and the more obscure facts that may have escaped the reader. The topics include what we know of his most anguished love affair with Josephine von Brunsvik.

I shall also describe, briefly, the three stylistic periods in Beethoven's music, as well as recall a most privileged moment in my own life with regard to Beethoven, when I came possibly as close to being physically alone with him as is possible in our time.

From the day in 1778 when he gave his first public performance at the age of seven[51], the pressure was on little Ludwig van Beethoven to 'become the next Mozart'. His first three piano sonatas were published when he was eleven and a master painter chose – or was commissioned – to paint a portrait of him in oil when he was twelve. In that portrait, we see a distinctly ugly boy with a broken nose, streaks of blond hair and dark eyes that are too large for his small face. He seems disturbingly too wise for his age. He does not smile. This boy has witnessed suffering too early. We see a grown-up market trader who does not expect kindness for its own sake. But we also see a boy who knows he is special. He looks down on his portraitist. Outside the painter's studio in the provincial capital of Bonn in the Rhine valley, we hear that his alcoholic father sees him as his only hope to wealth. They say he locks the boy in a room for up to eight hours a day to force him practice, on the violin.

The boy's grandfather, Lodewijk, a Dutch immigrant of Spanish descent, has risen to be director of music or Kapellmeister at the court of Prince Clemens August. But the prince is miserly in treating his servants and so the Kapellmeister has developed a wine merchant's business on the side. This enables him to hold his head high on the streets and to subsidise the life of his only son, Johann, a tenor in the orchestra. Johann is morose and falls into fits of depression. He is young Ludwig's first teacher. But seeing the child's startling talent early, the family soon employs more prestigious teachers to train him. These include the court organist Christian Gottlob Neefe, who, apart from teaching his young charge musical theory, also instils in him a love of the classics, the philosophers and the poets, a love that will last him all his life. Most importantly, all this happens in the heady years immediately after the

French revolution. The whole of Europe, is ablaze with the ideals of equality and the injustice of being subject to parasitic aristocrats. This is particularly so in the Rhine Valley, which is next door to France and has for some time looked up to Paris as the intellectual capital of the world.

Young Ludwig soon begins to work as a viola player in the orchestra and observes what makes a particular composition succeed or a fail. He impresses the royal eye with his own virtuoso playing and compositions, so that when he is 16, he is sent to Vienna, with a letter of introduction from the prince himself, to be a student with the great Mozart. But he stays there only a few weeks or months and returns home to be with his mother in her last months of tuberculosis. He stays in Bonn for five years after her death to look after his two younger brothers. With his grandfather also dead now and his father quite unable to act responsibly, he has to go to court to claim half the man's salary to help him feed his brothers.

Most scholars believe that Mozart, while impressed greatly by the young man's talent, had not been able to accept him as a student because he, Mozart, was overwhelmed by work and becoming clearly ill. It sounds convincing. Beethoven never met Mozart again, but held him in deep reverence for the rest of his life. When he returned to Vienna in 1892, armed with another clutch of princely recommendations and a small stipend, Mozart had died a year earlier.

While still at home, Beethoven had met the second-most revered composer of the day, Joseph Haydn, who had been on his way to London for his first long residence there. Haydn had met him again on his return from England and promised to teach him in Vienna. Thus when the young student arrived in the glittering capital of the Austrian Empire, the musical capital of the world, all door were flung open to him. Despite a provincial accent and somewhat rough manners – made worse by only a modest height and an arrogance born of insecurity – his seemingly divine command of the piano soon dazzled all. Half the women, young and old, of the aristocratic houses which competed for his presence at their soirées could, in the coming years, be said to be in love with him. On one occasion at the palace of Prince Lichnowsky in the late 1790s, we hear that the elderly 'Countess Thun went on her knees in front of Beethoven who reclined on the sofa, begging of him to play something, which he refused to do'.

There is yet another story that shows the extent of his adoration by his public. It is said that at the end of some recitals, when he had reduced many women in the hall to weeping, he would suddenly throw up his hands in the air and burst out laughing at them.

But a key factor in his survival in his new city – where an estimated 300 pianists competed desperately for the favours of the educated classes – was acquiring new sponsors at the highest level of society, the level of the archdukes and the princes. Among these were Archduke Rudolph, the emperor's youngest son who took lessons from him on composition and dedicated one of his own works to Beethoven, and the Russian ambassador, Count Andreas, later Prince, Razumovsky, to whom Beethoven dedicated his opus 59 string quartets. They made certain he did not need to succumb to the efforts of the king of Westphalia – a brother of the French emperor Napoleon – who wanted to poach him for the prestige of his own court.

Despite the sponsorships, however, and despite his growing income from the sale of his compositions all over Europe and revenue from concerts, Beethoven was always short of money, to the extent of having to borrow money to survive. This was partly due to his having to keep up appearances among his new friends. It was also due to his developing a taste for the good gifts of life, such as expensive wines, spending months every summer in the more agreeable climate of Hungarian spa towns, and hiring his own apartment in order to escape the stifling atmosphere of palaces whose protocols caused him to throw tantrums. These had forced Archduke Rudolph to issue a circular to his palace staff that Beethoven could behave in whatever manner he wished while at the palace.

Beethoven loved and hated it, but mostly loved it. For years he even let pass a rumour that he was himself a nobleman, albeit the illegitimate son of the king of Bavaria in whose palace his mother had served. Eventually, he refuted it, asserting that his mother has been a woman of 'complete integrity', but he allowed it to persist far too long. Certainly his two younger brothers, with whom he had a stormy relationship because he disapproved of their wives, felt at times that he had deserted them, that he had fallen completely under the spell of his new friends.

In his painful 'Heiligenstadt Testament', the letter of 1802 to his brothers where he contemplated suicide, he refuted the charge and, later, he brought them both to Vienna to act as his business assistants. But his wooing of the wealthy really did constitute one of the weaker sides of his personality. If we knew more of his life than we do, perhaps we would find it easier to forgive him for it.

One central cause of his depressions was, of course, his growing deafness. Coming on top of his abdominal pains that had afflicted him in his mid-twenties, this was one affliction that, of all people, musicians needed least. Furthermore, it was worse that deafness as generally imagined: a total silence. It began as a severe form of tinnitus, a loud ringing in his head through which he had to imagine the music he was composing. Eventually, it did become a total inability to hear sound, from around the age of 35, when he had to resort of 'conversation books'. These were notebooks in which his visitors wrote their questions or statements, which necessarily meant that he was confined only to practical or basic exchanges with his friends. For a man who was gregarious by nature and who had been among the foremost intellectuals of his time, this was a most abominable loss.

Yet another cause of frustration was that most of the women with whom he fell in love either rejected him before marrying wealthier titled men, or were, else, forced by their families to reject him for his lack of noble blood. Among the hundreds of letters that have survived into our time from Beethoven, there is a dearth of love letters. Understandably so, for they could have compromised the reputations of their recipients. But 13 letters have survived that are clearly addressed to the tragic Countess Deym, Josephine von Brunsvik, who was one of his most devoted students. Another, the much-studied 'Immortal Beloved' letter of July 1812, does not mention to whom it is addressed. It was found among Beethoven's belongings after his death, with the possibility that it was never posted, or that it was returned to him. It is a harrowing letter, hurriedly-written, over three days while Beethoven was in the Bohemian spa town of Teplitz, waiting for the mail coach to arrive. Beethoven tells the lady that he is aware of her suffering and that, soon, after his return, they would find a way of living together. It is worth quoting in large chunks to show the confused, even traumatised, state of his mind at the time:

> My angel, my everything, my very self. – only a few words today, and in pencil (yours) – I shall not be certain of my rooms here until tomorrow – what an unnecessary waste of time – why this deep grief, where necessity speaks – can our love exist but by sacrifices, by not demanding everything. Can you change it, that you are not completely mine, that I am not completely yours? Oh God, look upon beautiful Nature and calm your mind about what must be – love demands everything and completely with good reason, <u>that is how it is for me with you, and for you with me</u> – only you forget too easily, that I must live for myself and <u>for you as well</u>, if we were wholly united, you would not feel this as painfully, just as little as I would …
>
> We will probably see each other soon, … Oh – There are moments when I feel that language is nothing at all – cheer up – remain my faithful only darling, my everything, as I for you, the rest is up to the gods, what must be for us and what is in store for us. … You are suffering, you my dearest creature … Oh, wherever I am, you are with me, I talk to myself and to you, arrange it that I can live with you. What a life…. as it is…. without you … I weep when I think that you will probably not receive news of me until Saturday. However as much as you love me – I love you even more deeply, but – but never hide yourself from me … Oh God – so near. so far. Is not our love a true edifice in Heaven – but also

as firm as the firmament. ...

While still in bed my thoughts turn towards you my Immortal Beloved, now and then happy, then sad again, waiting whether fate might answer us – I can only live either wholly with you or not at all, yes I have resolved to stray about in the distance, until I can fly into your arms, and send my soul embraced by you into the realm of the Spirits – yes unfortunately it must be – you will compose yourself all the more since you know my faithfulness to you, never can another own my heart, never – never ...

– O God why do I have to separate from someone whom I love so much, and yet my life in V[ienna] as it is now is a miserable life – Your love makes me at once most happy and most unhappy – at my age I would now need some ... regularity .... can this exist in our relationship? ... be patient – only through quiet contemplation of our existence can we achieve our purpose to live together ... Be calm; for only by calmly considering our lives can we achieve our purpose of living together. – be calm – love me – today – yesterday – What yearning with tears for you – you – you my life – my everything – farewell – oh continue to love me – never misjudge the most faithful heart of your Beloved
Forever thine
forever mine
forever us.[52]

One Beethoven specialist, Maynard Solomon, believes it more likely that the object of Beethoven's adoration in this particular letter was not Josephine von Brunsvik, but Antonie Brentano, the wife of a Frankfurt merchant and friend of Beethoven. A possible miniature portrait of her was found in a concealed drawer after Beethoven's death. But although she had married only out of obedience to her father and was probably still unhappy after producing several children, she was not so unusually desperate as to justify the description in the letter. To be seen as the cause of her separation and loss of custody of her children would have also stamped a strong social stigma on Beethoven's head. By contrast, Josephine von Brunsvik had, at the time, separated from her second, disastrous husband and was in financial difficulty. It seems unlikely that her mother would have again vetoed a union between her and Beethoven.

A puzzle is why, after writing such a passionate letter and making ardent promises to end her suffering soon, Beethoven decided not to return to Vienna until September. Could it be that, on long reflection, he decided that his art was more important to him than his personal happiness, that Josephine was now too needy and too depressed not to require all his time? Unlike Solomon and his supporters, most scholars think of Josephine as the most likely candidate as the recipient of the Immortal Beloved letter, even though they have less forensic evidence to show than Solomon has detected in his researches. For whatever little it is worth, I belong to their camp.

In any case, even if Brentano was the addressee of the letter of July 1812, the fact remains that Josephine von Brunsvik was the main love of Beethoven's life. His relationship with her lasted for about five years before it was ended in 1809 on the orders of her mother, far longer than the nine months from the autumn of 1811 to the summer of 1812 implied in the Immortal Beloved letter.[53] Two moving excerpts from the later diary of Josephine's elder sister, Therese, bear witness to it:

'Beethoven. It is like a dream, that he was the friend, the confidant of our house – a beautiful mind. Why did not my sister Josephine, as widow Deym, take him as her husband? Josephine's soul-mate. They were born for each other. She would have been happier with him than with Stackelberg. Maternal affection made her forgo her own happiness'. ...

'I was so lucky to have been acquainted with Beethoven, intimately and intellectually, for so many years. Josephine's intimate friend, her soul mate. They were born for each other, and if both were still alive, they would be united'.

Whatever the details of all the letters, though, Beethoven's constant search for, and continued failure to find, a suitable wife deepened the calamity of his deafness. Debt, the fickleness of some sponsors, the cold reception by the public of some of his innovative compositions, and a long, costly legal wrangle over the custody of his young nephew Karl, whom he wished to make his own son, were other causes of anguish. By the end, in the half-dozen years before he died in March 1827 at the age of only 56, he was at times a nervous ruin, neglecting his appearance, talking to himself in the streets, forgetting to pay for his restaurant meals, losing his temper with loyal friends, fearing that the whole world was plotting against him.

Yet fortunately, there were also times of frivolity and elation. In his 'late period', the last dozen years of his life, he was regarded everywhere as the greatest living composer of Europe and, of course, the whole world. For example, the Philharmonic Society of London made him an advance payment of £50 for his next symphony – which was to be the unsurpassed Ninth, the Choral –, the king of France awarded him a gold medal that was 'a large chunk of gold', and the Royal Swedish Academy of Music granted him honorary membership. He also had a growing circle of devoted friends – including useful sycophants ready to run errands for him. These crowded around him at every opportunity to entertain him or represent him in negotiations with publishers, etc. For their mid-day meal, they would gather at a tavern and were sometimes worried by Beethoven's outspoken criticism of the government, even of the emperor himself. This was during a reign of terror instituted by chancellor Metternich and his omnipresent secret police.

Sometimes in these years, he would make a little fool of himself in his enthusiasm. A singer, Madame Schroder-Devrient, many years later recalled that once:

> The last rehearsals were set when I heard that Beethoven had asked for the honour of conducting the work himself to celebrate the day. With a wild expression and unearthly inspired eyes, waving his baton back and forth with violence, he stood in the middle of the musicians and didn't hear a note. The inevitable happened. The deaf master threw the singers and the orchestra completely off the beat and into the greatest confusion. No one knew any longer where they were.[54]

In those years – in fact, throughout his career – Beethoven was also pursued everywhere by portrait painters, including ones commissioned by archdukes, and even wax impressions of his face were made to give posterity an exact likeness of him. In short, he was adored by tens of thousands of ordinary lovers of music and revered by the best among the educated of Europe, with the odd exception, of course, of a Goethe or Hegel who refused to divert their gaze from the past. His old master and mentor Haydn is said to have been jealous of him. But this seems exaggerated. Hayden in fact took pride in him as a musical son and seems to have been quite convinced of his superiority over himself.

Beethoven's last three months were particularly excruciating, with hugely swollen feet suggesting kidney failure and extreme abdominal pain that made him bend over. Such diseases as lead poisoning, syphilis and hepatitis A can be ruled out, even though the latter might explain the serious damage to the liver that was found during his autopsy. Alcohol poisoning is more likely to have been the cause of the latter damage, for he routinely had a bottle of wine with every meal in his last years. Having read all that has been written about his illnesses, one is tempted to incline towards a combination of alcoholism and an infection that affected his kidneys in December 1816 as the immediate cause of death. Eventually he died in a coma during a thunderstorm. His gradually deepening deafness that became serious around 1800, when he reached the age of 30, may well have been due to an immunological defect, or so at least it appears from studying modern medical opinion.

In those three months of acute illness, when his doctors would forbid him alcohol, he made periodic recoveries and was again his usual, lucid self. During one such remission, he was told that the Philharmonic Society in London (the present Royal Philharmonic Society) had sent him a gift of £100 towards his medical costs[55]. He sent them a grateful message and the orchestra promised them another symphony or an overture on his recovery. On another occasion he sent another message to London saying that he hoped, one day, 'to make a success of my life, after all.'

A brutal question poses itself for us here. Now that Beethoven's whole-life suffering is nearly two centuries in the past, would we wish it to have been less painful to him, apart from the agony of his non-productive last three months, of course? Would the whole of humanity for millennia not have been the loser if he had found happiness in love, or had been cured of deafness? Surely it is possible that he might have been diverted by domestic contentment from expressing his pain in his music. Recalling his occasional failings, yet another question confronts us. To what extent should we forgive great artists their moral deficiencies? Are we perfect ourselves? It is an issue that will inflict itself on Mankind for as long as civilisation survives.

*

In the spring of 1983, I found myself in a London hospital struck down with a brain tumour. By coincidence, the editor of The Times, Charles Douglas-Home, who had recruited me to write on the Middle East for him, was also being treated there and so, feeling sorry for me and my young family, he visited me on some evenings to reassure me that I would not die. He was in much greater pain than I was, from what he said was sciatica, and walked with a crutch. In fact, he was suffering from cancer which killed him a couple of years later. He took a Walkman cassette player out of his pocket and said that he was being sustained by Beethoven's piano sonatas. At that time I had not really discovered these, for I had been taking cello lessons[56] and concentrating my efforts in that direction. I nodded, as if I was familiar with all of them, and merely said that I knew the pianist Stephen Bishop – more commonly known as Stephen Kovacevich and hailed as one of the greatest interpreters of Beethoven in modern times.[57] This impressed 'Charlie' enough, though he said that he preferred Alfred Brendel when it came to Beethoven.[58]

I am grateful to Charlie for implanting in my mind the idea that the piano sonatas – of which there are 32 – might be a greater achievement than the string quartets, of which there are 16 (according to Beethoven, that is, but 16 ½, according to me.). I cannot say that I am wholly convinced, but after Charlie's death, I remembered his remark and turned to the sonatas. Since then, they have helped to sustain me, too, alongside the quartets, through some dark corridors of my own.

They were written over the whole length of Beethoven's productive life, and so display the enormous range of his experimenting and developing, though most musicologists are not fond of classifying his music according to style, such as the traditional classic, Romantic or Heroic. Instead, they prefer to divide his creative life roughly into three periods, the Early, Middle and Late.

Yet, being mere admirers without a reputation for accuracy to defend, we can allow ourselves the liberty of doing so and even go further, announce that we love Beethoven the more for writing inspirational, rousing, 'heroic' music. We can see that until about the middle of 1803, when he is 32 years of age and begins to accept that he is going deaf, young Beethoven remains under the spell of Mozart and Hayden. While he is showing signs of diverging from his idols to find his own feet, he is still not confident enough to be radically different from them. Or perhaps he has not had time to decide who he is. This is most obvious in his first two symphonies. To this period also belong the set of six string quartets of Opus 18, the first two piano concertos and the first dozen piano concertos, including the much loved Pathétique, Opus 13.

But then listen to symphony number 3 of 1804-5 and suddenly a dazzling new sun has been born. The 'Eroica' symphony, twice as long as the innumerable symphonies of Mozart and Haydn, many of which were scarcely distinguishable from one another, shocks the old wigs and makes them sway their heads in disbelief, also no doubt muttering 'republican', 'ungrateful', 'traitor', for it was known that Beethoven had meant to dedicate it to 'the enemy', Bonaparte. On hearing in May 1804 that the First Consul of France had declared himself an emperor, a monarch, Beethoven had scratched out the dedication, but still published it as 'A heroic symphony: In memory of a (once) great man'. Now disillusioned with revolutionaries, Beethoven dedicated the result of his latest toil to his friend Prince Lobkowitz and received the fee that he would otherwise have lost. It received only a lukewarm reception in Vienna in 1805, but nearer our time, Leonard Bernstein described its first two movements as 'perhaps the greatest in all symphonic music'. If you wish to be lifted to the seventh heaven, the quickest route may well be to turn to the Eroica.

This is the start of the Middle Period of a dozen years or so until 1815, produced such other heroic symphonies as the 5th and the last three piano concertos. But it also produced such distinctly unheroic symphony as the 6th, the Pastoral, or the lyric 7th and the playful 8th. It coincided with the turmoil of the long and tearful love affair with Josephine von Brunsvik, as well as the occupation and bombardment of Vienna by the French. It was hugely productive despite the upheavals, or perhaps because of them. The Earth was moving around society's ears, and around Beethoven's in particular. His chief friend and sponsor, Archduke Rudolph, had to abandon the city for a time, other sponsors died or returned to Russia, the French occupation made certain that the first staging of his only opera, Fidelio, was a failure.

The Late Period is depicted as the last dozen years or so of his life. While some German musical journals were by then tempted to write him off as a spent force, he rose to astound them with such immense and epoch-making efforts as the 9th symphony, the Missa Solemnis (for Archduke Rudolph), the last five piano sonatas and the last string quartets. In them all, we hear the message that humans are special, that we are fragile and vulnerable and yet, able to rise to aspire to sacredness as much as a broad, non-dogmatic interpretation of that word would permit. Beethoven the old man is now a biblical prophet preaching through music, albeit a prophet of uncertain religion, but one who is convinced that there is an impenetrable mystery at the root of the question why we are here. He calls that mystery God.

*

The reader will hopefully forgive me here if I recall a moment of special elation in my life with regard to Beethoven, for I once came as close as it is possible in our time to being in his physical presence. It happened in 1992. For the first time since it had been sent to him as a gift, 'the most valuable piano in the world', certainly the most prized possession of Beethoven's life and the intimate companion of his unhappiest last years, was returning home to England for repairs and I found myself, unexpectedly and unofficially, being asked by a group of BBC journalists to photograph it for their house journal. In the few minutes I was left alone with the instrument, I was so overcome emotionally by the silence and nearness of Beethoven that I could not resist placing my right palm on the keys, keys that my idol had pressed in the myriad moments of his own loneliness.

A word is appropriate on what 'the Broadwood' meant to Beethoven and on its history since. In the spring of 1818, the English piano maker Thomas Broadwood visited Beethoven in Vienna, almost as a pilgrim visits a living saint. On his return to England, Broadwood commissioned five musicians to go round his factory and choose the best. This being done, the musicians' names were engraved inside the pianoforte and the instrument was sent by sea to Trieste, and whence by cart to Vienna, where it arrived slightly damaged. The voyage had taken eight months.

Much sturdier than the Viennese pianos Beethoven had hitherto possessed, it immediately became the star exhibition of his apartment. It is said that he played it so violently – in the hope of hearing at least its vibrations – that the instrument was unplayable a year or two later. Beethoven himself would not have known that. It is the subject of an evocative watercolour painting of his room a few days before his death.

The piano found its way to Liszt some 20 years after Beethoven's death, by which time it had been surpassed by more modern instruments. He took it to his great house in Weimar as revered relic of Beethoven. After his death, it was given to the national museum of Hungary where it has been on display since.

Returning to Beethoven, it is tempting to believe that if he had lived beyond his mere 56 years, he might have created even more astounding works. This is, of course, possible, for nothing about Beethoven should surprise anyone. But, fortunately for us, I do not believe that we would have seen any new creation by him that would have enriched us significantly beyond the gifts he has bestowed on us, as of now. We know that he planned to write at least one more symphony and one more opera. But that symphony would have, in all likelihood, been in a style we already have of him, a choral one, for example, like the 9th, or another pastoral, as with the 6th. It might even have been another heroic symphony, as with the 5th. As for operas, for many years, especially after the last and highly successful revision of Fidelio, he had searched exhaustively for a subject that inspired him, but failed.

Thus we can rejoice that his legacy is on a vast scale and feel rather confident that he would not have been able to change the course of musical history a second time. It is sometimes said – was it Bertrand Russell? – that all philosophy is footnotes to Greek philosophy. I believe that all music after Beethoven – if it does not aspire to his example, as do, for example, the creations of Schubert, Brahms and Richard Straus – is mere entertainment. After hearing Beethoven's last string quartet of the winter of 1825, the Opus 131 in C sharp minor, Schubert is reported to have been so overwhelmed that he asked: 'After this, what is there left for us to write? And when Schubert himself was about to die, five days before his death, his last musical wish was that, not one of his own great quartets, but Beethoven's Opus 131 be played to him.

# Darwin

*The unpromising boy who became the most famous Englishman of all time*

59

To my deep mortification, my father once said to me, 'You care for nothing but shooting, dogs and rat catching, and you will be a disgrace to yourself and all your family'. But my father, who was the kindest man I ever knew and whose memory I love with all my heart, must have been angry and somewhat unjust when he said such words.[60]

I have heard it said that the success of a work abroad is the best test of its enduring value. I doubt whether this is at all trustworthy, but judged by this standard my name ought to live for a few years.[61]

It is dogged as does it.

*

I know that I ought to be ashamed of admitting this, but I am not. I believe that, as the sins of the father should not be met upon the children, neither should his glory be inherited by them. I hope that most of my readers will understand. I was recently excited a little more than I would normally have been, not just because a number of agreeable friends were coming to lunch on a bright and crisp Sunday, but also because among those friends was a Darwin. This was clearly a case of reflected affection and, I suspect, it afflicts most of us, explaining why, even in mature Western democracies where difference is supposed to be dead, political parties find it irresistible to advance the candidacy for elected office of famous names. It may suggest also that there was more to the worship of relics in the Middle Ages than meets the eye. It was not only to appeal to a saint for a redemption of kinds. You went to a shrine to 'praise famous men'.

In my case, of course, the relic was no skeletal remainder of a dead saint, but a noisy and animate friend whose friendship I had made long before I knew of his descent. But his first visit to my home had an emotional impact that no honour bestowed on me by any of the princes of England could possibly approach. My friend carried a fragment of the flesh and blood of one of the greatest men who had ever lived, someone who shed so much light on our view of ourselves that it is hard to imagine anyone else emulating him for as long as our species walks on this planet, and I had adulated him since my middle childhood. Now Charles Darwin had been dead for almost a century and a half, but one of his descendants[62], whom he had envisaged lovingly in the autobiographical notes he had addressed to them, was coming to my home to 'break bread' with me and mine. And surely, Darwin himself would have liked to be there with us. He loved conversation, though in his last years his nervous ailments made any excitement disturbing to bear, and he would have been most curious to watch his descendant and to learn of his life. I must look it up. Darwin probably even knew my Sussex village. Down House, his home in the second half of his life, is not too far away. Perhaps he came here with friends to shoot partridges?

Why dare I say that Charles Darwin has been – and will perhaps for ever be – the most famous Englishman in the world, when England has produced more than her fair share of glittering names in history and is likely to go on doing so? Her stellar names of the past two millennia include King Alfred the Great, the man whose encouragement of his native tongue in the ninth century laid the first stone for English to be today the common language of Mankind (see the chapter on Boethius); Shakespeare, the greatest dramatist ever who outshone Sophocles and Euripides; an array of great philosophers from Bacon to Russell; Newton, the law-giver of gravity, Rutherford, the finder of the electron, the building brick of all modern communications; commanders of men of the daring of Nelson and Wellington, statesmen of the influence of Churchill. How could a reclusive gentleman of Kent who suffered almost constant ill health and who spent most of his time in the company of tortoises, birds, barnacles and earthworms compete with any of those other stars of England's sky?

The answer is simple. Go into any humble school in any poor village in the remotest corner of the world and ask the children how many Englishmen have they ever heard of. They are likely to mention only one, from their elementary biology class, and the revolution that Charles Darwin set in motion in our understanding of ourselves with the publication of his Origin of Species in 1859 continues to enrich every generation anew.

Please note that I did not claim that Darwin was the greatest Englishman who ever lived. Were we to judge by intellectual brilliance or the ability to give pleasure to others, I have no doubt that Shakespeare would be a far greater man. There is also an element of chance involved in scientific discovery, and it has to be said that Darwin delivered a psychological shock to our self-esteem. He degraded us in our own eyes. Previous to him, we were convinced that we were the sole purpose of the existence of the Universe, that there was not the slightest link – apart from a few visual resemblances – between us and the beasts of the countryside, that those beasts, even the stars in the skies, had been made to serve us only, that we had been created in a single, separate act by God in His own image. Darwin explained how we had ourselves descended from beasts. He showed us that we were no more than the cleverest of the apes, even though incomparably more clever than any ape.

But then, if we were to ask most people whether it was better to be realistic about ourselves or else, to day dream, to put ourselves outside and above the rest of the Universe, the they are likely to fall silent. In the longer term, our false view of ourselves as semi-divine beings would have held us back. This is not to say that the evolution of Man is not the greatest occurrence in the history of the Universe as we know it. It may well be. The radio silence that we observe in the skies points in that direction, and nor has the discovery of the mechanism of our evolution diminished the awe that we feel in beholding our own ascent, intelligence, creativity, altruism, the love that we show towards our families and friends. In other words, none of the greatest fears that Darwin's critics harboured about his turning most of us into amoral monkeys has come about. I would by far live as the lowliest worker in the scientific and emancipated welfare state of today than be a middle class professional in Darwin's own time, let alone in the serfdoms of the eternity before him.

*

Charles Robert Darwin was born in April 1809 into one of the most fortunate families of England when England was itself one of the most fortunate countries in the world, in fact the world's acknowledged superpower, despite Napoleon still holding sway in large parts of Europe. He was born into both substantial wealth and intellectual pedigree. His father Robert was a successful doctor in the town of Shrewsbury, in the county of Shropshire, and had grown rich through investing his earnings in the booming infrastructure of the industrial revolution, particularly roads. But probably more important to the social ambitions of his children was that he had been elected to the Royal Society, the oldest scientific institution in the world while still a young man. His own father, Erasmus Darwin, too, had been a member of that august gathering and had, in his time, produced a book, Zoonomia, on his view of how living species had evolved. Both Erasmus and Robert were agnostics, probably atheists, though in the interest of their financial dealings – and for domestic peace with their devout wives and relatives – they would not admit it.

Young Charles became an orphan when he was only eight years old. His mother, Susannah, a member of the Wedgewood pottery family, had developed stomach pains and died when she was 52. Robert did not marry again and so Charles' three older sisters became his substitute mothers.

Interestingly, and unusually for a man who would prove so brilliant in his middle years, he did not show promise at school. 'When I left school', he would write later, ' I was for my age neither high nor low in it; and I believe that I was considered by all my masters and by my father as a very ordinary boy, rather below the common standard in intellect'. Today we might describe him as a 'late developer'. He was interested in too many things outside the school curriculum to concentrate on his, admittedly uncharismatic, masters or devote enough time to his homework. Nor did the ever-present prospect of idle talk and sport on the estates of his Wedgwood relatives help. Nevertheless, his father did not give up and despatched him to Edinburgh university to train in medicine. There Charles disappointed the family again by asking to leave after only two years and transferred, instead, to Christ College, Cambridge, to study for a general degree in the classics. This would prepare him for further theological studies and the life of a country clergyman in the Church of England, where strong conviction was not a requirement. He did obtain a B. A.

degree at Cambridge, with distinction, but only among 'the oi polloi or crowd of men who do not go in for honours'.

> At Cambridge I used to practice throwing up my gun to my shoulder before a looking-glass to see that I threw it up straight. Another and better plan was to get a friend to wave about a lighter candle and then to fire at it with a cap on the nipple, and if the aim was accurate the little puff of air would blow out the candle. The explosion of the cap caused a sharp crack, and I was told that the tutor of the college remarked, 'What an extraordinary thing it is, Mr Darwin seems to spend hours in cracking a horse-whip in his room, for I often hear the crack when I pass under his windows'.[63]

One explanation that he gives for his seeming idleness in his youth is that, while at Edinburgh, he thought he would inherit so much property from both his parents that he would not have to earn his own living. His expectation was to prove justified, but we see him at Edinburgh and Cambridge not quite as idle as others saw him. As well as spending many evenings with 'a sporting set, including some dissipated low-minded young men', he sought, and was admitted to, the company of older men of impeccable moral character and high academic achievement. They included professors of moral philosophy, geologists and botanists, and these rekindled in him his boyhood obsession with the natural world: 'I remember one of my sporting friends who saw me at work with my beetles, saying that I should someday be a Fellow of the Royal Society, and the notion seemed to me preposterous'. At Cambridge, his reading also convinced him of the truth of Christian doctrine, with a new twist woven into it by the scientists that God was sufficiently patient to work through natural laws, rather than create new species or intervene in the flow of the world daily. It was vague, but appeared plausible enough, or was at least the best explanation available.

In his memoirs, Darwin tells us that a second reading of his grandfather's book, Zoonomia, on evolution through the exertion of will by animals, disappointed him. It was meagre on facts and speculated too much. He also emphasises that he did not consciously abandon his plan to become a vicar. It came about as a result of events. A friend, a professor of botany at Cambridge, nominated him to be the unpaid naturalist on board a survey ship, HMS Beagle, that would soon leave for the tropics. The voyage would last only two years. His father disapproved. His uncle Josiah Wedgewood interceded. His father relented. The ship left Plymouth two days after Christmas, 1831, but would not return until October 1836. It circumnavigated the globe. History was made, on a grand scale.

Considering how fiercely I have been attacked by the orthodox, it seems ludicrous that I once intended to be a clergyman. Nor was this intention and my father's wish ever formally given up, but died a natural death when, on leaving Cambridge, I joined the 'Beagle' as naturalist. If the phrenologists are to be trusted, I was well fitted in one respect to be a clergyman. A few years ago the secretaries of a German psychological society asked me earnestly by letter for a photograph of myself; and some time afterwards I received the proceedings of one of their meetings, in which it seemed that the shape of my head had been the subject of a public discussion, and one of the speakers had declared that I had the bump of reverence developed enough for ten priests.[64]

The story of the voyage of the Beagle, which Darwin described rightly as the most important event of his life, is likely to be familiar to readers, and so is how he arrived at the theory of natural selection as the main mechanism of organic evolution. But several points connected to both the voyage and the theory may help illuminate Darwin's character and explain his subsequent suffering.

First, Darwin remained silent on his conviction as to the truth of the theory for two decades before he was forced to announce it; second, the suspicion that species changed over time was not new, and, third, the severe sicknesses that dogged the naturalist for the rest of his life are nowadays attributed by most doctors to an illness that he brought back with him from South America. His happy marriage to his first cousin, Emma Wedgewood, also deserves a brief examination.

When the Beagle returned in the autumn of 1836, Darwin was a changed man, still young but exhilarated on two counts. He found himself the rising star of the scientific sky without expecting it, and he remained under the spell of the great new world he had experienced in South America, the Pacific and Australasia:

> The glories of the vegetation of the Tropics rise before my mind at the present time more vividly than anything else, though the sense of sublimity, which the great deserts of Patagonia and the forest-clad mountains of Tierra del Fuego excited in me, had left an indelible impression on my mind. ... I also reflect with high satisfaction on some of my scientific work, such as solving the problem of coral islands and making out the geological structure of certain islands, for instance St Helena. ...

During his absence, some of the letters he had written to the clergyman, geologist and botanist John Stevens Henslow at Cambridge had been printed and circulated without his knowledge and these had created an appetite for more writing by him on his return. Thus he threw himself into debilitating work on his journals, and on cataloguing and classifying the numerous specimens and fossils he had collected. He called these his 'museum'. But he also began a new notebook devoted entirely to his secret notion that he might have stumbled on exactly how and why a species evolved into another, or indeed into a whole family of new species. At the time, while increasing numbers of scientists were concluding that species were not stable, church and state both insisted on that core doctrine of the Christian faith. Many years later, he would tell a friend that publishing his discovery was 'like confessing to a murder'.

While on board the ship, and during his many rides into the interior of South America in the company of gauchos and settlers – where he was disgusted by their treatment of their slaves – he had fallen ill on many occasions. Now, seemingly due to overwork, he became ill again and was ordered to take a complete, long break. His ailments were various. They included palpitation, which went back to before he had left for South America. But the others were new. He vomited, trembled, had severe pain in the stomach, and he had boils and headaches. These in a man who had not yet reached the age of 30.

As more papers were read at conferences and journals published, honours were showered on his head, though none would ever come from Queen Victoria's palace. In June 1938, he was elected to the Athenæum club, along with Charles Dickens, having had to be on the waiting list only 14 months[65], and in the following January, he was elected to the Royal Society, the best of wedding presents, as he and Emma were married a few days later at the Wedgewoods' magnificent seventeenth-century mansion, Maer Hall, in Staffordshire.

His courtship of Emma similarly sheds light on his character and on his attachment to science. Clearly with Emma in mind, he had in the previous spring contemplated, on two pieces of paper, the advantages and drawbacks of marriage. On one sheet, there were the gains of settling down, such as 'a constant companion and a friend in old age, better than a dog anyhow'. Advising against wedlock were 'less money for books and a terrible loss of time'. With these thoughts dividing him, the love of cousin Emma, who was a few months older than he was, won the day and he discussed the idea with his father. Father approved – perhaps he and his close friend Josiah had had it in mind for many a year – but cautioned his son not to reveal his thoughts on transmutation to her. He did so, anyway, when in July he went north to see her, but he could not bring himself to propose, though it would have, no doubt, been quite clear to her why he had come. Eventually when he did propose, she accepted, but prayed also that God would not separate them on their deaths for his blasphemy.

Despite his clear hesitation to choose between wedlock and science, their marriage would prove a most romantic and happy one, to the extent that it seems unlikely that he would have achieved half of his success without Emma's constant nursing of his illnesses and her ruling over a large house with eight servants and eight children. She gave birth to ten. Two died in infancy and one, a daughter, at the age of ten, a catastrophe that took Darwin close to mental ruin.

Darwin worried continually about money, though his books sold so well that they often had to be reprinted within days of publication. He also inherited a fortune from his father in 1848, and so had Emma earlier in 1843 from the Wedgewood estate. He was justified – to a certain extent – in this insecurity. His four sons needed allowances at university to keep up with fellow gentlemen and his three daughters needed substantial dowries to ensure suitable matches. Furthermore, investments could fail suddenly and there was never any guarantee that his health would allow him to finish another book. Nevertheless, his nervousness appears extreme and may have been yet another symptom of his illnesses. At the end of 1875, Emma's accounts showed a surplus of £4658, or roughly twice the price of their house if it were to be put on the market. Even though that year, Darwin set up his faithful butler of 40 years, Parslow, in the village with a pension of £50 a year and the rent of a cottage, he could have afforded to pay his cook, groom, maids and at least two gardeners more generously.

Against this must be mentioned a host of generous donations to charity and interventions on behalf of acquaintances who had fallen on hard times. One example concerns Alfred Russel (sic) Wallace, the naturalist whose coincidental discovery of natural selection in 1858 had forced Darwin to publish his own, older writings on the subject. At the end of 1888, Darwin wrote to prime minister Gladstone about Wallace's 'love of natural history', failed investments in the depression and poor health due to tropical diseases to appeal for a state pension for him. Gladstone, who was no fan of natural selection, but who yet had visited Darwin at Down House, arranged for the naturalist to be paid £200 a year. Darwin wrote to Wallace personally to give him the good news on his 58th birthday. This intervention was against the advice of both Emma, who resented its interrupting Darwin's own work, and friends who were disappointed by Wallace's wallowing in spiritualism and astrology.[66]

The Darwins were liberal in the upbringing of their children, with him remembered as never having raised his voice to admonish any of them. On one occasion he found one of his sons jumping up and down on a sofa in the drawing room, damaging its springs. He told him: 'Oh, Lenny, Lenny, That is against all the rules'. To this, Lenny answered: 'Then I think you'd better get out of the room'. Lenny would be the only one of his four sons who would not later be elected to the Royal Society. He became a eugenicist. After their father's death, one daughter recalled:

Our father and mother would not even wish to know what we were doing or thinking unless we wished to tell. He always made us feel that we were each of us creatures whose opinions and thoughts were valuable to him, so that whatever there was best in us came out in the sunshine of his presence.

Yet another indication of Darwin's gentle mind is his reluctance to give his support to the militant atheists of his time. Towards the end of his life, a man who would soon become son-in-law to Carl Marx asked him for an interview with the aim of drawing out his beliefs. Darwin did not wish to see the man, yet he felt it impolite to refuse him. Emma struck on the ruse of inviting him to lunch, but together with the parish vicar, to impose a subdued air on the questioning. In the end, the man persisted and succeeded, almost. In a telling remark that pointed to his lack of religious conviction, Darwin replied:

> I am a strong advocate for free thought on all subjects, yet it appears to me that direct arguments against Christianity and theism produce hardly any effect on the public, and freedom of thought is best promoted by the illumination of men's minds, which follows from the advance of science. It has therefore been always my object to avoid writing on religion and I have confined myself to science. I may, however, have been unduly biased by the pain which it would give some members of my family in I aided in any way direct attacks on religion.

It is now thought that Darwin's ill health was the result of a number of illnesses. As mentioned earlier, as far back as the autumn of 1831, when he was awaiting calmer weather in Plymouth for the Beagle to set sale, he had severe chest pain and palpitation of the heart. While he eventually did die of heart failure, over 40 years later, a poor heart was not the main cause of his suffering. His stomach pains, vomiting and trembling that forced him to become a virtual recluse from society are nowadays said to have been due to the parasitic 'chagas' disease. It occurs in South America and is carried, among others of the Triatomine sub-family of blood-sucking insects, by the benchuca bug of Argentina. We may even hazard a guess as to the exact date when he caught it. In the entry in his journal on the 26th of March 1835 he wrote of an uncomfortable night in a village near Mendoza in western Argentina:

> [Last] night I experienced an attack (for it deserves no less a name) of the Benchuca (a species of Reduvius) the great black bug of the Pampas. It is most disgusting to feel soft wingless insects, about an inch long, crawling over one's body. ... When placed on the table, and though surrounded by people, if a finger was presented, the bold insect

would immediately draw its sucker, make a charge, and if allowed, draw blood. No pain was caused by the wound. ... This one feast, for which the benchuca was indebted to one of the officers, kept it fat during four whole months; but after the first fortnight, the insect was quite ready to have another suck.

However, whole medical conferences have been devoted to speculating about Darwin's illnesses and no consensus has been reached.

Darwin died on April 19, 1882 at the age of 73, still a controversial, though increasingly accepted, figure, with many theologians discovering that God had not really meant what he had said in the Bible regarding creation. The news spread rapidly and it made his club, the Athenaeum in Pall Mall, the centre of events for a week or so. A number of his friends and disciples there, and at a few doors away at the Royal Society, who called themselves 'the X Club' and who revolved around the biologist Thomas Huxley, sprang into action immediately and conspired with the Cannon of Westminster to organise a parliamentary petition to bury the great naturalist at the Abbey. In this, they were helped greatly by the sense of patriotism of former enemies on the leading newspapers of the day. These were propelled forth by pride as telegrams poured in to report the leading articles of the European and American press. No freethinker had previously been buried in such hallowed ground.

The conservative newspaper, the Daily Telegraph, pointed out that the king of Prussia had bestowed on Darwin his country's Order of Merit a full 15 years earlier, while England had kept 'her first son' a plain 'Mr.' England had 'failed to honour herself' by such neglect.

Amends have to be made before it is too late. Britain must not be outdone by her foreign rivals. Comparisons with the immortal Newton will ring hollow unless it is acted upon. Newton's honour has to be Darwin's. The State must take and enshrine the body.

Another conservative paper, the Standard, pleaded as follows with the naturalist's wife, Emma, and their children to consent to a burial at the Abbey:

Darwin died, as he had lived, in the quiet retirement of the country home which he loved; and the sylvan scenes amidst which he found the simple plants and animals that enabled him to solve the great enigma of the Origin of Species may seem, perhaps, to many of his friends the fittest surroundings for his last resting place. But one who has brought such honour on the English name, and whose death is lamented throughout the civilized world, to the temporary neglect of many burning political and social questions of the day, should not be laid in a comparatively obscure grave. His proper place is among those other worthies whose reputations are landmarks in the people's history, and if it should not clash with his own expressed wishes or the pious feelings of the family, we owe it to posterity to place his remains in Westminster Abbey, among the illustrious dead who make that noble fane unrivalled in the world.

The family did concede, and the great man's body was brought to London on a funeral carriage drawn by four horses. Queen Victoria and prime minister Gladstone stayed away, but Parliament emptied and the populace flocked to the Abbey. Prominent clergymen of the Church of England outdid one another in trying to prove that there was no conflict between the Origin of Species and the Bible. The Times, which had lost few opportunities to slight 'the Devil's Chaplain' in the past, thundered thus:

> The Abbey needed (Darwin's body) more than it (the body) needed the Abbey. This saintly man gave the Abbey an increased sanctity, a new cause for reverence. ...... The Abbey has its orators and Ministers who have convinced reluctant senates and swayed nations. Not one of them all has wielded a power over men and their intelligence more complete than that which for the last twenty-three years has emanated from a simple country house in Kent.

Alfred Russel (sic) Wallace, the cranky but generous naturalist who had so closely to Darwin the accolade of discovering natural selection, was invited to the ceremony and two dukes and an earl from among cabinet ministers displeased Victoria to be among the pall bearers. Darwin's eyes would have filled with tears repeatedly to see any of it, but perhaps especially to his simple old butler, Parslow, brushing shoulders with the United States' ambassador. Emma stayed behind in Downe.

The villagers were disappointed to lose his body to London. The publican especially. He sulked of the loss of the trade that would have been his if Darwin had been buried at nearby St Mary's church to make his grave a shrine to science. But the village did not lose him for ever. Down House has since 1998 been a museum open to the public, with the study and the other rooms restored faithfully to their original arrangement. The 'Sistine Chapel of Biology', as a wit has called it, now draws tens of thousands of grateful visitors from around the world each year and many of them flock to the pub for lunch or refreshments.

There are many consolation that go some way to make up for Darwin's neglect by his own country during his life time. His club, the Athenaeum, the Royal Society and Cambridge university bestowed their highest honours on him. The Athenæum in particular became a second home to him for many years whenever he came to London. He dined there almost daily, though he and Emma stayed at the large house that his elder brother Erasmus ('Raz' or 'Eras') owned in Queen Ann's Gate, across St James's Park from the club. He wrote about the Athenæum:

'feel like a gentleman, or rather like a lord, for I am sure the first evening ... I felt just like a Duke. ...... I enjoy it the more, because I fully expected to detest it. ...... I am full of admiration for the Athenaeum. ...... one meets so many people there that one likes to see.'[67]

Despite his physical and nervous ailments, Darwin exerted himself to be involved in the world. He even travelled occasionally. He had coaches and horses of his own, which eased the journey to the nearest railway station eight miles away, and from there Emma made certain he was inconvenienced as little as possible, to the extent that she once hired a train for their exclusive use across London to avoid the usually noisy and chaotic road journey between two rail terminals.

At home in Downe, Emma regulated his life meticulously. Routine and uninterrupted work were what he needed to function. According to the later recollections of their son Frank ('Francis'):

He rose early, chiefly because he could not lie in bed, and I think he would have liked to get up earlier than he did. He took a short turn before breakfast, a habit which began when he went for the first time to a water-cure establishment. ...

After breakfast alone about 7.45, he went to work at once, considering 1 ½ hours between 8 and 9.30 one of his best working times. At 9.30 he came into the drawing-room for his letters – rejoicing if the post was a light one and being sometimes much worried if it was not. He would then hear any family letters read aloud as he lay on a sofa.

The reading aloud, which also included part of a novel, lasted till about half-past ten, when he went back to work till twelve or a quarter past. By this time he considered his day's work over, and would often say, in a satisfied voice, 'I've done a good day's work'. He then went out of doors whether it was wet or fine; Polly, his white terrier, went with him in fair weather, but in rain she refused or might be seen hesitating in the veranda, with a mixed expression of disgust and shame at her own want of courage; generally, however, her conscience carried the day, and as soon as he was evidently gone, she could not bear to stay away.

Newspapers he read to himself, and so did he scientific books and journals of which he bought or received large numbers. He did not think highly of

Nature. In the evenings, beside reading novels to him and playing two games of backgammon with him – of which he kept records – Emma would also play on the piano for him while he lay on a sofa, before going to bed for more readings aloud until he fell asleep. Above all, however, he longed to be able to be among his books and experiments, and if one of the children helped with the experiments, all the better. His last project was an investigation of movements in plants, at which Frank assisted him. His biographers Adrian Desmond and James Moore have given us a memorable description of his study towards the end of his life:

> This, too, was a labour of love. Spring (1878) turned the study into a pungent jungle, with seeds sprouting in biscuit tins on the chimneypiece, cabbages and runner beans in flower pots, and nasturtiums, cyclamens, cacti and telegraph plants scattered on tables. Darwin was in his element, infatuated with every rootlet and blossom. All these were his companions; he had a feeling for their 'aliveness.' He talked to them unselfconsciously, praising their ingenuity or twitting 'little beggars' for 'doing just what I don't want them to'. Sometimes a flower caught his eye, and he would stroke it gently, childlike in his love for its delicate form and colour. The plants moved him, like the romances Emma read aloud [to him] in the afternoons.[68]

His last days and hours were a continuation of the story of love never-ending. He had suffered a heart seizure on a visit to the Lake District a couple of years earlier and had been diagnosed with angina. Emma exhausted herself nursing him and had at least two doctors on call. The seizures gradually became more frequent and more intense. When the end loomed, in early April 1883, she sent telegrams to the children and most were able to come. He suffered wretchedly, vomiting blood, becoming nauseous and fainting regularly. In between the faints, he would say that he was not afraid to die, but why did it take so long? A sip of whisky or brandy revived him momentarily. At 4pm on the 19th, he drew his last deep breath, with his head resting on Emma's breast and she swaying gently with her eyes closed.

# Mark Twain

*The clown who grew up*
*America's Omar Khayyām*
*The writer of humour who published best-sellers in three centuries*

69

There is one notable thing about our Christianity: bad, bloody, merciless, money-grabbing and predatory as it is—it is still a hundred times better than the Christianity of the Bible, with its prodigious crime—the invention of Hell. Measured by our Christianity of to-day, bad as it is, hypocritical as it is, empty and hollow as it is, neither the Deity nor his Son is a Christian.

You don't know about me, without you have read a book by the name of 'The Adventures of Tom Sawyer', but that ain't no matter. That book was made by Mr. Mark Twain, and he told the truth, mainly. There was things which he stretched, but mainly he told the truth. That is nothing. I never seen anybody but lied one time or another, without it was Aunt Polly, or the widow, or maybe Mary. Aunt Polly – tom's Aunt Polly, she is – and Mary, and the Widow Douglas is all told about in that book, with some stretchers, as I said before.

Now the way that the book winds up is this: Tom and me found the money that the robbers hid in the cave, and it made us rich. We got six thousand dollars apiece – all gold. It was an awful sight of money when it was piled up. Well, Judge thatcher he took it and put it out at interest, and it fetched us a dollar a day apiece all the year round – more than a body could tell what to do with. The Widow Douglas she took me for her son, and allowed she would sivilize me; but it was rough living in the house all the time, considering how dismal regular and decent the widow was in all her ways; and so when I couldn't stand it no longer I lit out. I got into my old rags and my sugarhogshead again, and was free and satisfied. But Tom Sawyer he hunted me up and said he was going to start a band of robbers, and I might join if I would go back to the widow and be respectable. So I went back.

The widow she cried over me, and called me a poor lost lamb, and she called me a lot of other names, too, but she never meant no harm by it. She put me in them new clothes again, and I couldn't do nothing but sweat and sweat, and feel all cramped up. Well, then, the old thing commenced again. The widow she rung a bell for supper, and you had to come to time. When you got to the table you couldn't go right to eating, but you had to wait for the widow to tuck down her head and grumble over the victuals, though there warn't really anything the matter with them ...

\*

These opening passages of Mark Twain's most successful novel, The Adventures of Huckleberry Finn, the book that made him rich, were my introduction to him many years ago and they caught me immediately, as they had millions previously elsewhere. Apart from the hugely creative and comic talent they unveil, they shout from the rooftop that they can be from America only, a continent of various temperaments and climates united perhaps by one thing, the English language. While this remains true today, despite the moulding – and the mauling? – of many decades of formal, unifying education, we may only imagine how much more diverse the 'country' was in the early 1840s –

before the great civil war and still in the age of slavery – when young Sam Clemens first became conscious of the world around him, centred on the great Mississippi. His little village of Hannibal on the river's edge had not yet acquired a rail road to New York and the east coast. It had to reach civilisation by horse-drawn stage coach, almost as if it were in the Roman empire.

The life of Samuel Clemens/Mark Twain was touched perhaps more regularly, and perhaps more often, by personal tragedy than were the lives of any other of the exemplars I have examined in this narrative so far. But fortunately for him, and for us, the bright and boisterous boy, Sam Clemens, inside the later, grown up observer of the world, Mark Twain, rose each time to triumph over tragedy to enable him to endure and, as a result, to bring light and laughter and enlightenment to the lives of the multitudes, in and out of America. He has often been described as 'the father of American literature'. He rose to be a figure on the world stage, too, the honoured guest of a thousand institutions and dinner companion to many heads of state.

How did he stand up to calamity?

\*

Samuel Langhorne Clemens was born on the last day of November 1835, two weeks after Halley's comet had begun one of its periodic, close approaches to the Earth. This is relevant to the story of 'a writer of humour', for towards the end of his life, he said that while he had come into the world with Halley's, he wanted to leave with it also. He would be most disappointed, he said, if the comet left him behind. He was not disappointed. He died on April 21, 1910, aged 74 years, when the comet was again streaking across the night sky.

The curricula vitae of America's greatest literary son is easily accessible 'online', as we have learnt to say recently. But a handful of facts on his childhood and early youth may serve here to explain his later development and greatness. Why did he so thirst after worldly success – a trait not much admired in this book – and what might explain his extraordinary resilience in the face of difficulty? What lay behind his unusual respect for European culture and the classical Greek tradition?

Sam Clemens was born into a household that struggled to feed itself. His father, John, had trained as a lawyer in Kentucky, but had been forced to abandon that state to escape the debts left behind by his stepfather. He had subsequently hopped westwards and northwards from one small town to another in search of steady work, but found none. He was tenacious. Beside the law, he had tried his hand at several other jobs. He had been shopkeeper, railway agent, postmaster. He had failed each time. Thus when he and his wife Jane arrived in 1835 in the town of Florida in the state of Missouri, where their fifth child, Sam, was born, the sum total of their wealth amounted to a cheap carriage, four undernourished horses and a slave girl, Jeanie. The eight of them shared a two-room shack in a poor corner of town with no running water or lavatory. They endured there for four years.

But then fortune smiled on them. In little Hannibal on the Missouri side of the Mississippi, John found regular work as a lawyer and earned enough, eventually, to buy a two-storey house of which respectable citizens would not be ashamed. Unfortunately, though, this was not to last. He died 10 years later from pneumonia, when he was 48 and become the little town's only judge. His death plunged the family into hardship once more. The children had to leave school to help their mother make ends meet.

John had inherited from his wealthy Virginian father – and possibly from the family's earlier origins in Cornwall, England – an ambition to rise in the world, together with a love of reading. This trait he passed onto most of his offspring. Thus his eldest son Orion became a cub reporter with a local newspaper while Sam, at the age of 12, became a printer's apprentice, graduating soon to writing occasional articles for his brother's journal.

A romantic attachment to the printer's craft would in later years drain Twain's huge earnings and be a factor in his going bankrupt. For the time being, though, it was a gateway to the glamorous world of writing and writers.

But it was only a matter of time before the great Mississippi would claim him for its own for several years, until the ruinous civil war of 1861-64 interrupted trade on the river. He learned the intricacies of 2000 miles of the shall edges of the river to become a steamship's pilot, a job that brought in a dazzling salary of $3000 a year and surpassed in prestige the rank of the ship's captain. It was at this time that another tragedy struck the family, perhaps more hurtful than the death of his father. He had persuaded his younger brother Henry to join him as an apprentice pilot, but the lad was killed when his steamship exploded. The accident left Sam with a strong sense of guilt for the rest of his life and drove him superstitious for a time, for he had dreamt of Henry's death a month before it occurred.

But his years working on the river would also provide much of the fodder of his future career as a writer. He loved and remembered every scrap of gossip, foible, hilarity and adventure he witnessed, and the river abounded with every type of human character one could imagine, from entertaining criminals to the ordinary sharp and shifty, and from downcast slaves to dreamy captains who recited Shakespeare to while away the hours. They would later give rise to such of his books as Life on the Mississippi.

The slang of the pilots gave him his future pen name. The pilot shouted 'mark twain' to warn the captain that the boat was now only two fathoms – 12 feet – above the bed of the river.

When war broke out, he and a close friend joined a local unit of the Confederate army, even though Orion worked for the office of President Lincoln. But his heart was clearly not on the side of the southern slave traders and he quit after two weeks. Then followed quite a number of years of more adventurous, and precarious, living, including a spell as a failed gold miner in the far west.

His first success as a writer came in San Francisco, where he worked as a reporter, and he never looked back to any other occupation. A story by him by the name of The Celebrated Jumping Frog of Calaveras County was published in a New York Magazine and earned him a reputation as a promising writer of humour. In 1867, it was published in book form with other tales and won him national fame. In the same year we find him setting off for Europe and Palestine as a travel writer for a local newspaper and the publication, two years later, of his reports in The Innocents Abroad established him firmly on the American publishing scene as a talent with the potential to earn large sums of money. But his surviving photographs of those years, albeit formal studio portraits, do not betray any sign of the gregarious joker of a young man that he clearly was. Perhaps it was the tragedies he had already witnessed. Thus we read that when, after his return from Europe in 1868, he was elected to a secret society, The Scroll and Key at Yale University, its motto of 'Fellowship, moral and literary self-improvement and charity', appealed to him. His flamboyant moustaches fronting serious eyebrows began to be a familiar sight in gossip magazines.

As for his personal life, 1971 saw the beginning of one of the happiest marriages one may hope to find in the history of writers. After a long courtship and a first date at a reading by Charles Dickens in New York, Twain eventually won the hand of a rich and beautiful, but also sickly, heiress, Olivia Langdon, daughter of a religious, but liberal businessman. Olivia introduced Sam to prominent abolitionists, 'socialists, principled atheists and activists for women's rights and social equality', and Mr Landon's wedding gift to the new couple was a whole house in the city of Buffalo, at the head of the Niagara Falls, complete with servants. Thus began a whirlwind of a social life in which Twain's large income combined with Olivia's wealth financed many a glittering gathering of artists and intellectuals. But Twain also drove himself, at times to exhaustion for a still young man.

After the publication of Sawyer in 1876, America could almost not have enough of him. The new nation's increasing literacy and multiplying numbers needed entertainment and it also needed to tell the mother civilisation, Europe, particularly England, that it deserved to have broken away. It now had culture of its own. After the publication of Sawyer's sequel, The Adventures of Huckleberry Finn, Twain's writings became obligatory reading among the informed classes in Britain and, in translation, in the rest of Europe. In the winter of 1891, which he and Jane were spending in Berlin, Kaiser Wilhelm recognised him in a park. A few minutes later, the two men left their companions behind to walk off 'arm in arm'. Then it was dinner with the Kaiser and breakfast with the Empress. Wilhelm especially liked his Life on the Mississippi and found his essay On the Awful German Language 'one of the funniest pieces of humour ever written'.

Twain visited England several times and once stayed two years, hiding from reporters. He had filed for protection from bankruptcy and needed to be away from America, even though he had sworn he would pay all his debts. For many years, he had invested heavily in inventions and new technology, particularly in the development of printing machines that promised to make him even richer. Almost invariably they drained his resources. But what broke the camel's back was a publishing company he had set up for a relative. It was during his longest stay in London that he made his most-quoted remark. After rumours had spread that he had died, an American reported traced him to a modest rented house in Tedworth Square, Chelsea. He asked the great man what he should say. In the words of his friend, secretary and biographer, Albert Bigelow Paine, Twain regarded the reporter gravely. 'Then, in his slow, nasal drawl, he said: 'Say – that the report of my death – has been grossly – exaggerated', a remark that, a day later, was amusing both hemispheres'.[70]

But though arthritis and other ailments began to plague him with increased age, he could not remain idle for long. His stays in England, for example, produced numerous essays and two books, The Prince and the Pauper, a commentary on social injustice, and A Connecticut Yankee at King Arthur's Court, a fantasy that does not work well. His new works, as well as the continued massive sale of his previous writings, enabled him not only pay all his creditors, but to become a most wealthy man once more. 'For once', he wrote, 'it gives me more pleasure to pay out money than it gives me to bring it in'. Thus when he returned to America for the last time, the newspapers discovered that the legendary Sir Walter Scott, the writer of Waverley, had acted as their own literary lion had done. He had paid all his debts after bankruptcy. The truth was, however, that Twain had always had a strong moral conviction. He had quietly supported many charities whenever he had had cash in the bank.

But as Twain grew older, in what is the reverse of the normal trend, his political and religious stances became similarly more rebellious, more left-wing, and often passionately so. Observe, for example, what he wrote towards the very end of his life on reading, for the last time, one of his bedside books:

[When I read] Carlyle's French Revolution [for the first time] in 1871, I was a Girondin; every time I have read it since, I have read it differently—being influenced and changed, little by little, by life and environment ... and now I lay the book down once more, and recognize that I am a Sansculotte. And not a pale, characterless Sansculotte, but a Marat.[71]

And although he continued to attend Presbyterian church services, his essays on organised religion became virtually unpublishable. He even struck at the very foundations of faith. 'Faith', he wrote, 'is believing what you know ain't so'.

In politics, he became the vice-president of the Anti-Imperialist Society to oppose the proposed American annexation of the Philippines.

At times, he refused to write for the major journals, even though they offered him colossal fees of up to a dollar per word. Instead, he wrote for many obscure publications without any remuneration. He also used several other pen names beside Twain and, for this reason, it will probably be impossible to trace all his writings. His biographer reports that it sometimes seemed as if no public meeting of any worth in New York would be complete without Twain being present to address it. Most such speeches went unrecorded.

Age also made him reflective on the transience of life. He was so moved by Edward FitzGerald's Rubaiyat of Omar Khayyām that he even wrote his own version, The Rubaiyat of Mark Twain. But his version is, unlike FitzGerald's philosophical but joyous poem, is sombre and dwells on death, rather than life. Here is a sample:

Sleep. for the Sun that scores another Day
Against the Tale allotted You to stay,
Reminding You, is Risen, and now
Serves Notice – ah, ignore it while You may.

The Joy of Life, that streaming through their Veins
Tumultuous swept, falls slack – and wanes
The Glory in the Eye and one by one
Life's Pleasures perish and make place for Pains.

Think – in this battered Caravanserai,
Whose Portals open stand all Night and Day,
How Microbe after Microbe with his Pomp
Arrives unasked, and comes to stay.

O Death, sole Precious Thing in This World's gift,
Behold us in this shabby Life adrift.
Have Thou our Worship – unto Thee,
Best Friend of Man, our tired Hearts we lift.

Myself when young did eagerly frequent
Some shady Houses, and heard Argument
About It and about; but evermore
I liked It well, and often in I went.

Behold – the Pen is mightier than the Sword,
That leapt from Sheath at any heating Word
So long ago – is peaceful now and calm,
And dreams unmoved of ancient Conquests scored.

They say that He who dyed his Hair and wrought
To keep his youth by Falsities, and bought
Sham Calves and such – why, that Wild Ass.
The Lizard dances on his Grave – and ought.

Rheumatic Gout. – a momentary Taste
Of being dipp'd in Hell full to the Waist, –
And lo, the mortal Misery has reached
The Limit of Endurance – O make Haste.

Apparently because they deem these verses too poor in quality, the directors of the Mark Twain Project at the University of California have decided to omit it from his collected works.[72]

Twain did not suffer from the kind of depression to which most writers of humour seem to be predisposed. His growing sombreness may well, therefore, have been the product of the many tragedies that befell those closest to him, as well as the deficits in social justice he perceived in society at large.

His personal tragedies had begun a long time ago. They began with the premature death of his father John Clemens and the accidental death of his younger brother Henry. Then followed the death from meningitis of a beloved niece, Orion's only child, at the age of ten. Together with Orion and his wife, Sam had prayed and stood vigil by the child's bed for days.

These early tragedies, nevertheless, did not affect his morale irrecoverably. He was young and resilient. The most serious of them was, without any doubt, the death, again from meningitis, of his eldest daughter Susie, when she was twenty-four years old and he sixty-one. She was specially devoted to her father and showed literary promise. So serious was the effect of her sudden passing that Twain and his wife, Olivia, abandoned the great house in which she had grown up.

The next death in the family was that of Olivia herself at fifty-eight and after thirty-four years of an unusually happy marriage. By then their middle daughter Clara had married and gone to live in Europe, leaving Twain alone in a large new house with her youngest sister, Jean. But Jean suffered from epileptic fits and had to spend months at times in asylums for what passed as treatment for the affliction in the 1900s. When she returned home for the last time, she established herself quickly as a tireless manager of her father's correspondence, accounts and domestic servants. But then, suddenly, on December 24, 1909, when she had prepared a massive heap of Christmas presents for the household and friends, she too died. It devastated Twain beyond the possibility of repair, it seemed. Four months later, he was dead.

Fortunately for him, he had in recent years acquired, a new friend who almost passed for a son. Albert Bigelow Pain was a writer in his 40s who had persuaded Twain to let him write the great man's biography. Twain dictated to a stenographer in Paine's presence his recollections of his life, on the condition that many parts of it would remain unpublished for a hundred years until everyone mentioned in them would be safely dead. In the meantime, immediately after Twain's death, Paine would be free to publish his own biography of him. (The autobiography was unveiled in two volumes in 2012 and 2013 and became an instant bestseller, giving its author the accolade of being the only writer known to have produced bestsellers in three consecutive centuries.)

Albert Paine became, in time, Twain's friend, secretary, neighbour and partner in endless games of billiard for which Twain would invent new rules to increase the fun. He gave Paine his spare billiard table and Paine said he would extend a study he planned to build to accommodate it. 'Now that will be very good', Twain replied. 'Then when I want exercise, I can walk down and play with you, and when you want exercise you can walk up and play with me.' He also gave Paine a piece of land so that the dividing line between their estates would be straight.

Though Twain grew visibly depressed in his last year, due both to the ferocity of his angina and the pain of Jean's death, he remained interested in public affairs and would sometimes write letters – under pseudonyms – to the press to participate in the political and philosophical controversies of the time.

Nor was he pompous about the quality of his own work. 'My books', he wrote once, 'are water. The books of the real geniuses are wine. Everyone drinks water'. If there is one exception to that, it is his Joan of Ark. The book, which is an imagined biography of the French heroine as told by one of her companions, he regarded as his best. He said that he dedicated it to his wife because it was the only one of his books that was worthy of her.

The following long extract from the New York Times' report of Twain's death in April 1910 is only about a third of the report which that important journal printed to inform America of the final passing of its foremost humourist[73]. I repeat it here, not just because it is charming enough to deserve a fresh reading, but mainly because it shows what Twain's death meant to millions of people in the English-speaking world:

## MARK TWAIN IS DEAD AT 74

### End Comes Peacefully at His New England Home After a Long Illness

### CONSCIOUS A LITTLE BEFORE

### Carlyle's "French Revolution" Lay Beside Him – "Give Me My Glasses" His Last Words

### SURVIVING CHILD WITH HIM

### Tragic Death of His Daughter Jean Recently Did Much To Hurry His End

---

*Special to The New York Times*

DANBURY, Conn., April 21 – Samuel Langhorne Clemens, "Mark Twain," died at 22 minutes after 6 to-night. Beside him on the bed lay a beloved book – it was Carlyle's "French Revolution" – and near the book his glasses, pushed away with a weary sigh a few hours before. Too weak to speak clearly, "Give me my glasses" he had written on a piece of paper. He had received them, put them down, and sunk into unconsciousness from which he glided almost imperceptibly into death. He was in his seventy-fifth year.

For some time his daughter Clara and her husband, Ossip Gabrilowitsch, and the humorist's biographer, Albert Bigelow Paine, had been by the bed waiting for the end which Drs. Quintard and Halsey had seen to be a matter of minutes. The patient felt absolutely no pain at the end and the moment of his death was scarcely noticeable.

Death came, however, when his favorite niece, Mrs. E. E. Loomis, and her husband, who is Vice President of the Delaware, Lackawanna & Western Railway, and a nephew, Jervis Langdon, were on the way to the railway station. They had left the house much encouraged by the fact that the sick man had recognized them, and took a train for New York ignorant of what happened later.

**Hopes Aroused Yesterday**

Although the end had been foreseen by the doctors and would not have been a shock at any time, the apparently strong rally of this morning had given basis for the hope that it would be postponed for

125

several days. Mr. Clemens awoke at about 4 o'clock this morning after a few hours of the first natural sleep he has (sic) had for several days, and the nurses could see by the brightness of his eyes that his vitality had been considerably restored. He was able to raise his arms above his head and clasp them behind his neck with the first evidence of physical comfort he had given for a long time.

His strength seemed to increase to allow him to enjoy the sunrise, the first signs of which he could see out of the windows in the three sides of the room where he lay. The increasing sunlight seemed to bring ease to him, and by the time the family were about he was strong enough to sit up in bed and overjoyed them by recognizing all of them and speaking a few words to each. This was the first time that his mental powers had been fully his for nearly two days, with the exception of a few minutes early last evening, when he addressed a few sentences to his daughter.

For two hours he lay in bed enjoying the feeling of this return of strength. Then he made a movement and asked in a faint voice for a copy of Carlyle's "French Revolution" which he has always had near him for the last year, and which he has read and re-read and brooded over.

This book was handed to him, and he lifted it up as if to read. Then a smile faintly illuminated his face when he realized that he was trying to read without his glasses. He tried to say "Give me my glasses", but his voice failed, and the nurses, bending over him, could not understand. He motioned for a sheet of paper and a pencil, and wrote what he could not say.

With his glasses on, he read a little and then slowly put the book down with a sigh. Soon he appeared to become drowsy and settled on his pillow. Gradually he sank and settled into a lethargy. Dr. Halsey appreciated that he could have been roused, but considered it better for him to rest. At 3 o'clock he went into a complete unconsciousness.

Later Dr. Quintard, who had arrived from New York, held a consultation with Dr. Halsey, and it was decided that death was near. The family was called and gathered about the bedside watching in a silence which was long unbroken. It was the end. At twenty-two minutes past 6, with the sunlight just turning red as it stole into the window, in perfect silence he breathed his last.

### Died of a Broken Heart

The people of Redding, Bethel and Danbury listened when they were told that the doctors said Mark Twain was dying of angina pectoris. But they say among themselves that he died of a broken heart. And this is the verdict not of popular sentiment alone. Albert Bigelow Paine, his biographer to be and literary executor, who has been constantly with him, said that for the past year at least Mr. Clemens had been weary of life. When Richard Watson Gilder died, he said: "How fortunate he is. No good fortune of that kind ever comes to me".

The man who has stood to the public as the greatest humorist this country has produced has in private life suffered overwhelming sorrows. The loss of an only son in infancy, a daughter in her teens and one in middle life, and finally of a wife who was a constant and sympathetic companion, has preyed upon his mind. The recent loss of his daughter Jean, who was closest to him in later years when her sister was abroad studying, was the final blow. On the heels of this came the symptoms of the disease which was surely to be fatal, and one of whose accompaniments is mental depression. Mr. Paine says that all heart went out of him and his work when his daughter Jean died. He has practically written nothing since he summoned his energies to write a last chapter, a memorial of her, for his autobiography.

He told his biographer that the past Winter in Bermuda was gay, but not happy. Bermuda is always gay in Winter and Mark Twain was a central figure in the gayety. He was staying at the home of William H. Allen, the American Consul. Even in Bermuda, however, Mr. Clemens found himself unable to write and finally relied on Mr. Allen's fifteen-year-old daughter Helen to write the few letters he cared to send.

His health failed rapidly and Mr. Allen wrote to Mr. Paine that his friend was in a most serious condition. Mr. Paine immediately cabled to Mrs. Gabrilowitsch, his surviving daughter, who was in Europe, and started himself on April 2 for Bermuda, embarking with the humorist for the return to New York immediately after his arrival...

Mr. Paine said to-night that Mark Twain had put his affairs in perfect order and that he died well off, though by no means a rich man. He leaves a considerable number of manuscripts, in all stages of incompleteness and of all characters. ...

\*

My books are water. The books of the true geniuses are wine. Everyone drinks water.

# Russell

*The painfully shy boy who became the Delphic oracle of his age*

74

*Bertrand Russell*

Three passions, simple but overwhelmingly strong, have governed my life: the longing for love, the search for knowledge, and an unbearable pity for the suffering of mankind. These passions, like great winds, have blown me hither and thither, in a wayward course, over a deep ocean of anguish, reaching to the very verge of despair.[75]

I do not know who my biographer may be. But I should like him to report 'with what flourish his nature will' something like this: 'I was not a solemn stained glass saint, existing only for purposes of edification; I existed from my own centre, many things that I did were regrettable. I lied and practiced hypocrisy, because if I had not, I should not have been allowed to do my work. I hated hypocrisy and lies: I loved life and real people, and wished to get rid of the shams that prevent us from loving real people as they really are. I believed in laughter and spontaneity, and trusted to nature to bring out the genuine good in people, if once genuineness could come to be tolerated'.[76]

It is not the nature of most men to be happy in a prison, and the passions
that shut us up in ourselves constitute one of the worst kinds of prison.
Among such passions, some of the commonest are fear, envy, the sense of sin,
self-pity and self-admiration.[77]

Most people prefer not to think. They would rather die, and they usually do.[78]

*

If nothing but a short book of such excerpts were to survive into the future
from Bertrand Russell's vast collection of writings, it would still be possible
to describe this last great name in British empirical philosophy as one of the
wisest sages in history. Fortunately all his work is available to all of us in a
hundred languages and although, as with all other human beings who are not
'solemn stained glass saints', his beliefs changed occasionally and evolved over
time, his core thinking and sentiments were consistent and will be cherished
for a long time, possibly as long as Man will read. As a great thinker, he had
a major advantage over his predecessors: He was born into the age of modern
science and modern science is expected to suffer fewer revolutions now.

For the purposes of this short profile, I shall try to show how this sensitive
man, this most influential philosopher of his time[79], guarded his sanity tossed
about on his 'ocean of anguish'. He was not misguided in his anxiety. Many
contemporaries shared it with him. The First World War, the killing of large
numbers of young men for the sake, as they saw it, of assuaging the pride of the
princes of Europe, drove him to the verge of a nervous breakdown and resulted
in his expulsion from the cherished circles of his colleagues and friends. He
was even imprisoned for his opposition to that slaughter, that most tragic of
upheavals that culminated in still greater suffering at the hands of Bolshevists
and Nazis.

A few decades later, with the invention, use and development of nuclear
weapons, it appeared to Russell as if mankind was on course for even more
catastrophic carnage, a carnage that, this time, might end in the extinguishing
of civilisation altogether, or at least for centuries. He was imprisoned again,
though briefly on account of his frailty, despite having previously been awarded
the highest honours that his own nation and the world could bestow on anyone.

Bertrand Russell 'lied and practiced hypocrisy', or so he said; but that
enables more of us to identify with him the more easily, for we too have feet of
clay. More importantly, he had his heart and mind in the right place on many a
great issue more than most other thinkers did, and he inspired millions to show

greater courage and, in the process, to better themselves in their daily lives. He entertained us, too, with his unfailing wit.

As a man, Russell was lucky in his country, his social rank, his timing and his genes. He was born into one of England's top aristocratic houses, he enjoyed robust health for most of his life and he lived for almost a century. He was born before the invention of the telephone, but died after seeing men on the moon. He lived through one of the most exciting eras of the whole history of the world, with achievements in medicine, nutrition, communication, transport and education that could hardly have been imagined by his parents, let alone earlier generations. As a thinker, he was equally lucky. His early mastery of mathematics enabled him to keep up with the progress being made in the other fields of knowledge such as quantum mechanics, relativity, biology, psychology and astronomy. Thus he did not suffer from the crippling scientific blindness of earlier philosophers, or even of those contemporary philosophers who came to philosophy from the classics, not mathematics.[80]

To crown his array of lucky stars, Bertrand Russell was also possessed of an extraordinary talent for language. This made him not only efficient in what he wished to communicate, but a joy to read and to hear. They awarded him the Nobel prize for literature, presumably because there is no such prize for philosophy. But I believe that the designation can be justified. The poetry of his expressions and his wit have made many of his books classics of the English language that will be read long into the future. Without the striking lucidity of his tongue, I doubt if he would have attracted much attention beyond narrow academic gatherings.

*

Bertrand Arthur William Russell was born on May 18, 1872[81] in Wales the youngest child of John Russell, Lord Amberley, the elder son of the Liberal prime minister Earl Russell. He had earlier advocated birth control and been forced to abandon a career in Parliament that had seemed promising. His wife Kathrine was also brought up in a reformist family, that of Lord Stanley of Alderley. After she had addressed a gathering in London on women's suffrage, Queen Victoria had said of her: 'Lady Amberley ought to be given a good whipping'. But there was even greater scandal in store. The Amberleys converted to the idea of open marriage, to the extent that when the sickly tutor of their elder son seemed destined to die celibate, they decided that Kathrine should 'let him live with her'. The tutor was the brilliant, self-made biologist Douglas Spalding, the discoverer of imprinting in animals. Thus he may – or may not. – have contributed his share to baby Bertie's dazzling brain, although, as far as I know, none has raised this possibility elsewhere.[82]

Be that as it may, Bertrand's mother and elder sister died of diphtheria when he was two, and his father died of grief 20 months later. They had appointed Spalding and another freethinker as wards over him and his elder brother, Frank, but Lord Russell, the patriarch who was used to being visited at home by Queen Victoria and the Shah of Persia, among others, forced the two men to give up their legal claim over his grandchildren. Thus the boys came to live under his wing in a rambling house in Richmond, west London. Pembroke Lodge proved ideal for them, for it had extensive gardens, a sense of importance and a throng of servants and animals.

The two boys were of vastly different temperaments. Whereas John, who was always called Frank and was eight years older, had been unruly from his earliest days, Bertrand was cheerful and cooperative, just like 'Spaldie' had been.[83] Frank was sent away to a boarding school, but Bertrand, everyone's favourite, was educated at home under a succession of governesses and tutors. He was given the impression that he had been born in the mould of his illustrious grandfather and that, one day, an 'equestrian statue' would be erected in his honour. This was not to be, for at the age of eleven he raised his first case of philosophical doubt. Frank tried to teach him the basics of the geometry of Euclid one day, but Bertie demanded proof for the assumptions that lay behind it. Frank said that they could not continue if Bertie disagreed with the ancient Greek. So the lesson continued and it was love at first sight, with geometry and mathematics.

Although he would in the future describe his childhood as happy, he would also say that it was a lonely existence: 'I spent all my spare time reading [Shelly]', he wrote in his autobiography, 'and, learning him by heart, knowing no one to whom I could speak of what I thought or felt, I used to reflect how wonderful it would have been to know Shelley, and to wonder whether I should meet any live human being with whom I should feel so much sympathy.' He wrote a diary, with Greek characters to disguise it as exercise.

His grandmother, the first Countess Russell, towered over his childhood. She was puritanical and stern in her Presbyterianism, despite her acceptance of the truth of Darwinism. But she made every effort to make Bertie feel loved. Inside a copy of the Bible she gave him later, she wrote: Thou shalt not follow a multitude to do evil'. This advice was to guide the philosopher to the end of his life. He would always be wary of mobs and, for this reason, would be accused of being an elitist, not without some justification. He is on record as having said, though perhaps partly in jest, that 'one Darwin' was worth '30,000 ordinary men'.

The seclusion of his childhood may well have nurtured his genius, but it did not prepare him for the real world. This is painfully shown by his first stay at Trinity College in Cambridge in 1889, when he was 17. He had been called there for a few days to be examined for a scholarship in mathematics. He was so shy that he could not ask a student or a porter the direction to the toilets. So twice a day he walked for miles to the city's railway station for the purpose.

Once, however, he had begun life as a student, 'everything went well with me', he wrote. He found almost religious fulfilment in the contemplation of the perfection of mathematical formulae, and he found ecstasy in the company of The Apostles, a 'secret' society of the cleverest students at the university who had, half a century earlier, included the now-lionised poet laureate, Lord Tennyson.

The story of Russell's four marriages is easily accessed elsewhere and would make this account too long, though I should later examine the accusation levelled at him as a womaniser. For the moment, the main intellectual and political events of his life that propelled him to prominence by the outbreak of the Great War in 1914 should concern us most.

As we might expect, a whirlwind of fellowships and accolades followed as the extent of his brilliance became known in the circles in which he moved. For example, in 1896, only six years after he began his studies at Trinity, we find him lecturing at the new London School of Economics, and he makes, shortly afterwards, the first of his many journeys to the United States to conduct classes, this first time on non-Euclidian geometry. By then it has also become clear that the heritage of the Russells as champions of political and social reform weighs heavily on his shoulders. After all, grandfather Russell had pushed through Parliament the Great Reform Bill of 1832. In that same year of 1896, taking advantage of his fluent German, he toured Germany to meet political leaders and thinkers there. The result was his first book: German Social Democracy.

In the first two decades of his life, the bulk of his work leans in the direction of mathematics and philosophy, including the massive Principia Mathematica which took him and his collaborator Alfred North Whitehead ten years of hard concentration.[84] These early publications challenged Frege, the German logician who is often regarded as the greatest since Aristotle, and they were of such importance that they established his name as the most revolutionary logician of modern times, as well as placing him firmly in the line of renowned British empiricist philosophers such as Hobbes, Hume and Mill, the latter his own lay godfather. He made highly influential contributions to the philosophy of language, metaphysics and epistemology. Then followed such titles as Principles of Social Reconstruction, Why Men Fight, Justice in War-Time, Political Ideals, Mysticism and Logic and Proposed Roads to Freedom, all of which published during the war of 1914-18. These turned him into perhaps the most influential political thinker of the early 1900s.

The frenetic pace of work that Russell set himself during the war helped to save his mind. His abhorrence of suffering, his daily witnessing of the train-loads of young men, including some of his own students, who were sent to the slaughter fields of the Somme and Verdun, and his acute awareness of the other costs that the war was inflicting on the society and civilisation of Europe, drove him to that 'verge of despair' that he mentions in his memoirs. Beside the books, he also travelled widely to address anti-war gatherings and, though not a pacifist in the absolutist sense of the word, he wrote regularly for pacifist journals.

Yet another benefit of the work was the camaraderie it gained him of the men and women who shared his views. One such friendship soon blossomed into a deep love affair. It was with Lady Ottoline Morrell whose 'aristocratic habits of mind' he habituated by the fact of his own birth. Her letters inspired him for the rest of his life and a framed photograph of her he kept on his desk to his last days.

After the affair with Ottoline Morrell had faded, due to 'the sense of failure' that her inability to stimulate him intellectually instilled in him, he fell in love with another aristocrat, the actress Colette O'Neil, Lady Constance Malleson, who was similarly active against the war. In a letter to her of September 29, 1916, he reveals an important aspect of what he thought makes us feel good in ourselves:

> You are already where I have struggled to be, and without the weariness of long effort. I have hated many people in the past. The language of hate still comes to me easily, but I don't really hate anyone now. It is defeat that makes one hate people – and now I have no sense of defeat anymore. No one need ever be defeated – it rests with oneself to make oneself invincible. Quite lately I have had a sense of freedom I never had before … I don't like the spirit of socialism – I think freedom is the basis of everything.
>
> … there is a world of peace, and one can live in it and yet be active still over all that is bad in the world. Do you know how sometimes all the barriers of personality fall away, and one is free for all the world to come in – the stars and the night and the wind, and all the passions and hopes of men, and all the slow centuries of growth …

At the end of the war, he was imprisoned for six months for claiming that American troops in Britain would be used as strike breakers. Fortunately, some of his friends stood by him. The Foreign Secretary Lord Balfour arranged for him to receive all the books he wanted in prison and so Russell went back to mathematics to while away his hours of enforced isolation. He wrote Introduction to Mathematical Philosophy in a period of few weeks.

More generally, he would later write that the war transformed his life:

The war of 1914-18 changed everything for me. I ceased to be an academic and took to writing a new kind of book. I changed my whole conception of human nature. … Through the spectacle of death I acquired a new love for what is living. … I grew suspicious of all purposes demanding stern discipline. Being in opposition to the whole purpose of the community, and finding all the everyday virtues used as a means for the slaughter of Germans, I experienced great difficulty in not becoming a complete Antinomian. But I was saved from this by the profound compassion that I felt for the sorrows of the world.[85]

His suspicion of stern discipline imposed by governments to achieve implement their policies would reveal itself most starkly in his next book, which he wrote in 1920, after visiting the new Soviet Union and interviewing its leader Lenin. The Labour Party delegation of which he was a member included such other luminaries as Bernard Shaw. But unlike Shaw and the others, Russell was not impressed. While earlier in 1917 he had welcomed the Bolshevik revolution as a liberation for the various peoples of the vast Russian empire, he now saw that it had concentrated all political and economic power in the hands a few ruthless men, and that it was far worse that any such concentration that a capitalist class could acquire. He returned to England still a 'socialist', but with a deep sense of foreboding for Russia. His analysis of the Soviet state in The Theory and Practice of Bolshevism lost him many friends on the left wing of politics, but proved prescient of even greater horrors to come under Stalin. It has remained in print ever since and been a powerful influence on the side of the West against Communism and all other kinds of totalitarianism in the world at large.

For at least two reasons, the switch away from academic philosophy towards writing popular books was inevitable. While at Cambridge before the war, he had given away most of his inheritance to charity and to friends in need. So when he was expelled from Trinity as a result of his activities against the war and lost his only income, his salary, he had no other way of earning his livelihood. Had it not been for his physical stamina and for the astounding fluency of his mind that enabled him to dictate several thousand words a day to a secretary on intricate subjects, he would have been reduced to penury quickly.

Another reason was the clamour of publishers for quick short books by him on a variety of lighter subjects that were, nevertheless, serious in their content. There was also the attraction and ease of the new medium of broadcasting that made him known to, and loved by, millions of new people. He was similarly in demand to go on more lecture tours in America and elsewhere. In 1929, he even made a dangerous journey to China where he was moved by the yearning for new knowledge of the students and faculty of the University of Peking. He almost died from pneumonia there and read his own obituaries in the newspapers. He also read that the obituaries had brought an un-Christian sigh of relief to the bosom of many a church potentate.

By the time the second world war began in 1939, there was not the slightest trace remaining of Bertrand Russell, the pacifist. He became a vociferous supporter of a robust response to Hitler's ambition to conquer Europe, but found himself physically stranded in America and in the middle of a binding contract to deliver a series of lectures there. On the other hand, his American years proved lucrative and ensured his freedom from want in the long term. Despite a ferocious campaign in the press, based on his book Marriage and Morals, that forced the City College of New York to withdraw a proposal of employment to him, other contracts enabled him to write his History of Western Philosophy, a book that would, alone, make him financially independent for the rest of his life.

Russell returned to Britain on board a naval convoy a year before the war ended, with his family following later. He volunteered to speak to the troops to boost their morale, but found that an army regulation forbade lecturers who were civilians. Thus he found, to the amusement of the former pacifist in him, that he had been made an honorary colonel.

Further consolidation of this unaccustomed position at the heart of the ruling class followed quickly. For a brief period when America had the monopoly of nuclear weapons, he thought it justifiable for the West to wage a short war against Stalin's Russia to deprive it of the ability to acquire the same destructive power. His old college, Trinity, which had expelled him in disgrace for his opposition to war, now gave him Newton's apartment in which to live and, in 1949, the king offered him a personal gift, elevation to the exalted Order of Merit of which there were only 24 members from across the whole of the British Empire. A year later, the highest honour in the world for any intellectual arrived. The king of Norway pinned on his breast the Nobel Prize for Literature.[86]

Surely, it was time to go to prison again?

This he 'achieved' in 1961, in his 90th year, at the end of an arduous campaign against the possession of nuclear weapons by Britain. He advocated civil disobedience and brought on his head allegations that he had gone soft on the Communists by urging negotiations with Russia, albeit after Stalin. The chronology and details of these years are accessed easily elsewhere. They included the famous Russell-Einstein statement in favour of world nuclear disarmament, his setting up, with Joseph Rotblat, of the Pugwash conferences of the world's most distinguished scientists, his starting of the Committee of 100 to organise civil disobedience, and his attempt to persuade America's president John F Kennedy and Russia's leader Nikita Khrushchev to negotiate an end to their confrontation during the Cuba missile crisis of 1962. Russell was not deluded about his influence over the great powers, even though both Khrushchev and Kennedy broadcast their replies to him so that the public could judge for themselves. He said that Khrushchev only complied with his wishes if he had already decided that it was in his interest to do so.

There are signs that the passage of time has absolved Russell for these years. We can also conclude that he was himself the chief sufferer for his acts. They made him appear ridiculous at times, and he alienated many of his admirers by allowing – for lack of money, he said – one of his employees, his political assistant Ralph Schoneman, to take advantage of his name in the service of his own ego and extreme left-wing ideology.

As a newly arrived student from a remote corner of Kurdistan in 1960, I watched with disapproval on the streets of London some of the marches that Russell organised. I thought that if the British government took his advice and disarmed unilaterally, it would weaken the West against Communism. Now I believe that it would have set a good example to the world without making a significant difference to the protection that America's nuclear armament extended to itself and the rest of the West. I can also see that his defiance of his own government inspired dissent on the other side of the Iron Curtain, in the hearts of such brave thinkers as Andrey Sakharov, the 'father' of Russian's nuclear arms, as well as bringing to the attention of hundreds of millions of people all over the world the grave threat that nuclear weapons posed – and still pose – to civilisation.

A telling little event from 1961 may be recalled here. As the 89-year-old Russell was released from his week's detention – in a prison hospital – in London, his cousin the duke of Bedford thought it might be advisable for the frail old man and his wife Edith if they took a brief rest at Woburn Abbey before they made their long journey back home in Wales. Russell was sentimental about his relatives and used to describe the current duke as 'the head of my family', even when the incumbent was younger than he was. So he was tempted to take up his cousin's kind offer. It would have also provided the world's newspapers with the amusement of reporting how a criminal was able to transfer straight from one of Her Majesty's prisons to one of England's greatest palaces. But unfortunately it could not be. He had to return home immediately to begin the task of replying to tens of thousands of messages of support and good will that he had received while in detention.

Speaking of Edith Russell, this may be a good place to examine the charge of womanising that is sometimes levelled at Russell by his critics. While each one of us may come to a separate conclusion after reading several tomes on his life, to this writer the accusation appears unjust, or at least feeble. It is true that Russell had a sex drive that was overly strong in his youth and middle years. But my many years of reading about him – and indeed conversing with his last secretary Christopher Farley – suggest that he was never indiscriminate in his pursuit of women. No-where do we see any report that he sought the love of a woman who did not attract him as an intellectual first, and as we examine the distance in time between his love affairs, we have to admit that many of us would not have been as good as he was. By the time, for example, that he concluded he was no-longer in love with his first wife, Alys Pearsal Smith, the marriage had not been intimate for eleven years. It was after that traumatic realisation that, eventually, he started his next liaison, with Lady Ottoline Morrell. It is also important to point out that all his women – to my knowledge – loved him for as long as they lived? It is true that 'Colette' – Lady Constance Malleson – once sent him an angry letter saying that he had thrice made her 'the centre of his life, only to expel her again'. But she changed her mind quickly and sent him a bunch of red roses every May for his birthday for the rest of his life. These, Edith would place on his desk and he would always answer them with new professions of love. Indeed such was the sense of nearness that Russell had for the women he had loved that Edith felt it necessary to write to Colette immediately after his death to inform her of the manner of his passing.

Although Russell's contributions to purely philosophical thought, as opposed to his ethics, fall outside the purposes of this book, a brief overview here may not be out of place. His contributions range from the fundamental in some fields to mere improvements in others, but they are in some instances significant enough to go on being taught at universities for centuries, perhaps millennia. They fall largely in three fields: mathematical logic, the theory of knowledge and the conception of reality, i.e., metaphysics . In logic, he and Whitehead broke from Aristotle in their architectonic Principia Mathematica by devising a special notation and by achieving a greater generality in their system. He was a founder of the now-dominant new school of thought, Logical Analysis, and paved the way for the Logical Positivists' declaration that metaphysical statements were 'not even false, but literally meaningless', even though his student Wittgenstein was a more direct influence here.

In the words of his most respected commentator and admirer, the late Sir Alfred Ayer of Oxford[87]: 'with the possible exception of his pupil Ludwig Wittgenstein, there is no philosopher of our time who has made such a large difference, not only to the treatment of particular philosophical problems, but to the way in which the whole subject is pursued'[88]. In the opinion of the American philosophical couple Robert Solomon and Kathleen Higgins, there were 'two primary architects' of the new world of philosophy, Russell and

Husserl, the latter in Germany. But there is no doubt which of the two thinkers the couple esteem more highly. In their opus magnum of 1996, A Short History of Philosophy, they sprinkle their section on Russell with such phrases as 'the philosopher's philosopher', 'a paragon of intellectual integrity', and a true empiricist successor to 'his illustrious predecessor Hume'. While Solomon and Higgins do add that both Russell and Husserl were 'surpassed' by their own most brilliant students – Wittgenstein in Russell's case and Heidegger in Husserl's – 'who would take their work in very different directions, they also say that the trend had proved a matter of passing fashion, and that in Russell's case, he was here to stay. They write: '[Russell's] ontological hard-headedness, combined with his dazzling tools of the new logic, would transform philosophy in England and America. Those logically demanding, minimalist tendencies remain. Indeed, for many professional philosophers the only thing in the game that has changed dramatically is the location. Whereas once the primary playing field was in Cambridge (England), it has now moved to Cambridge (Massachusetts), Pittsburgh, Chicago and Berkeley.'[89]

*

Let me include in this profile a few personal memories concerning Russell that speak as much of his position in the world at the height of his popularity in the 1960s as they do of the inevitable ambiguity in the support that some of his many millions of admirers and supporters showed him when I was a raw youth in the 1960s.

Despite my anxiety that Russell's advice for Britain to give up its nuclear arms would weaken the West's defences against Communist Russia, I joined the Peace Foundation that he set up to promote co-existence between nations. As a young man of strong Kurdish patriotic feeling, I was constantly aware of the cruelties that several Middle Eastern states inflicted on my people, and I was pleased that Russell raised his voice against those states, Turkey, Iran, Iraq and Syria. On one occasion, I received from him a message to be read by me at a student rally in London that urged Israel to be more accommodating towards the Palestinians. But a few days after the rally, I was surprised to find that, unlike me who regarded himself as of the Left, a prominent British left-winger seemed virtually unable to hear the very name of Bertrand Russell. I had gone to the offices of the New Statesman magazine regarding the suppression of Iranian democrats, among them a childhood friend of my father's, Dr Karim Sanjabi, who was the leader of Iran's liberal opposition to the shah's autocracy. In order to impress the editor, Paul Johnson, I produced out of my pocket the letter from Bertrand Russell with his squidgy signature at the bottom. It was a red rag to a bull. Johnson almost threw the letter back at me and waved me out of his office. I understood later that he had recently quarrelled with Russell. It also transpired, a few years later, that Johnson was at the time undergoing a change of mind from the left to the right of British politics. He would therefore have hated Russell for his own reasons. But for me, apart from achieving nothing in my errand, the main result was that I lost my precious letter from the greatest philosopher of my time. I was so startled by Johnson's behaviour that I left the office without collecting my letter.

Another cherished memory is that my father, though a revered mystic and a holy man who disapproved of atheists, nevertheless felt some admiration for the great champion of peace in our world. So, on hearing that I had a tenuous link with the philosopher, he had visited a famous craftsman and commissioned him to make the finest possible pipe that he could make. But when the handsome pipe of matured cherry wood arrived for me to send on to Russell, I saw that it was too large to be of any practical use. Its ball was the size of a large man's fist and had probably been fashioned for Kurdish hashish dervishes. In jest, I told Chris Farley, Russell's secretary, of it and he, after talking to Wales, suggested that I should travel there to make the presentation in person. It would please Russell greatly, he said, and I could also talk to him about the Kurds and about Iran. On reflection, I decided not to go. I told those around me that I might give the great man a cold and kill him in his ancient condition. But I was in truth afraid of having no conversation to interest his mighty intellect. Now I wish that I had gone. He died of influenza a few months later.

*

Despite witnessing more horrors than was his 'fair share' in the twentieth century, Bertrand Russell made an effort not to forget that we, Mankind, had many attractive and admirable aspects to our nature. Examples are our tendency to cooperate, our abhorrence of seeing pain in others, our thirst for knowledge, an ability to love deeply family and friends – and even sometimes estrangers – that goes far beyond the needs of replicating our genes, and a craving for art that reflects reverence for the Universe: in short all the products of human consciousness. He also loved the beauty – as conceived by Man, of course – of the nature around us: landscapes, plants, skies, the stars, sunsets. One of the last things he said to Edith was: Oh, I do hate to leave this world.

*

An example of Russell's brilliance as a story teller cannot fail to move the reader. The following is from a little book entitled Unpopular Essays:

Mr Gladstone was, in private life dominated by the power of his eyes, which was quick and piercing and calculated to inspire terror. One felt like a small boy in the presence of an old-fashioned schoolmaster, a constant impulse to say 'please, Sir, it wasn't me'. Everybody felt like this. I cannot imagine a human being who would have ventured to tell him a story even in the faintest degree risqué. His moral horror would have frozen the narrator to stone. I had a grandmother who was the most formidable woman whom I have ever known. Other eminent men invariably quailed before her. But once, when Mr Gladstone was coming to tea, she told us all in advance that she was going to set him right on his Irish policy, of which she strongly disapproved. He came, and I was present throughout, waiting breathlessly for the expected clash. Alas. My grandmother was all softness, and said not a syllable to start the lion roaring. No one would have guessed that she disagreed with him about anything.

*

Finally, I would say this of Bertrand Russell, or at least of what he means to me: When you hold a book by him, you do not hold just a compilation of facts and opinions made by a wise man. You partake of the companionship of Bertrand Russell, a companionship that is unlikely to be surpassed any time soon. For me, he was the best of Man and, and since Man is the pinnacle of nature – as far as we know – he represented the highpoint of the Universe for me.

Thus if my readers are threatened with exile on a desert island, but allowed to take a book with them, I urge them to opt for Bertrand Russell's History of Western Philosophy. That great work will not only give them his wisdom and his wit, his companionship. It will also give them the best history of the West, which happens to have been the most important – because the most innovative – chunk of the world. In its readable and joyous pages, we have on display how the ancient Greeks took up the rudiments of learning from the Babylonians and, with astounding speed, raised it to such an advanced stage that dominates our thoughts to this day. We also see how the rise of ideology in the shape of Christianity stifled that innovation for centuries, how the churches and noblemen nevertheless preserved some of that ancient learning, and how, with the coming into being of mercantile classes in small city states in Italy in the period we call the Renaissance, the old learning was taken up once again in public and took off to sponsor true science to result in the liberation of our minds in the modern world.

But if the reader is allowed the luxury of taking two books with him on his exile, I should insist on his choosing Russell's Autobiography. That book tells the story of the bulk of the twentieth century, one of the most brilliant eras in the story of Homo Sapiens. It will also at times move them to tears with the love he felt for those around him and even for those he did not know in person, including the generations to come. Such has been Russell's influence over our social lives today that, at least in the advanced democracies, we are all Russellians now.

You burned for me, the estranger:
In your limbs you felt the pain of my wounds.
You lit up the world to help me heal.
Long after your last flicker,
You lighten the gloom of my nights.

So, live on, Bertrand Alfred William.
You were 'no solemn stained glass saint',
As you confessed.
You lived from your own centre.
You lied, you hated, broke a few hearts.

But you also loved,
You shone and you warmed.
You believed in my tending to be good.
You thought me noble,
You thought me rare.

So, live on, Bertie:
Burn on, my beacon.
Ease my darker nights.
Zarathustra Socrates Seneca.
You roll their candles into one for me.

# Boris Pasternak

*The Russian whose identification with European civilisation
helped destroy the Soviet Union*

90

**By his father Leonid in 1910**

In me are people without names,
Children, stay-at-homes, trees.
I am conquered by them all
And this is my only victory.

Although the artist will die, the happiness of living which he has experienced
is immortal. If it is captured in a personal and yet universal form, it can
actually be re-lived by others through his work.

I think that most plays should be cut for staging. I admire the English for
knowing how to cut Shakespeare, not just to keep what is essential, but rather

to emphasize what is significant. The Comédie Française came to Moscow recently. They don't cut Racine and I feel it is a serious mistake. Only what is expressive today, what works dramatically, should be staged.

French writers, when they commit themselves to political causes, are particularly unattractive. Either they are cliquish and insincere or, with their French sense of logic, they feel they have to carry out their beliefs to their conclusion. They fancy they must be absolutists like Robespierre or Saint-Just.

\*

Can you ever hope to portray a poet accurately, even in a tome of a book?[91] Poets are unstable mentally, given to moods, sensitive, tossed about on a heaving sea of emotions by the event of the moment. And they speak in signs. Often, they themselves do not understand quite what they meant in a cryptic phrase that made sense long ago. And what if that poet has seen many deaths, fallen in, and out, of love many times, lived through two revolutions and three wars, brief months of hope and elation to be followed by years of censorship and terror, friends abducted in the middle of the night never to be seen again, lovers banished to distant prisons to punish him, the constant danger of his livelihood being taken away to plunge his family into penury? How lucky those of us are who have not been tested to even a fraction of that horrendous length.

Boris Pasternak was such a poet, and was tested to that length. What made him rare was that he resisted and eventually overcame the mountainous weight of a totalitarian state determined to crush his spirit to enslave him. He lived, on the whole, a life of integrity and remained loyal to his friends and principles. It helped that that he had a grand plan. He knew he had an epochal story to tell and he knew that it was essential to survive long enough to tell it, the story of his blighted people in one of their darkest centuries. Eventually he achieved his aim, despite the ever-present, lethal danger of being found writing it. By bearing the humiliation of appearing weak at times, by making concessions to his oppressors at the expense of his pride, he proved mightier than they were. His life's work undermined the Huns and helped to prepare their titanic fall. He also, in the process, managed to write enough poetry to be recognised by all as one of the greatest poets of the Russian language, a language that was already well endowed in magnificent poetry.

Boris Pasternak was one of the main, psychological architects of the eventual fall of the regime founded by Lenin and his thugs, and he will be read outside Russia, too, for as long as there will be men to read.

\*

It is early 1914 and, in Moscow, you are being urged to honour the forthcoming 25th anniversary of your marriage in style. You have many friends and colleagues. You can afford it. You are a successful Impressionist painter and a leading professor at the empire's central School of Painting, Sculpture and Architecture. You count among your intimate friends famous writers, artists and aristocrats, with Scriabin and Rachmaninov regular visitors to your dinner table. Your wife, Rosalia Kaufmann, is equally successful, even more talented than you are, by your own admission. She is a famous concert pianist and professor of music at the Conservatory. You have four bright, handsome and eligible children who would enjoy showing off the occasion to their peers. Boris, the eldest at twenty-four, is especially promising. He has composed a passable piano sonata and studied philosophy in Germany. He has published a collection of brilliant poems. Some predict a mighty future for him. Furthermore, now that social reform is in the air – the serfs have already been freed – and your own Jewish community feels at last that all doors in Russia are being flung open to it, the celebration would be doubly justified. So, what do you do?

After some soul-searching, you decide to throw a great ball and large numbers accept your invitation. The day eventually arrives. The children take over the opening ceremony. The two boys are immaculate in their formal evening coats, and the two girls are beautiful in their dresses and bouquets. Boris leads them and declaims a poem of his own to honour you. You are immensely proud. Later, you paint them to record the scene for ever.

Unfortunately for the Pasternaks, or the whole of Europe, for that matter, this idyll did not last. At the end of July, the great war of 1914-18 broke out and landed Russia into the lap of uncouth Bolshevik revolutionaries who had no time for 'bourgeois' culture.

Despite the seeming tumbling down of their world, however, the Pasternaks clung on to their country. The did not join the other hundreds of thousands of their class who left for western Europe. Even more admirably, they wished the revolution well and dared hope that its leader Lenin would lead them to democracy, when all citizens would be equal before the law and welcome to participate in politics. This was, of course, naïve, and a bitter civil war soon made matters worse. That lasted till 1922. Moscow starved and the Bolsheviks began to see enemies everywhere. Good people began to disappear.

Leonid and 'Rosa' bore the hardships cheerfully until the summer of 1921. But then, when they went to Germany for surgery on Leonid's eyes, taking the two girls with them, they decided not to return. Boris and Alexander remained, determined to make a success of themselves in the new, exciting Russia, with its ferment of innovation in all branches of the arts. Boris, who was then thirty-one, found himself being admitted to the circles of famous poets like Anna Akhmatova. Alexander practiced as an architect. While Boris could sell books to buy bread, Alexander knew which beams in the roof to cut away for fuel without bringing the house down.

On the whole, the opening years of the 1920s were the years of hope. Lenin was still alive and Trotsky, a Jew, seemed the next most powerful man in the government. So in 1922, when Boris took his bride to meet his parents and sisters in Berlin, he returned. In 1926, the couple went to Berlin again, this time with their infant son Evgeni, and stayed several months. But then the nightmare began in earnest: the replacement of Lenin's New Economic Policy after his death in 1924 with Stalin's 'Socialism in One Country,' and particularly Stalin's forced collectivisation of agriculture appeared to have the dimensions of a great genocide. Some ten million peasants were to die before 1934. There began also the purging of the intelligentsia in show trials and the sending of millions of others to their deaths in Corrective Labour Camps. Even the grand old man of Soviet letters, Maxim Gorky, would be shown no mercy.

Boris, as a prominent member of the Union of Soviet Writers, was now trapped, having remain silent in the face of every atrocity Stalin's brutes committed in the name of the cowed masses. But the Party did not seemingly take his silence for granted, for it tried to entrap him in luxury. In 1935, he was sent, though ill, without his family and reluctant to represent Soviet Russia, to Paris to take part in an 'anti-fascist' conference which he thought futile – while his Jewish parents and sisters were finding life hard in the new Germany of the Nazis – and he visited friends in London for two days.[92] A year later, he was given a medium-sized house in Peredelkino, a colony for writers that Stalin had set up on the estate of a former aristocrat near Moscow, and his poems and prose writings were allocated scarce resources for their publication.

Despite his privileges, however, Pasternak began to raise the ire of the leadership of the Writers' Union. He refused, for example, to sign a petition by them urging Stalin to execute 19 generals he had put on a show trial. He persisted even when the whole executive committee of the Union travelled to Peredelkino to plead with him. They feared for their own safety for not being able to convince him. On other occasions, he interceded with Bukharin and Stalin on behalf of detained friends, sometimes apparently successfully, before their eventual re-arrests, murders or suicides. On night, he received a terrifying telephone call from Stalin himself. The monster first asked why Pasternak had not informed on his close friend Osip Mandeslstam and then, when Pasternak waffled any knowledge of misconduct by Mandelstam, accused him of cowardice for not 'sticking by a comrade'. Mandelstam would soon die during transportation to a camp in Siberia.

What can only arouse our deepest admiration is that, throughout these years of horror met upon his friends and on the people of Russia at large, Pasternak was also able to concentrate on his art. He writes poetry that even anti-Communist émigré Russians applaud, and he completed a long list of translations from European classics, particularly the plays of Shakespeare, and he wrote plays of his own. Perhaps it was due to Stalin's grudging admiration for his work that he, allegedly, once struck Pasternak's name out of a list of suspects proposed to him for elimination. He is said to have uttered: 'Leave that cloud-dweller alone'. Those years were also a time of personal emotional turmoil for him. He had left his wife and son and lived with friends. He had heard of his parents' and sisters' second uprooting in 1938, from Nazi Germany to the safety of London, and he had fallen in love again and began a new co-habitation.

In the summer of 1938, Stalin suddenly unleashed on the world the shocking surprise of his non-aggression treaty with Hitler and his carving up of Poland with the hitherto 'fascist enemy'. So this is where the idealistic revolution of 1917 that had meant to liberate the whole of the world's oppressed, toiling masses, had ended up: in bed with a raging, racist devil to plunge humanity into a second global war, so soon after the industrial slaughter of the previous. Soon, it would appear as if Hitler's shadow had cast itself over his parents and sisters in England. How ardently and secretly must have he, therefore, wished every moment of every day and night in the summer of 1940 when those brave young men of the RAF attempted to thwart the Nazi's apparently unstoppable Luftwaffe over the skies London.

In June 1941, having been defeated in those skies, Hitler turned his hounds on his ally and Stalin, just as suddenly, changed his tune to woo over to his side the millions of Russians he has alienated. So, the former nationality-free champion of the working class, the man born and brought up in Georgia, became an old-fashioned Russian nationalist. He invoked the examples of Russia's medieval princes to instil purpose in his soldiers, and he relaxed his repression of the intelligentsia. This gave Pasternak new hope. The monster had learnt his lesson. He wrote some rabble-rousing patriotic poems of his own and recited them to assemblies of soldiers near the fronts. But the sojourn did not endure. Stalin unleashed his second reign of terror even before his armies had entered Berlin in the spring of 1945 and imposed his will over half-a-dozen new nations in eastern Europe. Pasternak, the sincere patriot that he was, said later that that he wished the Western powers had over-run Russia, too, to save it from the new suffering and to impose democracy on it.

The year of victory was both prolific and eventful for Boris. His father died in Oxford, not having seen his son for twenty-two years and disappointed that he, Boris, had abandoned Judaism. Beside other work, Boris translated Shakespeare's Henry IV, parts I and II, and supervised the publications of Othello and two verse collections. He also, in November, began the writing of Doctor Zhivago, the novel whose idea had for some time become the new motive force of his life.

Looking back on those years later, Pasternak wondered how he had managed to survive the men of the NKVD who had periodically bundled his neighbours in Peredelkino into waiting vans. His own work had come under attack from no-less an apparatchik as secretary-general of the Writers' Union, and one whole collection of his poetry had been pulped: 'It is surprising that I remained whole during the purges', he wrote in 1954. 'you cannot imagine the liberties I allowed myself. My future was shaped in precisely the way I myself shaped it'. Paying no attention to any warning sign, he recited some of early chapters of Zhivago to friends in Peredelkino and Moscow. Determined that the work should survive in safety, he had sent copies to confidantes inside the Soviet Union, as well as outside it, to his sisters in Oxford, with the stricture that if they leaked into public view, they would pronounce his end. The poet Nadezhda Mandelstam, Osip's surviving and persecuted widow, had her own view of Pasternak's survival. It was due, she said, to a combination of sheer luck and Pasternak's 'incredible charm'.

Stalin's sudden death in the spring of 1953 may well be regarded as the first crack in the wall of Communist tyranny in Russia. It is said that when he was found dead by his servants, fear of him still so cowed his minions in the so-called leadership of the Communist Party that they and his doctors did not, for several days, to approach his corpse in case he were merely asleep. The first result of the great event for Pasternak was that, a couple of months later, his lover Olga Ivinskaya, who had been taken virtually hostage by the state to intimidate him, was released from her Gulag prison as part of an amnesty.

Three years later, in February 1956, Stalin's successor Nikita Khrushchev denounced his former boss as a vengeful tyrant at the twentieth congress of the Party and promised that the he and his colleagues would henceforth listen to the country. The speech shocked the whole of the Communist world when it was leaked to the West and further raised hopes that a degree of tolerance might now be shown to those more moderate Communists who felt that the system needed to be reformed. In June, Pasternak signed over the non-Russian rights to Zhivago to an Italian publishing company and, to make certain that the company which had Communist sympathies would not bend to Soviet pressure, also gave a copy to Isiah Berlin, the Russian-born British philosopher and former diplomat, to smuggle it out to Britain.

To this day, speculation continues as to how the original manuscript fell into the hands of British and American intelligence. Most researchers agree that Berlin, by then no-longer a diplomat but a philosopher at Oxford university, had tried to persuade Pasternak not to publish the novel in his lifetime. He had been so worried for Pasternak's life and for the safely of those close to him that, after a long night of reading and 'weeping' over the novel and realising its greatness, he had made a second trip to Peredelkino to dissuade Pasternak. But Pasternak had insisted. 'This is my last word', he had told him. He was prepared for all consequences and wanted the world to read the greatest fruit of all his toils. Berlin continued his efforts to frustrate Pasternak's wish after his return to England. 'Just because someone is prepared for a martyr's crown', he wrote to a friend, 'that doesn't give one the right to push it on his brow. The whole thing really is revolting'.[93]

It is believed that Berlin, knowing not how to smuggle the large manuscript through Moscow airport himself, had entrusted it to his friend the British ambassador in Moscow for inclusion in the diplomatic bag, and that the embassy had made micro-film copies of it. The British government had then given a copy to the United States, upon which the Americans had – illegally – printed it in Belgium through a CIA front publisher for distribution inside Russia. This was the height of the cold war and the West found it hard to resist the propaganda lure presented by one of the soviet Union's own most famous writers.

In the event, the Italian Communist publisher Feltrinelli resisted heavy Soviet pressure to suppress the book, and brought out a faithful Italian translation in November 1957. Immediately, feverish work got underway to translate the novel into dozens of other languages, and the response from readers was tremendous. In October the following year, seeing the original Russian version published, the Swedish Academy had no doubt in granting Pasternak the Nobel Prize for Literature. Pasternak was delighted and telegraphed his gratitude to the Academy, only to see the full force of the state's media being brought down upon his head.

The authorities had held back from providing the book with publicity of their own. They had been content with warning Pasternak to recall the rights he had given Feltrinelli, forbidding any of their own publishing institutes to which Pasternak had offered the novel from publishing it, and sending envoys to Italy to intercede with Feltrinelli. None of that had stopped Pasternak. So now they had to counter-act the continuous news of the disaster that western radios poured into most Soviet homes each morning and each night. Their campaign of vilification began. Pasternak was expelled from the Writers' Union and denounced in the press as a class enemy and traitor to Russia. He was a 'mangy sheep', a 'literary weed', 'a pig who has soiled where he has eaten', beside much else.

Pasternak apparently became suicidal and Olga was summoned to be told, among other things, that she must prevent him from taking his life, for that would show the Party in a bad light abroad. The summons served also as a blatant warning to Pasternak that he would not be the only one to suffer if he did not cooperate. So a few days after he had accepted the accolade with such enthusiasm, he telegraphed Sweden again to decline it. His eldest son Evgeni later recalled that he did not recognise his father when he called at the house that evening. 'Pale, lifeless face, tired painful eyes, and only speaking about one thing: Now it all doesn't matter; I declined the prize'.

Rumours also circulated that Khrushchev was inclined towards deporting him, presumably on his own or with his wife alone. Olga pressed him to plead with Khrushchev to let him remain.[94] He wrote to the prime minister to say that he would die if deported, that he could not imagine being away from Russia. Olga later wrote in her autobiography that she was sorry to have persuaded him to do so.[95] Western medicine might have caught his cancer in time.

Pasternak married twice and continued to live with his second wife to the end, but it was Olga who was the most important woman in his life, his muse and source of strength in the years of his toil over Zhivago. He had fallen in love with her at first sight in the autumn of 1946 at the offices of Novi Mir, the literary journal for which he wrote. She worked there as a sub-editor and was a widow at the age only of 34 years, bringing up two children on her meagre salary. When the apparatchiks in charge of the journal chose to punish him by harassing her, he persuaded her to resign to become a translator and his part-time secretary. In July 1950, she was arrested and sentenced to five years in the Gulag when she refused to bear witness against him. Pasternak would later write of that atrocity: 'She was put in jail on my account, as the person considered to be closest to me. They hoped that by means of a grueling interrogation and threats they could extract enough evidence from her to put me on trial. I owe my life, and the fact that they did not touch me in those years, to her heroism and endurance.'

\*

In an act of revenge that should for ever go down as a damning indictment of the last years of the Soviet tyranny, Olga was arrested again, a short while after Pasternak's death, in May 1960, this time with her daughter, and accused of converting foreign currency – presumably some of his Western royalties – on the black market. The two women were not made to serve the full length of their sentences, but the state also seized most of her papers, especially her correspondence with Pasternak, to stop her publishing them in an autobiography. It did not succeed. Her memoirs, A Captive of Time: My Years with Pasternak, came out in 1978, including again in a masterly English translation by the late Max Hayward. A measure of her love for Pasternak can be gleamed from a passage, addressed to Pasternak, in her closing pages:

My love. I now come to the end of the book you wanted me to write. When we first met, I was only just thirty-four years old[96]. Now, as I write these final lines, it is my sixtieth birthday ... The greatest part of my conscious life has been devoted to you – and what is left of it will also be devoted to you.

Life, as you know, has not been kind to me. But I have no complaint against it: it bestowed on me the great gift of your love, and our friendship and closeness. You used to say to me that life treats us more gently, with more compassion, than we generally expect. This is a great truth and I never cease to be mindful of your words to me: 'One must never, in any circumstances, despair. In misfortune, it is our duty to hope and to act'.

Olga Ivinskaya lived long enough (she died in 1995) to see the fall of the system that had blighted her life and those of countless others. But she is assured of a much longer literary life. Apart from her moving memoirs, which will be read as long as Zhivago will be read, she helped give birth to that great novel. She inspired its creator to persist and became his model for the character of Lara.

*

I first read Zhivago in the early 1970s, for a poor grasp of English had defeated my earlier attempts to do so. To me, it is now really a long poem, as well as a long story. Every great novel is thus. They are love letters to the vulnerable flocks of human beings wondering how to live the life left to them. Long after the death of its creator and the downfall of his oppressors, Zhivago is also to me the sympathetic tale of the lives of ordinary human beings in extraordinary times. That in the process, it tells the story of the Russian revolution of 1917 and shows its particular band of revolutionaries to have been foolish, though well-meaning, enthusiasts who later found themselves trapped in the web of a psychopathic monster is of secondary importance, even though it was its creator's central, motivating force. Altogether, Zhivago is, beside a long poem, an attempt to celebrate our good qualities and to understand our weaknesses.

*

You are young:
The world lies at your feet.
Tall, handsome, in black coat and white tie,
You lead your siblings to recite a poem
To honour your parents at a ball.[97]

Do you know what lies in store for you?

You exude confidence, as you should.
Rich, bright, well bred,
Among Russia's chosen,
You embody her hopes for a European future;
You shall liberate her masses from their yoke of ages.

Let me tell you:
Your revolution will come.
There will be wars, also.
You will starve, weep and hate,
You won't dare say whom you love.

But you will live on to shine once more:
You will shout your dreams from the rooftops;
You will burst upon the whole world
To make it weep for Russia,
To urge her on to hope again.

The Huns will tremble at your name:
Their emperor wears no clothes;
Their castles will tumble down.
Russia will resume her fitful journey,
And she will remember you.

# Hannah Arendt

*The woman whose world collapsed thrice*
*The witness to the twentieth century who saw a potential*
*exterminator in most of us*
*The Jewish refugee who forgave her Nazi betrayers*

98

I shall either study philosophy or drown myself.

What will happen once the authentic mass man takes over, we do not know, although it may be a fair guess that he will have more in common with the meticulous correctness of Himmler than with the hysterical fanaticism of Hitler, and that he will more resemble the stubborn dullness of Molotov than the sensual vindictive cruelty of Stalin.[99]

The banality of evil

Compared to the eleven wise men I have studied so far, Hannah Arendt has perhaps inspired few people to rise above themselves, although this may change, given that recently a part of her life has been turned into a glamorous Hollywood film. For now, she remains no hero of world repute, and she continues even to attract some criticism. According to a number of her detractors, she had a chance to shake off the grip of Romantic German metaphysics when, in the second half of her life, she found herself in the more clear-eyed world of Anglophone philosophy, but she did not.

Be that as it may – for one philosopher's profound insight is sometimes another's utter waffle – Hannah Arendt was endowed with rare qualities. Beside her dazzling intelligence, her capacity to forgive was of an unusual dimension. It extended not only to Martin Heidegger, her former teacher and lover who had betrayed her by joining the Nazis, but also to many others, such as the playwright Bertolt Brecht who refused to denounce the barbarities of Stalinist communism. She was courageous and did not allow herself to be intimidated by the herd. Even though she had been in the leading ranks of the struggle to save European Jewry from annihilation, and even though she was devoted to the survival and prosperity of the new state of Israel, she alienated Israel's leaders the moment she detected in them the signs of common nationalism, indications that, as survivors of the Holocaust themselves, they did not sympathise sufficiently with the suffering of the Palestinians for whose displacement they had been partly responsible. She tried to mobilise public opinion in her new country, the United States, against visits from some of the most extreme of those leaders, the terrorists of the Irgun and Stern gangs, and, even more famously, when Israel's pursuit and punishment of the Nazi arch-criminal Adolf Eichmann fell short of the highest standards of Western justice, she raised her voice in protest. She was almost excommunicated for it and lost many personal friends.

Hannah Arendt's generosity in friendship similarly remains an inspiring example and proved a saviour in the darkest hours of her own life. Her voluminous correspondence with the novelist Mary McCarthy will be read long after us, as will some of her books on political theory.

She also had stamina and tenacity in plenitude. In the end, however, a life that had been abrim with grief and stress took its toll. She died from heart disease at the age of sixty-nine, early for an affluent academic living in the New York of the 1970s.

*

Hannah Arendt was born in 1906 in the district of Linden, in today's Hanover, before her family moved to their ancestral Konigsberg, today's Kaliningrad in

Russia. German Jewry flourished at the time and had reasons to be grateful for its deliverance from centuries of insecurity and discrimination. Though traditional anti-Semitism survived at the level of the street, enlightened laws had been enacted to grant all citizens full equality and Jews served the empire at the highest levels of government and were prominent in the professions. Her father, an engineer, was a respectable member of Konigsberg society and presided over a secular household, where Judaism was not the primary badge of identity.

Even when, in the course of the first world war, the family had to abandon Konigsberg and moved to Berlin, the future promised hope still. Hannah's father had died by then and her mother had remarried and given birth to another daughter. Hannah shone at school and decided to study philosophy, no doubt inspired by the fame of Konigsberg's most famous son, Immanuel Kant. She would later recall that the future course of her life was set when she first began to browse in the family's home library. 'I would either study philosophy', she said, 'or drown myself, so to speak'.

But the peace was not to last. Though Germany was now a democracy, the war of 1914-1918 had plunged it into defeat, bankruptcy and political chaos. As a consequence, a rising tide of anti-Semitism put an end to the progress made. The Jews were made to feel unwanted aliens in the towns and cities they had come to think their own.

Young Hannah had been traumatised by the slaughter and waste of the war and by its consequences, and her bourgeois mother had come to admire Rosa Luxemburg, the Marxist revolutionary leader who was murdered in 1919 by right-wing militia. But in spite of the drama around her in the early 1920s as she prepared to go to university, Hannah showed no interest in politics. She did not join any factions or parties, whether the Social Democrats or the Zionists.

Thus when she went to the university of Marburg in 1924, she had a high expectation of her philosophy teachers and one of them, Martin Heidegger, answered that longing in more senses than one. At 35 years of age, he was seen as a rising star of German philosophy, expected to become a successor to the last of the greatest, Nietzsche, and – what was to be fateful for the eighteen-year-old Hannah – he was also handsome, and a womaniser. Within a year, he was her lover.

As Heidegger was married, with young children, and also keen to avoid any scandal in the service of his career, the affair could not be divulged to any but Hannah's closest friends. Nor did she have his exclusive attention. Unknown to her, he was having a similar affair with another of his students. So there were periodic breakups during the four years between 1924 to 1928 that it lasted. In the wake of one such breakup, she transferred to the university of Heidelberg and began the writing of her doctoral theses there, under the supervision of a good man, this time, Karl Jaspers, who was married to a Jew. Tellingly, Hannah had chosen to research the concept of love in the thought of St Augustine, both under the influence of Heidegger and as an indication of her own temperament and future behaviour.

The theses was published in 1929 and she hoped to follow it up with a higher doctorate to enable her to teach at a university. But by then the streets had become a battleground between militias of the left and right and Adolf Hitler had become a powerful political presence. The spread of ideological anti-Semitism to the press and body politic barred Hannah's way. Jewish students were openly banned from pursuing higher studies and even established Jewish professors were losing their seats.

From several years back, Hannah had seen the disaster looming and so, despite not belonging to any Zionist or ever social democratic party, had begun to work informally for the welfare of victims of the new persecution. In 1933, the year Hitler became chancellor, she was caught gathering evidence of anti-Semitism in the press and governmental institutions for publication abroad. She was lucky. The Nazis had not yet consolidated their hold on the police and she was let out on bail after only two weeks. She fled illegally across the frontier into Switzerland and joined the already large community of German Jewish and leftist exiles in Paris.

There, she devoted herself wholly to the welfare of destitute refugees from the new German Reich. In particular, she helped gather funds for Jewish children who had been separated from their parents in order to send them to agricultural cooperatives, Kibbutzim, in Palestine. It was there that she learned Heidegger had joined the Nazis and been installed by them as the new rector of the university of Freiburg, and it was there that she learned he was sacking Jewish teachers and professors from that university with the zeal of a convert. The unfortunate included Heidegger's own former mentor, the phenomenologist Jewish philosopher Husserl. 'I felt sick in the stomach when I heard the news', she told Heidegger years later.

In this her first exile from home, which was to last until Hitler grabbed France, too, it was inevitable that she would live at the centre of the gloom that was the collapse of civilisation in Germany. It had been the civilisation about which she cared most and which she held above all others, though, in the latter years, she had been forced to emphasise her distinctness as a Jew. Jaspers had once told her that, of course, she was a German. She had replied: 'I am not. Just look at me'.

There was the relentless nature of her work to keep her sane, and there was the companionship of some of the most dazzling intellectuals of Europe in which to glow. She became friends with Raymond Aron, the French critic of Marxism, one of the seminal political thinkers of the twentieth century, and she became close to Walter Benjamin, the Marxist writer and critic who would later commit suicide in Spain to avoid being handed over to the Gestapo.

Hannah was lucky to be able to cheat the Gestapo a second time. While being detained in a women's camp for aliens in southern France in 1941, and as the French prepared to hand over their charges to the Germans, she evaded the guards with a few other women and reached Portugal. Her visa had been issued by an American diplomat acting against his neutral government's directives, and another American, a philanthropist, had paid for her voyage across the Atlantic. Harrowing recollections of her fellow inmates who could not escape and perished in concentration camps in eastern Europe haunted her for the rest of her life.

Thus she arrived in New York in 1941 a refugee, thirty-four years of age and penniless, with little knowledge of the language of her hosts. Fortunately she had her devoted husband, a German philosopher and former Communist, with her, and she had her mother, too, even though a frail and distraught old lady by now. Husband and mother did not much like one another and the accommodation they were given, a small apartment in a run-down block, did not help. Nevertheless, they were safe and felt welcome, and they could throw themselves into work for other refugees and push for America to join the war. Another consolation came from the knowledge that her sister, four years her junior, was safe in British Palestine. She had been sent there as far back as 1934, 'the year after Hitler'. But countless friends, relatives, neighbours and acquaintances had sunk without trace.

The impression one gets of those years for her is one of back-breaking activity: English classes, refugee work, numerous political gatherings, writing a column in German for a Jewish émigré journal. Altogether, it seems to have been easier for her than it was for her husband Heinrich. It would take years for him to get a job in his own speciality, teaching philosophy. But Hannah was soon publishing political and academic essays in English, with the help of American friends. By 1944, when it was clear that the end of the Nazi nightmare was assured, she was director of a new organisation devoted to rescuing Jewish cultural treasures stolen by the Nazis or hidden all over occupied Europe. The work would take her back to the home continent, as would a new job, the chief editorship of a publishing firm, Schocken Books, Kafka's publisher in pre-war Berlin which had transferred to New York.

By 1948, we find that Arendt has already got herself into trouble with some sections of the new state of Israel. We find her name alongside Einstein's and those of other prominent Jews and Americans in a letter to the New York Times. They object to the visit to the United States by Menachem Begin, the former leader of the Jewish terrorist gang Irgun. The writers do not shy away from using strong words. They describe Begin's new party, the Freedom Party, as 'closely akin in its organization, methods, political philosophy and social appeal to the Fascist and Nazi parties'. The first stone is thus thrown to alienate Arendt from many fellow Jews and Israelis who regard the former anti-British and anti-Arab terrorists as heroes. They will not forgive her, and will achieve vengeance in 1963 when Arendt publishes Eichmann in Jerusalem.

This was a consequence of Israeli agents finding and abducting the former Nazi transportation chief hiding in Argentina a couple of years earlier. As soon as Arendt heard that the animal was going to be tried before an Israeli court, she volunteered to cover it for the widely-read and influential New Yorker magazine. As she was now the famous author of two heavy-weight books, The Origins of Totalitarianism and The Human Condition, she was immediately accepted. But when her report eventually came out in book form, the Jewish community, and even some mainstream Americans, found them aghast. How could a Jew, especially one so prominent and proven, claim that the new and idealistic state of Israel had resorted to staging a show trial for ulterior purposes? She received sacks of hate mail and even threats to her life as a traitor, even as a German nationalist. Friends of many years abandoned her. Her own sister in Israel could not understand.[100]

Fortunately some of her closest friends, such as Mary McCarty, stood by her, and her employers – colleges and publishers – rescinded their requests that she resign when told she might fight them in the courts. But the couple had a hard time of it and it exacerbated her husband's poor health. He died in 1970 after an earlier heart attack. Heinrich's death plunged her into a new period of gloom and loneliness.

A comic, and yet also tragic, little story is worth telling here. Soon after Heinrich's death, the world-famous poet W. H. Auden who had become a close friend proposed marriage to Hannah to help fill the new void in her life. His determined homosexuality was no problem to either side. It would never be romance at their ages. But she later recalled for a a girlfriend one of her reasons for declining the offer. Auden never washed, she said. Despite his wealth, he refused even to buy himself a second suit so that the first one could be cleaned.

While telling tales of her life – and story-telling was esteemed by her as more effective than philosophy – another anecdote may help to shed light on her puzzling adoration of Heidegger. Her niece and heir, Edna Brocke, gave a lecture at the Hannah Arendt Center for Politics and Humanities at Bard College, Annandale-on-Hudson, New York State, in April 2012. She recalled that some six months before her aunt died in December 1975, she was with her aunt as she boarded an aircraft to visit Heidegger. The young women, who shared her family's distaste for Hannah's continued association with a Nazi, steeled herself and asked her, though as sweetly as she could, whether the trip was 'really necessary'? Hannah drew her niece close and whispered in her ear, in German: 'My dear, there are things that are more powerful than Mankind'. Asked by a student what Hannah had meant, Brocke said that she really did not know, for she had held her aunt in too much awe to continue with a follow-up question. Pressed again, Brocke added: 'I think she meant to say that this one thing was beyond her ability'. That reminds me of a sentence in one of her first letters to Heidegger after their reconciliation after the war. She wrote, possibly referring to their love: 'For something to endure, it must remain the same'.

To this day, certainly, her enduring relationship with Heidegger puzzles her biographers. After his betrayal – and he went on to pay his membership fee to the Nazi party until it fell apart after Hitler's suicide in 1945 – it was always Arendt who worked hard at keeping the friendship alive. She had made the initial contact with the marginalised philosopher, sending regular letters and food parcels, and she visited him every year despite the clear jealousy of his wife. In fact, she helped to rehabilitate his name in philosophical circles by arranging for the translation and publication of his works in English, and he certainly used her in his pursuit of that same aim. Tellingly, although she succeeded to tempt Jaspers to meet Heidegger for old times' sake, Jaspers eventually pulled back, finding it impossible to meet a cruel Nazi who, as rector in Freiburg, had inflicted so much pain on Jewish colleagues. He remembered that while he had himself been isolated and forced to flee his country to avoid possible extermination, Heidegger had featured regularly in Nazi journals praising 'the civilising mission of the thousand-year Reich' and the genius of the Fuhrer[101].

It is interesting that Arendt objected to being described as a philosopher. This is despite her voluminous writings on subjects that have always been classed as philosophy. She said that philosophy confined itself to Man in the singular, whereas she was concerned with him[102] as a member of society, as a political being. Instead, she preferred to be described as a political theorist. I suspect that this preference stemmed from her deep distrust of intellectuals. She had seen too many of them – including Heidegger – resorting to mental acrobatics to justify their gravitation towards the wielders of power under both Hitler and Stalin.

Will her work endure? This is not an easy question to answer. For while her main books continue to be in print and numerous academic seminars are annually devoted to her thought, much of her work is bound to its own time. Her first major work, The Origins of Totalitarianism, which saw many more affinities than differences between Soviet Russia and Nazi Germany, was most helpful in the 1950s and 60s, when the Soviet Union still inspired some Western idealists against the evidence of its barbarities leaking daily out of the gulags. But her claim that totalitarian states had not existed before our time is less convincing. We are bound to think, for example, of ancient Sparta or early Islam, both of which tried to control and mould the minds of their followers to the minutest degree.

Arendt's other tome, The Human Condition, remains her most influential work. It develops her theory of the superiority of political action over 'labour' or repetitive, life-sustaining production, and 'work', by which she meant the kind of creative, fulfilling activity that produces 'a human world'. The book also asserts her view that while Man has always lived in society, in a social environment, only a few societies initiated a common space that was conducive to the individual's freedom.

In yet another book, On Revolution, she asserts that the revolution in France in 1789 was a failure because it abandoned the pursuit of freedom to concentrate on compassion for the masses. By contrast, the Founding Fathers of the American Revolution of 1765-83 had made certain that liberty came first and was therefore a success. Unfortunately by now, power in the United States had receded by a great distance from the citizen and what was needed was human-scale local councils to correct the deviation. For this reason, Arendt has been accused by some of utopianism. She has been accused of harking to the first days of little Athens and republican Rome when citizens knew one another and gathered in public square to elect their leaders. This is unfair. Others have described her as a pessimist.

Some other of her works, such as Men in Dark Times, in which Walter Benjamin and Karl Jaspers feature, are moving narratives, while the unfinished Life of the Mind is too obtuse to be of interest to the general reader.

The collapse of the remaining totalitarian super-power in 1989 would, apparently, not have surprised Hannah Arendt. This is probably because she believed that states that felt insecure in their appeal to their citizens indulged in arming themselves too heavily and exhaust themselves. When one of her biographers[103] was asked this question in a radio interview in 2002, she imitated Arendt's booming voice and replied: 'Ach, vaat did you expect?' By the time Arendt died in New York in 1975, she had lived in an academic, English-speaking environment for 35 years. Yet she had not managed completely to master her new language and still spoke with a heavy German accent.

To sum up, whether Hannah Arendt's philosophical work endures is not yet to be determined. She is certainly regarded by some as the initiator of a new theory of politics which breaks from that which prevailed from Plato to our time. Others find the claim arguable. What is not in doubt is that she was a supreme interpreter of the twentieth century to itself, that she was a heroic human being of rare stature, and that she possessed a supreme ability to understand her fellow human beings, to love them and to forgive them. In my opinion, it was this ability to forgive, which was the direct result of her insight into us as emotional, fallible beings, that was Hannah Arendt's greatest achievement. It proved vital to her resilience. It provided her with an impenetrable armour against despair when surrendering to despair would have been the easier course. Her example will hopefully continue to inspire people long after our time.

For another view, I should direct the reader to the (almost) incomparable George Steiner. In a long article in the Times Literary Supplement on January 29, he reviewed some of Arendt's correspondence with Heidegger, then recently revealed. He made it clear that he did not hold Arendt's intellect in high esteem, and his attitude towards Heidegger was, of course, infused with revulsion. Nevertheless, suspecting that Heidegger was likely to mesmerise many people for a long time yet, he ended his article with the following pronouncement: 'It may well be that in centuries to come, the Abelard-Eloise letters and the Heidegger-Arendt Briefe will circle one another, reciprocally illuminating and mapping, in their intersecting orbits, a cosmography of the thinking heart.'

# Part Two

# Poems for Autumn

I had originally planned to exclude from this anthology any poems that invoked 'God' as a source of solace or strength. God would divide us, I thought. When science had come to rule the minds of most modern people, resorting to religious dogma would discourage some of my readers to read on, no matter how broadly we interpreted the word god. 'God' carries, for countless men and women still a heavy historical baggage. He has a well-defined image, the grandest of grandfathers watching over us benevolently, though dispensing stern justice when we die over how we lived our lives.

But then I thought that, for the average Western reader of a book of this nature, 'God' had come by now to be only a vague notion. He/She/It had shed its medieval character, along with its human features of love and hate. It had evolved – perhaps because we are too lazy or unable to substitute a more appropriate word for it – to stand merely for the mystery that continues to remain at the heart of the Universe for us. Why are we here? Why is there no oblivion, instead, an oblivion so utter that even the rule of oblivion itself cannot exist in it? 'I call that mystery God', some people say. Some philosophers had always said so when the priests had not been within earshot to admonish them.

Even the most up-to-date of our top scientists – including Peter Atkins, one of the contributors to this book[104], say that while they can calculate the progress of the world back to the first trillionth of a second of the 'Big Bang', some 13.7 billion years ago, they go blind at that infinitesimally short instant, for the laws of physics had not yet come into being. So the mystery does not appear about to be unravelled any time soon, if ever. Secondly, many of us non-scientists persist in asking an awkward question: What was the cause of the Big Bang? Surely there must have been something that had the potential to give rise to it? The question may appear to be an oxymoron to some, for Time, we are told, came into being with the Big Bang and there could, therefore, have been no 'before'. We are not convinced, and nor are all scientists. Surely things could not come out of nothing, we say. Lee Smolin is one living scientist who argues that Time has to be eternal, whatever the attribute 'eternal' means. On the other hand, some scientists, such as Peter Atkins, assert that the scientific method will solve that mystery, too. At the end of his famous little book A Brief History of Time, Stephen Hawking dreams of one day succeeding in doing just that, to be able to say why we are here. But then he seems to stumble. For want of a better expression, he invokes God again: '… it would be the ultimate triumph of human reason' he writes, 'for then we would know the mind of God'.

My change of mind to spread the net wider and include some God-informed poetry was further strengthened by another dear friend, Michael Alexander, the poet and former professor of English literature at the University of St Andrews. Michael is the author of many a large tome on the history of English letters and is admired worldwide among scholars of Shakespeare. He is also a practicing Christian, however non-dogmatic. He told me that, in fact, most of the greatest English poets were 'more Stoic than Christian'. To exclude the devout among them from the book would only impoverish it, he said. I surrendered.

I have divided the anthology into five sections in order of increasing hopefulness. They avoid proclaiming an unrealistic view of the darker hours of our autumns, let alone of our winters. Thus they begin with poems of loss and solace and end with poems of love and joy. Some have been nominated or written by friends. A few at the end of each section are mine. Most are by famous poets from a variety of national literatures. I hope to come back to them again and again, to reflect, to remember, to gain a little solace and, hopefully, to laugh also.

# 1

## *Poems of Loss*

**Four quatrains**
Omar Khayyām
Tr. HT

Alas, the story of my youth is told;
Alas, bold spring into autumn grew.
The songbird they called my carefree youth
Unloved it arrived, in haste it flew.

\*

Never of teachers did I go deprived.
Then more theorems I myself contrived.
Seventy-two years, day and night, I thought:
Only to conclude that I knew naught.

\*

Agreeable friends, where did they all go?
At the feet of Time, one by one fell low.
For a while we feigned brave defiance;
None prevails over this vale of sorrow.

\*

Those who conquered all science and letters,
And shone as beacons among their betters,
Did not find the thread of this Tangled Heap,
Only told a tale, and then fell asleep.


**On my first sonne**
Ben Johnson

Farewell, thou child of my right hand, and joy;
My sinne was too much hope of thee, lov'd boy
Seven yeeres thou wert lent to me, and I thee pay,
Exacted by thy fate, on the just day.
O, could I loose all father, now. For why

Will man lament the state he should envie?
To have so soone scap'd worlds, and fleshes rage,
And, if no other miserie, yet age?
Rest in soft peace, and, ask'd, say here doth lye
Ben Jonson his best piece of poetrie.
For whose sake, hence-forth, all his vowes be such,
As what he loves may never like too much.


## Dover Beach[105]
Matthew Arnold

The sea is calm to-night.
The tide is full, the moon lies fair
Upon the straits; —on the French coast the light
Gleams and is gone; the cliffs of England stand,
Glimmering and vast, out in the tranquil bay.
Come to the window, sweet is the night-air.
Only, from the long line of spray
Where the sea meets the moon-blanch'd land,
Listen. you hear the grating roar
Of pebbles which the waves draw back, and fling,
At their return, up the high strand,

Begin, and cease, and then again begin,
With tremulous cadence slow, and bring
The eternal note of sadness in.

Sophocles long ago
Heard it on the Ægæan, and it brought
Into his mind the turbid ebb and flow
Of human misery; we
Find also in the sound a thought,
Hearing it by this distant northern sea.

The Sea of Faith
Was once, too, at the full, and round earth's shore
Lay like the folds of a bright girdle furl'd.
But now I only hear
Its melancholy, long, withdrawing roar,
Retreating, to the breath
Of the night-wind, down the vast edges drear
And naked shingles of the world.

Ah, love, let us be true
To one another. for the world, which seems
To lie before us like a land of dreams,
So various, so beautiful, so new,
Hath really neither joy, nor love, nor light,
Nor certitude, nor peace, nor help for pain;
And we are here as on a darkling plain
Swept with confused alarms of struggle and flight,
Where ignorant armies clash by night.


## The First Day
Christina Rossetti

I wish I could remember the first day,
First hour, first moment of your meeting me;
If bright or dim the season, it might be
Summer or winter for aught I can say.
So unrecorded did it slip away,
So blind was I to see and to foresee,
So dull to mark the budding of my tree
That would not blossom yet for many a May.
If only I could recollect it. Such
A day of days. I let it come and go
As traceless as a thaw of bygone snow.
It seemed to mean so little, meant so much.
If only now I could recall that touch,
First touch of hand in hand. – Did one but know.


## The Voice
Thomas Hardy

Woman much missed, how you call to me, call to me,
Saying that now you are not as you were
When you had changed from the one who was all to me,
But as at first, when our day was fair.
Can it be you that I hear? Let me view you, then,
Standing as when I drew near to the town
Where you would wait for me: yes, as I knew you then,
Even to the original air-blue gown.
Or is it only the breeze, in its listlessness

Travelling across the wet mead to me here,
You being ever dissolved to wan wistlessness,
Heard no more again far or near?

Thus I; faltering forward,
Leaves around me falling,
Wind oozing thin through the thorn from norward,
And the woman calling.


**When you are old**
William Butler Yeats

When you are old and grey and full of sleep,
And nodding by the fire, take down this book,
And slowly read, and dream of the soft look
Your eyes had once, and of their shadows deep;

How many loved your moments of glad grace,
And loved your beauty with love false or true,
But one man loved the pilgrim Soul in you,
And loved the sorrows of your changing face;

And bending down beside the glowing bars,
Murmur, a little sadly, how Love fled
And paced upon the mountains overhead
And hid his face amid a crowd of stars.


**Hamlet**
Boris Pasternak
Tr. HT

I climb onto the stage.
All fall silent.
I listen for the faintest echo.
What does my future hold?
A thousand opera glasses pour on me
The darkness of the night.

Abba, Father, let this cup pass from me.
All is possible to thee.
I love your obstinate purpose.

I agree to all my parts.
But I yearn for another play.
Just this once,
Free me from the rules.

The acts are written.
The end cannot be spurned.

I am alone.
The world drowns in lies.
'Life is not a walk across a field'.[106]


## My Father's Signature
David Morphet[107]

The hand is steady
with each letter formed
in the mould of fifty years.
'A' starts off surely on its way:
The 'M' and 'o' curl confidently round'
stutter through 'r' into the dip of 'p'
and end up calmly 'h', 'e', 't'.

It shows no mutability.
I know what lies, for all that,
behind the hand's clarity.
Each day he would have looked
at such frail proof of identity
with mortal dismay,
waiting for death's eviction.

His life ran slow,
its end I did not see –
saw only his body and his signature


## Valley of my forefathers.
HT

Valley of my forefathers.
It is now forty years
Since I climbed your mountains,
Drank the scent of your orchards after a spring shower,

Caressed the parched earth of your summers.

It has been four decades now
Since I sat on that boulder,
The perch of my grandfather,
As he watched the tumbling river
And sang hymns to the wilderness.

Will I ever see you again?
If so, when?
When my back will be arched over?
When my steps will need propping?
When my eyes will be too dim to make out
The words on my father's tombstone?


**The water lily is no more**
HT

The water lily is no more.
Overnight,
The pond is a sheet of futile ripples.
Vanished is the darling daughter of the garden.

It happened yesterday,
Which began with such promise:
Even though late in October,
The sun shone, the wind stood still.

No-one expected it,
Least of all the gardener.
The solid man of the earth,
Wept in view of the crowd.

The pond is edged with ground ivy
And creeping roses.
Poplars and willows, ashes and oaks,
Shelter it on all sides.

Secure at the heart of its universe,
The star plant had bloomed.
It had spread its wings;
It greeted all passers-by.

The trees had, each morning,
Bent over in tribute,
Hailed the bride in their midst,
Renewed their vows of adoration.

Do not tell the gardener to grow another.
He would die of grief.
He thinks his love
Will suddenly reappear.

# 2

## *Poems of Solace*

**Four quatrains**
Omar Khayyām (d. 1131)

This Sea of Being has come out of naught;
No glimpse of its truth has anyone caught.
Many a clown has put forth his thought:
From the Other Side news cannot be sought.

Choose a bowl of wine over the land of Tūs,
The mace of Caesar, the ring of Kāvūs.
The roar of a drunk at dawn in the street
Beats for me the peace of the Holy Cheat.

My ashes, loved ones, disperse wide and far;
My many failings count at the bazaar.
Or else, from my clay fashion a brick,
To make a stopper for the vintner's jar.

This garden, this park, these broad skies,
Hillocks, waterfalls, meadows, butterflies.
Go send for my friends, those tingling wits
Who lighten my heart, who brighten my eyes.

**Oft , in the stilly night**
Thomas Moore (d. 1535)

Oft, in the stilly night,
Ere slumber's chain has bound me,
Fond memory brings the light
Of other days around me;
The smiles, the tears,
Of boyhood's years,
The words of love then spoken;
The eyes that shone,
Now dimm'd and gone,

The cheerful hearts now broken.
Thus, in the stilly night,
Ere slumber's chain hath bound me,
Sad memory brings the light
Of other days around me.

When I remember all
The friends, so link'd together,
I've seen around me fall,
Like leaves in wintry weather;
I feel like one
Who treads alone
Some banquet-hall deserted,
Whose lights are fled,
Whose garlands dead,
And all but he departed.
Thus, in the stilly night,
Ere slumber's chain has bound me,
Sad memory brings the light
Of other days around me.


**Fear no more the heat o' the sun**
William Shakespeare (d. 1616)
From Cymbeline, IV, ii

Fear no more the heat o' the sun;
Nor the furious winter's rages,
Thou thy worldly task hast done,
Home art gone, and ta'en thy wages;
Golden lads and girls all must,
As chimney sweepers come to dust.

Fear no more the frown of the great,
Thou art past the tyrant's stroke:
Care no more to clothe and eat;
To thee the reed is as the oak:
The sceptre, learning, physic, must
All follow this, and come to dust.

Fear no more the lightning-flash,
Nor the all-dread thunder-stone;
Fear not slander, censure rash;

Thou hast finished joy and moan;
All lovers young, all lovers must
Consign to thee, and come to dust.


**Farewell**
Anne Bronte (d. 1849)

Farewell to thee. But not farewell
To all my fondest thoughts of thee;
Within my heart they still shall dwell
And they shall cheer and comfort me.

Life seems more sweet that thou didst live
And men more true that thou wert one;
Nothing is lost that thou didst give,
Nothing destroyed that thou hast done.


**Rondeau**
Leigh Hunt (d. 1859)

Jenny kissed me when we met,
Jumping from the chair she sat in;
Time, you thief, who love to get
Sweets into your list, put that in.

Say I'm weary, say I'm sad,
Say that health and wealth have missed me;
Say I'm growing old, but add:
Jenny kissed me.


**They told me, Heraclitus**
William Johnson Cory (d. 1892)

They told me, Heraclitus, they told me you were dead,
They brought me bitter news to hear and bitter tears to shed.
I wept as I remember'd how often you and I
Had tired the sun with talking and sent him down the sky.

And now that thou art lying, my dear old Carian guest,
A handful of grey ashes, long, long ago at rest,

Still thy pleasant voices, thy nightingales, awake;
For Death, he taketh all away, but them he cannot take.


## Yes, I remember Adlestrop
Edward Thomas (d. 1917)

Yes, I remember Adlestrop –
The name, because one afternoon
Of heat the express-train drew up there
Unwontedly. It was late June.

The steam hissed. Someone cleared his throat.
No one left and no one came
On the bare platform. What I saw
Was Adlestrop – only the name

And willows, willow-herb, and grass,
And meadowsweet, and haycocks dry,
No whit less still and lonely fair
Than the high cloudlets in the sky.

And for that minute a blackbird sang
Close by, and round him, mistier,
Farther and farther, all the birds
Of Oxfordshire and Gloucestershire.


## Youth and June
Jean Blewett (d. 1934)

I was your lover long ago, sweet June,
Ere life grew hard; I am your lover still,
And follow gladly to the wondrous tune
You pipe on golden reeds to vale and hill.
I am your lover still; to me you seem
To hold the fragrance of the joys long dead,
The brightness and the beauty of the dream
We dreamed in youth, to hold the tears we shed,
The laughter of our lips, the faith that lies
Back in that season dear to every heart,
Life's springtime, when God's earth and
God's blue skies

Are, measured by our glance, not far apart

## The Explosion[108]
Philip Larkin, 1974

On the day of the explosion
Shadows pointed towards the pithead:
In the sun the slagheap slept.

Down the lane came men in pitboots
Coughing oath-edged talk and pipe-smoke,
Shouldering off the freshened silence.

One chased after rabbits; lost them;
Came back with a nest of lark's eggs;
Showed them; lodged them in the grasses.

So they passed in beards and moleskins,
Fathers, brothers, nicknames, laughter,
Through the tall gates standing open.

At noon, there came a tremor; cows
Stopped chewing for a second; sun,
Scarfed as in a heat-haze, dimmed.

The dead go on before us, they
Are sitting in God's house in comfort,
We shall see them face to face –

Plain as lettering in the chapels
It was said, and for a second
Wives saw men of the explosion

Larger than in life they managed –
Gold as on a coin, or walking
Somehow from the sun towards them,

One showing the eggs unbroken.

## Now or Then
Jon Swan[109]

We shall leave it all behind

as the saint his riches,
and go forth unencumbered.

We shall lie beside still waters,
listening like mothers for
a sound from the yet unborn.

From the trees we shall learn how to
climb both ways, up and down,
with the same daring and care.

We shall come to terms with the birds
whose language was foreign
to what was left of our ears,

while from the grouse and the woodcock
we shall learn to be still,
more still, then invisible.


**Dawn is not quite upon us**
HT

Dawn is not quite upon us.
London's river and I are alone together.
The street lamps of Bermondsey
Twinkle in the mirror of a low tide
To soothe me in Limehouse.

I see the white belly of a seagull
Gliding silently over the water,
As if it were Time itself
Treading thoughtfully,
The path it began many moons ago.

How many of my forefathers
Watched the same telling flight
Over a million rivers
Before a million dawns
And became their own forefathers for a moment?

## Autumn

HT

It's true, Autumn  does have its wasps:
Those dull, aching arms,
That hairline crack in the foot that takes many months to heal,
The heart that grumbles at dawn
When it ought to be at rest.

Sometimes there are hornets, too:
A child emigrating,
A lifelong friend calling no longer.
We lost Elizabeth this year;
We marked her birthday last night.
She would have been fifty-nine only.

But Autumn has its fruits, also:
Evenings by the fireside,
Listening to Radio Three,
Taking the Literary Review to bed,
The children visiting together,
Shiny ripe conkers by the grass edges.

Don't forget the greenhouse, either:
The peppers, aubergines and tomatoes
Shone brightly this year.
We had 15 sweetheart melons,
One still growing in mid-September.

I must move on.
I must bring some logs in.
The sky's gone sullen suddenly
And the winds are westerly again.

By the way, have I not told you?
John's invited himself over.
You don't mind, do you?
Pasta and salad will do.
Do we have fresh sheets for him?
He'll stay only a couple of weeks.

## Epitaph for the Common Man
HT

It's true.
He did his share of damage to the Earth.
He caused trees to fall early,
His body heat still shakes the reeds,
His body's other emanations go on
To nibble at the ozone layer.

But he meant well:
He patted dogs,
Made children laugh,
Greeted strangers, and –
St Peter will like this especially –
He held together the few around him.


## The Male Silverback
HT

A restlessness has,
Uninvited, all day,
Run through my veins,
Plagued my hands.

It's relieved at times,
By Beethoven,
Or a book review.
But returns,
And reconquers.

Is it a symptom of the years?
A wrench of conscience?
Resurrected guilt?
The rest of my days?

Whatever its cause,
I will not panic.
There is a cure,
If it lasts.

I shall learn from the male silverback:
When he's ousted by a younger brute,

He retires, quietly,
To the jungle and discovers:
The amazing art of watching.


**But ...**
HT

It was a lovely day today:
A real summers' day,
The first of August,
My birthday, my seventy-fourth.

Blackberries are early this year.
The barley and wheat sheaves, too,
Glow in the nearness of autumn.
Everywhere fledglings have gained confidence.

As we returned from Bewl Water,
The ewes of Sussex and their lambs
Had filled the shade of every large tree,
Claimed the nooks in every hedgerow.

The village dozed in the heat:
An ancient silence had fallen upon it.
An old brick wall told us
It was always thus when she was young.

Friends will come to dinner tonight.
We shall sit in the garden.
The food and wine will be excellent,
Tall flowers all around us will glisten in the candlelight.

But I look forward only
To our friends' late-night voices,
News of their children,
Weddings, new births, even funerals.

Is it because,
I fear,
The Time of Goodbyes
Draws near?

## Should my final months come into view
HT

Should my final months come into view,
I'll make a new set of resolutions,
My very last,
The last of many.

After asking my doctor not to call again,
– For his knowledge and care
Will be needed more usefully elsewhere –
I'll draw up my new action list as follows:

First,
I'll seek out my lovely old pipe.
It's gone unloved far too long;
It languishes in a drawer somewhere.
It's a work of art,
Cherry wood wrapped in part in fine leather.

I'll polish it till it gleams again.
I'll grasp her in both hands.
I'll apologise to her.
I jilted her under duress.

I'll then order
– In case the doctor is a pessimist –
A whole year's supply
Of Condor Aromatic pipe tobacco,
That strong, bronze Virginian,
Cured in honey, bacon fat and wood smoke.

I'll light up with my eyes closed.
I'll inhale the bouquet of a thousand essential oils.
How vastly superior it will be
To simple atmospheric air.

My next purchase will be:
A barrel of creamy, unsalted Somerset butter.
I'll spread it copiously,
Lovingly,
Over granary bread
And savour the two on their own.

Then my attention shall switch

To the life force of the grape.
No more cheap wines for me:
Life's too short (literally, this time).
I'll order a dozen crates of the best
That the vintners of St Emilion,
Bordeaux and Rhone can conjure,
After kneeling for years
At the feet of their revered grandfathers.

The last item on the list will be:
Give six dinner parties a week,
Till my last breath,
For everyone we knew:
Friends, family, old passers-by, too.

Talk of death will not be allowed:
It would be a waste of time.
We'll eat, drink and sing;
We'll hail the sun and the moon;
We'll thank the laws of physics
That brought us together.

The seventh evening I'll keep free,
For me and my woman only.
We'll sit down at dusk
To a simple supper,
By candlelight,
In silence.

It was good to be alive:
To caress dry earth,
To watch rain fall,
To hear human voices,
To know that love existed.

# 3

## *Poems of Hope*

### Integer Vitae
Thomas Campion (d. 1620)

THE man of life upright,
Whose guiltless heart is free
From all dishonest deeds,
Or thought of vanity;

The man whose silent days
In harmless joys are spent,
Whom hopes cannot delude,
Nor sorrow discontent;

That man needs neither towers
Nor armour for defence,
Nor secret vaults to fly
From thunder's violence:

He only can behold
With unaffrighted eyes
The horrors of the deep
And terrors of the skies.

Thus, scorning all the cares
That fate or fortune brings,
He makes the heaven his book,
His wisdom heavenly things;

Good thoughts his only friends,
His wealth a well-spent age,
The earth his sober inn
And quiet pilgrimage.

### A Prayer for Indifference
Frances Greville (d. 1789)

Oft I've implor'd the gods in vain,
And pray'd till I've been weary;
For once I'll seek my wish to gain
Of Oberon, the Fairy.

Sweet airy being, wanton sprite,
Who lurk'st in woods unseen,
And oft by Cynthia's silver light,
Trip'st gaily o'er the green:

If e'er thy pitying heart was mov'd,
As ancient stories tell,
And for the Athenian maid who lov'd,
Thou sought'st a wondrous spell;

O deign once more t'exert thy power.
Haply some herb or tree,
Sovereign as juice of western flower,
Conceals a balm for me.

I ask no kind return of love,
No tempting charm to please;
Far from the heart those gifts remove,
That sighs for peace and ease:

Far as distress the soul can wound,
'Tis pain in each degree;
'Tis bliss but to a certain bound,
Beyond, is agony.

Then take this treacherous sense of mine,
Which dooms me still to smart;
Which pleasure can to pain refine,
To pain new pangs depart.

O haste to shed the sovereign balm,
My shatter'd nerves new string;
And for my guest, serenely calm,
The nymph Indifference bring.

At her approach, see Hope, see Fear,
See Expectation fly.

And Disappointment in the rear,
That blasts the promis'd joy.

The tear which Pity taught to flow
The eye shall then disown;
The heart that melts for others' woe
Shall then scarce feel its own.

The wounds which now each moment bleed,
Each moment then shall close;
And tranquil days shall still succeed
To nights of calm repose.

O Fairy Elf. but grant me this,
This one kind comfort send,
And so may never-fading bliss
Thy flowery paths attend.

So may the glow-worm's glimmering light
Thy tiny footsteps lead
To some new region of delight,
Unknown to mortal tread.

And be thy acorn goblet filled
With heaven's ambrosial dew,
From sweetest, freshest flowers distilled,
That shed fresh sweets for you.

And what of life remains for me
I'll pass in sober ease;
Half pleased, contented will I be,
Content but half to please.


**The Choir Invisible**
By George Eliot

Oh, may I join the choir invisible
Of those immortal dead who live again
In minds made better by their presence; live
In pulses stirred to generosity,
In deeds of daring rectitude, in scorn
For miserable aims that end with self,
In thoughts sublime that pierce the night like stars,

And with their mild persistence urge men's search
To vaster issues. So to live is heaven:
To make undying music in the world,
Breathing a beauteous order that controls
With growing sway the growing life of man.
So we inherit that sweet purity
For which we struggled, failed, and agonized
With widening retrospect that bred despair.
Rebellious flesh that would not be subdued,
A vicious parent shaming still its child,
Poor anxious penitence, is quick dissolved;
Its discords, quenched by meeting harmonies,
Die in the large and charitable air,
And all our rarer, better, truer self
That sobbed religiously in yearning song,
That watched to ease the burden of the world,
Laboriously tracing what must be,
And what may yet be better, – saw within
A worthier image for the sanctuary,
And shaped it forth before the multitude,
Divinely human, raising worship so
To higher reverence more mixed with love, –
That better self shall live till human Time
Shall fold its eyelids, and the human sky
Be gathered like a scroll within the tomb
Unread forever. This is life to come, –
Which martyred men have made more glorious
For us who strive to follow. May I reach
That purest heaven, – be to other souls
The cup of strength in some great agony,
Enkindle generous ardor, feed pure love,
Beget the smiles that have no cruelty,
Be the sweet presence of a good diffused,
And in diffusion ever more intense.
So shall I join the choir invisible
Whose music is the gladness of the world.

**Ulysses (excerpt)**
Alfred, Lord Tennyson[110]

There lies the port; the vessel puffs her sail:
There gloom the dark broad seas. My mariners,
Souls that have toiled, and wrought, and thought
    with me—
That ever with a frolic welcome took
The thunder and the sunshine, and opposed
Free hearts, free foreheads—you and I are old;
Old age hath yet his honour and his toil;
Death closes all: but something ere the end,
Some work of noble note, may yet be done,
Not unbecoming men that strove with Gods.
The lights begin to twinkle from the rocks:
The long day wanes: the slow moon climbs: the deep
Moans round with many voices. Come, my friends,
'Tis not too late to seek a newer world.
Push off, and sitting well in order smite
The sounding furrows; for my purpose holds
To sail beyond the sunset, and the baths
Of all the western stars, until I die.
It may be that the gulfs will wash us down:
It may be we shall touch the Happy Isles4,
And see the great Achilles5, whom we knew
Though much is taken, much abides; and though
We are not now that strength which in old days
Moved earth and heaven; that which we are, we are;
One equal temper of heroic hearts,
Made weak by time and fate, but strong in will
To strive, to seek, to find, and not to yield.


**An Old Man's Almost Jubilant Meditations**
Feyyaz Fergar[111]

I am too old to run after new wisdoms,
To attend philosophy's surgery hours.
I am too old to handle the battering-rams
Of hard-hitting, snarling logic.
I've seen too many times too many pros and cons
Change places to try to make permanent sense of things.

Someone said two and two never saw eye to eye;
All I can hope to do is to guess
My way out of cruel corners.
But not at the cost of selling my mind
To pensionable servility. I am not a hermit crab.
I cannot inhabit borrowed silence.
Silence is not golden when silence dislodges speech.

A voice must stay true to itself,
Or be a puppet-straw to any sombre wind.

\*

Now I live with both hands, ageing but alert;
I hang on to life's every scrap and crumb,
Its every tatter and shred with grateful skill.
These are not the small coins of salvation,
But booming gifts that can sustain reach and scope
And add bone to shadow,
When shadows prey on one's breath.

Time's edge seems to be just round the corner:
I can take nothing for granted,
Not even the good behaviours of my heart.
But I don't carry in it
The embossed blueprint of death.

\*

Each night before I go to bed,
I wish well to all the parts of me
That keep me together in the stream of being
And make me belong to this world in which I live:
Not to gloat over every carat
Of success and possession, but to share
Undimmed, my power, my readiness
To love, to praise, to understand and to hope.
I commend my soul to no-one:
I want no complications.

\*

Every day now brings brightly
Something to wonder at, something to hold dear.
I put my jacket on, for instance,

And it is a season and a joy.
They sit well on my back.

I look at a woman
As if in timeless standing ovation
And it is another season, another depth.
Apple of my heart, she thrives
In the thrilling core of my eyes,
On her way to deepest stations of love.


## Testament
Feyyaz Fergar

There is no bad blood between death and me:
He can lay claims to my perishable goods,
My dust, my mistakes, my birthdays.

But when I die I shall leave behind
All the tools of my breath.
I shall leave behind
My eyes, my hands,
The results of my voice,
The roads that lived in my veins,
My habit of smuggling windows into houses
Under stark arrest.

I shall also leave behind
The light that stood by me
Against the sarcasms of the dark.

With all these I shall speak
For the Sun.
Turn your cemeteries off.
There is more to come.


## Looking Back
David Morphet

Nostalgia, now it's time to look
in your direction. Though your face
may be three parts false,

I should still like to run my hand
over its seductive surface.

Young men writing their dreams
will throw them in dark corners
for their ghosts to rediscover.
That kind of script is never worse
for being written in an unformed hand.

I ask if sentiment is worth the risk
of ridicule, and answer yes.
I know what I am looking for and seek,
in evidence of what I was,
the germ of what I still could be.


**Grandfather oak tree**
HT

The storm arrived as expected.
All through the evening it gathered pace.
'Grandfather' oak tree.
On your own, in the middle of the field,
Tall and broad in full leaf in October,
I worried about you.

Past midnight, the world still roared.
The wind and the rain,
With the weight of the Atlantic behind them,
Lashed the house,
Levelled younger trees,
Quashed street lights.
You held on.

Then, forty-eight minutes past two,
Above the growl of the tempest,
Through the sanctum of my walls,
I heard you.

Thus ended an age for me:
For years, you had been the confidant of my dawns,
The toast of my sunsets,
Hint of heaven to my friends,
Rock of everness to my young.

For four centuries and more,
You had watched over the village,
Lit many fires with your cast-off twigs,
Fattened herds of sheep on the bounty of your leaves.

It was St Jude's Day,[112]
The patron saint of the depressed.

The storm passed,
Light returned to the world,
I ran to the window:
You were there.
Shaken, bruised, shorn of some branches,
You stood tall as ever:
It had been a bad night.

Grandfather oak tree.
Friend of my mornings.
Toast of my evenings.
We're brothers now:
Chastened and wiser,
A little tired, having seen so much,
We shall tell one another:
It's only autumn.
Love can broaden yet.

# 4

## *Poems of Joy*

**Awake.**
Omar Khayyām
Tr. Edward FitzGerald[113]

Awake. for Morning in the Bowl of Night
Has flung the Stone that puts the Stars to Flight:
    And Lo. the Hunter of the East has caught
The Sultan's Turret in a Noose of Light.

Dreaming when Dawn's Left Hand was in the Sky
I heard a Voice within the Tavern cry:
    'Awake, my dear ones, and fill the Cup
Before Life's Liquor in its Cup be dry.'

And, as the Cock crew, those who stood before
The Tavern shouted – 'Op then the Door.
    You know how little while we have to stay,
And, once departed, may return no more.

**Since Venus and Mars …**
Omar Khayyām
Tr.HT

Since Venus and Mars trod the sky at night,
Than the juice of grapes naught has proved so right.
I ask my vintner, ask him often: Why?
Better than he sells, what hopes he to buy?

This garden, this park, these broad skies,
Hillocks, waterfalls, meadows, butterflies.
Do send for my friends, those tingling wits
Who lighten my heart, who brighten my eyes.

Today I will shed my robe of restraint:
Let trails of red wine my white beard taint.

No more piety. I am SEVENTY.
If not dance now, when might it then be?


**To thee, fair freedom.** (Written at an inn in Henley)
William Shenstone (d. 1763)

To thee, fair freedom. I retire
From flattery, cards, dice and din:
Nor art thou found in mansions higher
Than the low cott, or humble inn.

'It's here with boundless pow'r, I reign;
And ev'ry health which I begin,
Converts dull port to bright champaigne;
Such freedom crowns it, at an inn.

I fly from pomp, I fly from plate.
I fly from falsehood's specious grin.
Freedom I love, and form I hate,
And chuse my lodgings at an inn.

Whoe'er has travell'd life's dull round,
Where'er his stages may have been,
May sigh to think he still has found
The warmest welcome, at an inn.


**My Heart Leaps Up**
William Wordsworth

My heart leaps up when I behold
A rainbow in the sky:
So was it when my life began;
So is it now I am a man;
So be it when I shall grow old.
Or let me die.
The child is father of the Man;
And I could wish my days to be
Bound each to each by natural piety.

## Friendship
Dinah Maria Craik (d.1887)

Oh, the Comfort –
the inexpressible comfort of feeling safe with a person –
having neither to weigh thoughts nor measure words,
but pouring them all right out,
just as they are,
chaff and grain together;
certain that a faithful hand will take and sift them,
keep what is worth keeping,
and then with a breath of kindness blow the rest away.


## You are old, Father Williams.
Lewis Carroll, Alice's Adventures in Wonderland

'You are old, Father William,' the young man said,
'And your hair has become very white;
And yet you incessantly stand on your head—
Do you think, at your age, it is right?'

'In my youth,' Father William replied to his son,
'I feared it might injure the brain;
But now that I'm perfectly sure I have none,
Why, I do it again and again.'

'You are old,' said the youth, 'As I mentioned before,
And have grown most uncommonly fat;
Yet you turned a back-somersault in at the door—
Pray, what is the reason of that?'

'In my youth,' said the sage, as he shook his grey locks,
'I kept all my limbs very supple
By the use of this ointment—one shilling the box—
Allow me to sell you a couple?'

'You are old,' said the youth, 'And your jaws are too weak
For anything tougher than suet;
Yet you finished the goose, with the bones and the beak—
Pray, how did you manage to do it?'

'In my youth,' said his father, 'I took to the law,
And argued each case with my wife;

And the muscular strength which it gave to my jaw,
Has lasted the rest of my life.'

'You are old,' said the youth, 'one would hardly suppose
That your eye was as steady as ever;
Yet you balanced an eel on the end of your nose—
What made you so awfully clever?'

'I have answered three questions, and that is enough,'
Said his father; 'don't give yourself airs.
Do you think I can listen all day to such stuff?
Be off, or I'll kick you down stairs.'


**The Plotter**
Feyyaz Fergar (d. 1993)

I do not carry the greedy signs of your Zodiac
Tattooed on my skin
And I have no talent for the dark.

There is nothing to detain me
In these ziggurats of loneliness,
These huge gadgets of despair.

I am old
Yet watch me pick myself up
And move on with the dawn strong on my back.

I don't know about you
But I am plotting new windows.[114]


**Out of the omnidirectional kindness of my heart**
Feyyaz Fergar

Greetings to all the teams
Of new dreamers,
Greetings to all candidates,
Charming but not at all candid.
Greetings to all my laureate friends
Of the Petty-Larousse and verse contests.

But above all greetings

And top of the morning
To all kites and balloons
And those who fly or play in them.

I wish them the most cerulean,
The gentlest of all skies.


## Obsequy, with Satyr
Jon Swan[115]

Warren, I think, said it best,
at yesterday's obsequies,
when he rose in his dark suit
and, having cleared his throat,
said (and who could disagree?)
that each and every one of us
must in due course turn to dust.

So far, so good, but then went on
to say that we must now adjust
to what is likely to happen next:
not only shall we, one by one,
return to dust, but, soon enough,
the species as a whole: the lot of us.
This struck many as going too far.

There was a shifting in the pews.
Wives turned to husbands and
these to them in turn to judge
what they should do: leave or see
this ceremony through. Some rose
and stole away, giving Warren
time again to clear his throat,

and thrust his jaw forward as if
prepared to take whatever blow
might be in store. 'And where,'
he said, 'will that leave God when
none are left to worship a deity
brought to life through long belief?'
This struck some as going too far.

So once again there was a shifting

in the pews, and many rose and stole
away, their exodus giving Warren
time to compose himself and clear
his throat and jut his jaw as if prepared
to take whatever blow might
be in store when he went on to say:

'Not only God will go, but the rocks
and rills and all the hills and every
form of life that has endeared itself
to us, as, for example, goldfinches
and larks, fish and frogs and turtles;
they, too, one by one or two by two,
will, companionably, turn to dust.'

By now the pews were all but empty,
as people, singly or in twos, or more,
with averted faces rose and stole away,
holding the door for those who followed
softly after. Thus, I found myself alone
when he went on to ask which one of us—
as if there were now more than one –

would care to be the sole survivor of
our kind when all the rest were gone,
as happened to a satyr once in Greece,
roughly fifty years before the birth
of Christ when, as Plutarch tells us,
Roman soldiers found one sleeping
in a green dell – a satyr 'just like those

depicted by sculptors and painters,'
a creature no living man until that day
had seen except as figures on an urn
or vase, and there found sleeping
in a dell and brought to General Sulla.
'How would you, Jon, feel,' Warren said,
'if you, the last Mohican, as it were,

of humankind were roused from sleep
and hauled before some general whose
interpreters tried their languages on you
and they could not understand a word

197

you said because they had not ever heard
our language, which had disappeared,
taking Shakespeare and the Bible with it?'

Interrogated so, in the emptied church,
how could I respond except to say
that this dark scenario seemed unlikely.
There must be other satyrs somewhere.
And as I spoke I felt my limbs grow shaggy,
my feet as hard as hooves, and I could smell
the difference. And, asleep again, I dreamed.


## The Reprieve
Jon Swan

When I worked in New York all those
years ago, the office of diminishing returns
to which I reported wasn't exactly in
the bowels of the city, though more often
than not that's the impression one got.

The lungs of the city where one could
remove the jacket and loosen the tie
(this was years ago, remember) and
inhale and exhale as if reprieved by
the governor of green thoughts, were

a stone's throw away through glass walls.
'I love the way people enjoy parks here,'
said my wife who arrived from Holland
believing there were no trees in the city
and in the course of time brought the children

one by one to see the unbelievable trees.
That was then of course and now is now
and never the twain shall meet as we know,
unless walking hand in hand in the green
thought preserved in the heart of the city.

## Earliest Morning
HT

Earliest morning I love best:
The great river at low tide,
Gleaming, silent, waves at rest,
The ducks resting side by side
After a night's ceaseless quest
    For sustenance in mud and slime.

And then, there is the day to plan,
Gazing at the sun, coffee mug in hand:
To earn that million for the clan,
And compose that sarabande
I dreamt last night I began.
    Mornings are Man's plotting time.


## Limehouse Fly.
HT

He was a Darwinian dream,
A living flying machine,
Faster, for his weight, than a fighter plane.

As he shot through the air this late summer's day,
He had no care in the world,
Only a pleasant longing in his groin.

But, …
Alas, …
The next moment he flapped in my wine glass.

It is true to say,
Death was stalking him.
Autumn draws near.

Also, just before he died,
He tasted a fine Montagne St-Emilion,
The cherished gift of a dear friend.

I gave him a ceremonial send-off, too:
The whole glass of Chateau de Musset 2000, grand cru
Accompanied him, to the end of the Universe, into the Thames.

## I sipped white wine with Sir Alfred Ayer
HT (13 May 1987)

I had last night, a privilege rare:
I sipped white wine with Sir Alfred Ayer.
Helped by his 'good friend', Cynthia, Mrs Robert Kee,
He had just finished Thomas Paine's biography.

It's really nothing, he said,
All you have to do is 500 words a day.
That will give you 175,000 words a year;
You can have one or two books that way.
Of course, now that I'm seventy-seven,
I can't write philosophy that fast.
But Tom Paine's life was quite easy;
So many have written on him in the past.
Mind you, no new-fangled things for me:
People say I need an IBM PC.
What's wrong with longhand, I ask,
As long as you have a secretary?

I whispered to my friend, John of Killegar:
Don't let them out of sight;
This could be the start of a literary friendship,
Memorise the date of this night.

Replied John, slowly, earnestly:
I have one condition: Freddie for you, Cynthia for me.

But alas Sir Freddie had other plans.
Off to the Garrick for dinner went he,
Leaving me and John on the streets of South Ken,
Even though we, too, were SDP.


## You.
HT

You are this house's guardian angel.
Were it not for you,
The windows would never be thrown open,
The sun would be shut out,

The pot plants would die of thirst,
The house, as with me, would become a widower.

The garden would mourn you deeper still.
The lawn might be mowed every now and then,
But the roses would go unfed,
The magnolias would remain untrimmed.
The dahlias would be killed by frost,
Weeds would strangle the lavender bed.

So, hurrah for the house,
Hurrah for the garden,
Hurrah for the man.
But, first, my love,
Hurrah for you,
My whirlwind of a woman.

# 5

## *Poems of Love*

**Ah, Moon of my Delight …**
Omar Khayyām
Tr. Edward FitzGerald

Ah, Moon of my Delight who know'st no wane,
The Moon of Heav'n is rising once again:
How oft thereafter rising shall she look
Through this same garden after me – in vain.

Here with a Loaf of Bread beneath the Bough,
A Flask of Wine, a Book of Verse – and Thou
Beside me singing in the Wilderness –
And Wilderness is Paradise enow.

**Some bread, some meat …**
Omar Khayyām
Tr. HT

Some bread, some cheese, and a jug of wine,
With you beside me beneath a lush vine.
I know a great king who would, if he could,
Barter his crown for this day of mine.

Each tiny atom of earth, air and sea
Once moved another to write poetry.
This speck of dust on your hair was once:
As loved by someone as you are by me.

**The Passionate Shepherd to His Love**
Christopher Marlowe

Come live with mee, and be my love,
And wee will all the pleasures prove
That Valleys, groves, hills, and fields,

Woods, or steepie mountain yeelds.
And wee will sit upon the rocks,
Seeing the Shepheards feede their flocks,
By Shallow Rivers, to whose falls,
Melodious byrds sing madrigalls.
And I will make thee beds of Roses
And a thousand fragrant posies,
A cap of flowers, and a kirtle,
Embroydred all with leaves of Mirtle;
A gown made of the finest wool,
Which from our pretty Lambs we pull,
Fair linèd slippers for the cold:
With buckles of the purest gold.
A belt of straw, and Ivie buds,
With Coral clasps and Amber studs:
And if these pleasures may thee move,
Come live with me, and be my love.
The Sheepheards swains shall daunce and sing,
For thy delight each May morning:
If these delights thy mind may move,
Then live with me and be my love.


**That Time of Year**
William Shakespeare, sonnet 73

That time of year thou mayst in me behold
When yellow leaves, or none, or few, do hang
Upon those boughs which shake against the cold,
Bare ruin'd choirs, where late the sweet birds sang.
In me thou see'st the twilight of such day
As after sunset fadeth in the west,
Which by and by black night doth take away,
Death's second self, that seals up all in rest.
In me thou see'st the glowing of such fire
That on the ashes of his youth doth lie,
As the death-bed whereon it must expire
Consumed with that which it was nourish'd by.
This thou perceivest, which makes thy love more strong,
To love that well which thou must leave ere long.

## John Anderson my jo
Robert Burns

John Andeerson my jo, John,
When we were first acquent;
Your locks were like the raven,
Your bony brow was brent;
But now your brow is beld, John,
Your locks are like the snaw;
But blessings on your frosty pow,
John Anderson my Jo.

John Anderson my jo, John,
We clamb the hill the gither;
And mony a canty day, John,
We've had wi' ane anither:
Now we maun totter down, John,
And hand in hand we'll go;
And sleep the gither at the foot,
John Anderson my Jo.

jo, dear; brent, smooth; beld, bald; mony, many; pow, head; canty, pleasant; maun, must.


## The Confirmation
Edwin Muir (d. 1959)

Yes, yours, my love, is the right human face,
I in my mind had waited for this long,
Seeing the false and searching for the true,
Then found you as a traveller finds a place
Of welcome suddenly amid the wrong
Valleys and rocks and twisting roads. But you,
What shall I call you? A fountain in a waste,
A well of water in a country dry,
Or anything that's honest and good, an eye
That makes the whole world bright. Your open heart,
Simple with giving, gives the primal deed,
The first good world, the blossom, the blowing seed,
The hearth, the steadfast land, the wandering sea.
Not beautiful or rare in every part.
But like yourself, as they were meant to be.

## Daybreak
Boris Pasternak
Tr. Max Hayward and Manya Harari

You meant everything in my destiny.
Then came the war, the disaster.
For a long, long time,
No trace, no news of you.

After all these years,
Again your voice has disturbed me.
All night I read your testament.
It was like reviving from a faint.

I want to be among people,
In a crowd, in the morning bustle.
I'm ready to smash everything to splinters
And bring them to their knees.

And I run down the stairs
As though coming out for the first time
Into these snowy streets
With their deserted pavements.

All around are lights, homeliness, people getting up,
Drinking tea, hurrying to the trams.
In the space of several minutes
The town is unrecognisable.

The blizzard weaves a net
Of thickly falling snow across the gate.
They all scurry out to be on time,
Leaving their food half-eaten, their tea unfinished.

I feel for each of them
As if I were in their skins,
I melt with the melting snow,
I frown with the morning.

In me are people without names,
Children, stay-at-homes, trees.
I am conquered by them all
And this is my only victory.

**To Edith**
Bertrand Russell

Through the long years
I sought peace;
I found ecstasy, I found anguish,
I found madness,
I found loneliness,
I found the solitary pain that gnaws at the heart;
But peace I did not find.

Now, old and near my end,
I have known you,
And, knowing you,
I have found both ecstasy and peace;
I know rest
After so many lonely years.
I know what life and love may be.

Now, if I sleep,
I shall sleep fulfilled.[116]


**A Svelte Orchard Rememberd**
Feyyaz Fergar (d. 1993)

That year Summer was
In full sweeping swing,
Weaving into veins of trees
The hum of its textural verve.

That year means for me
Lillian and her shapely steps
Echoing through places
Like Wide Open and Pity-me-Not
In green wartime Geordie country.

I remember
Touching her
With hands full of songs.

That year was many seasons,

Many joys ago.


**Praise and Exile**
Feyyaz Fergar

'I love acrobats,' she said,
Out of the budding blue.
He who had never been able
Even to stand on his head
At the best of times and places past,
Swayed a bit, looked at her voice.
He felt something like gathering heights
Slowly, awkwardly gathering shape in him
And soaring with unfurled precision
Into octaves of flight,
Chisel in the air a priceless
Singing somersault.
'How lovely,' she said, 'this is pure Chagall.'

He, heart undone, he receding in lung and pulse,
Found himself scrapped in second-hand sky.


**Voices**
David Morphet[117]

Like an old lacquered seventy-eight
my memory goes crackling round
with sounds of voices long unheard –
perhaps for some now, mine is the sole recording.

Of these my little aunt comes much to mind.
Her vocal cords were badly tuned
in childhood when she toppled down
and broke the string of growth.

That midget voice
with its light rasp and quaver came
from a child's form,
peculiarly small.

As a young man I was her favourite.

I used to sit beside her kitchen range
and tell her my ambitions.
Her life was tethered down

and mine was taking flight.
In me she grasped at opportunity
vicariously, urging me on
with her scraped and piccolo words.

Her death came suddenly
when I was far away
in thought and place.
How much I wished I'd had

a chance to say farewell
to my tiny champion
before she laid aside
her apron and her homilies.

Silence falls all too quickly
on the voices that we love –
often before we know, let alone tell,
how much they meant to us.


**As we sat down to dinner last night**
HT

As we sat down to dinner last night
And I looked at you,
Across the table,
Between the candles,
I saw suddenly the young woman I had met long ago:
Your eyes flashed mischievously,
Your girl's voice was there, too.

I saw also
That I was countless man,
You countless woman,
Across the eras,
Over many seas,
Sitting down at dusk with voiceful eyes,
Exchanging silent poems,
Knowing the fate of ages.

I love you.


**Earlier this October evening**
HT

Earlier this October evening,
I sat by the fire,
While you cooked in the kitchen.
Streaks of red and ochre brightened the sky;
The ash tree on the left, the oak on the right,
Stood guard of honour to the setting sun.

Guilt bites at my arm.
All day I remained in my room,
Socrates and Seneca my excuses.
But you, my Lara of the Urals,
Cleared the wood shed of ivy and cobwebs,
Cut the grass, swept the yard of leaves,
Fashioned wonders from a poor larder.

Miracle of womanhood,
My walking stick,
My leaning wall.
How could I make up
For what I owe you
For this single day?

# Part Three

# Possessions for Autumn

# Between the Hermit and the Hoarder

118

If I had to live my life again, I would have made a rule to read some poetry and listen to some music, at least once every week; for perhaps parts of my brain now atrophied would thus have been kept alive through use. The loss of these tasks is a loss of happiness, and may possibly be injurious to the intellectual and, more probably, to the moral intellect, by affecting the emotional part of our nature.[119]

Some bread, some cheese, and a jug of wine,
With you beside me shaded by a vine.
I know a great king who would, if he could,
Barter his crown for that which is mine.[120]

*

– What Did we do before we had fire?

– We were ignorant brutes, but thinking brutes. So we were miserable.

– What did we do before we had goats, donkeys, the wheel?

– We began to have cooking, but we were still miserable, because we remained fearful of the future, of disease, childbirth, spirits.

– What did we do before we had electric lighting, the telephone, the gramophone, the radio, the car?

– We did much better, but we still had to wait for penicillin and brain scans.

– All right, All tight. You've made your point. No doubt you'll now say: what did we do before we had e-mail and the Internet?

– Do you have Eye-Fi Mobi?

– What's that?

– Oh, no. You don't know what you're missing.

These joyous cries of astonishment have been heard down the ages from the day we fashioned tools out of stone, and each generation has become accustomed to, and cherished, the tools and comforts it has inherited or invented, because they made life more capable of fulfilment. But the cries of joy have been redolent of anxiety, too, because those tools and comforts could always be lost, at least temporarily, and no matter how often wiser heads have reminded us that, even before we had hot meals, we had the ecstasy of a cool breeze on our cheeks in the heat of summer, and had the song of the birds, love, language and art, going back has not been possible except for a few religious hermits.

But there is no justification for going back, within reason. My latest joy, reading books on electronic tablets, is not going to destroy the planet. It just enables me to read more, because life is running out and I do not wish to confine myself to reading only a dozen books a year. E-book readers are easier on my failing eyes and they may even benefit the planet by saving a few trees.

Recently, a severe rain storm caused an interruption in our broadband Internet connection in the county of Sussex in southern England, where we live. My wife said that she could not imagine life without e-mails and the Web. I had to agree. It is remarkable how quickly happiness can become dependent on a new possession. While we did not have the connection, we still had electricity, the telephone, digital radio and television, even hundreds of orchestras in the form of compact discs sitting on shelves and ready to play the most sublime works of art we could wish to hear. Yes, we both became restless, casting anxious glances in the direction of a little black box called a 'router' to see whether it was no-longer blinking, showing that our new window on the world was open once more.

But as we become older and wiser, we will hopefully see that a good, fulfilled life does not depend on the quantity of objects and freedoms we possess, but on their quality. Thus a glamorous sports car loses its lustre (fortunately it never had any for me), and a slow broadband connection quickly becomes sufficient for sending e-mails and browsing the Web for information. It dawns on one, in fact, that we really need many fewer things that we thought we needed.

Before I elaborate on the minimum number of possessions that I, personally, would need for a good life in the modern age, let me enumerate them in a list. They make a presumption, of course, of reasonable health, an income sufficient enough to free us from the possibility of humiliation, an ability to do a little good in society, and a quiet home that allows us to pursue a modest hobby. Under such circumstances, and in order of importance, the following are all I would need, I think, to make me happy:

A conscience at ease;
A loving companion;
A few faithful and agreeable friends;
A free people with enlightened laws enforced by a powerful judiciary;
A dozen book shelves of philosophy, history and literature in beautiful print worthy of them;
An e-book reader for my failing eyes;
A microchip bearing the mature works of Bach, Mozart, Beethoven, Schubert, Richard Straus and – please do not tell anyone – Tchaikovsky, plus a thousand classic love songs;
An Internet connection to watch the madness of my fellow human beings;
A cello on which to make noises of my own;
A modest greenhouse in a climate with seasons;
A few hundred recipes of healthy, mostly vegetarian, dishes;
A calligraphic pen for writing letters to my friends and make diary notes for myself.
And a small cellar of good wines for my friends' visits.

I have always thought that a conscience at ease with itself is the greatest of riches. Without it, one could not respect oneself and without the feeling that you have not caused harm to others or been a parasite on the body of society, no happiness would come the way of a normal person.

The importance of a loving partner and a ring of close and tested friends does not need elaboration. Without them, life would be worthless to me. It would be a pit of loneliness to which only the nature of some solitary animals is suited.

But a country of enlightened laws with a political system that ensures the rulers cannot violate the rights of citizens is not within the reach of the majority of mankind. Thus those of us who live in mature democracies should throw our hats in the air thrice a day to celebrate our great good luck, our fortune of having attained what most of our ancestors dreamt of. Enlightened laws allow a citizen the dignity to which human consciousness has always aspired, the chance to live as a full member of society around one, to participate in the kinds of social discussion that make us human, to choose the managers of one's communal affairs, to enjoy innovative art, and to feel confident that, should one fall into poverty for no fault of one's own, we would not have to lower our heads before individuals for charity. A political systems that ensures that freely elected institutions are above the mightiest ruler in the land is vital to our happiness, for otherwise, no laws, enlightened or not, would mean much if they depended on the whims of rulers for their implementation.

The remaining items on my list may be described as 'the little things' that I would need to make my life enjoyable, as opposed to tolerable, for no matter how loving my partner and friends and no matter how good the laws and the political system under which I lived, I would be a burden upon my loved ones if I did not possess those smaller possessions that brought a smile to my face. Fortunately, though, they do not need to cost the Earth and, hopefully, some of my readers will be morally superior to me and need even fewer of them than I do. They also show that it is possible to live on a planet with a dangerously warming climate without leaving what is called a large 'carbon footprint'.

One item on my list may raise eyebrows. Does one really need a cellar, no matter how modest, of good – that is, relatively expensive – wines to complete one's happiness? I would answer that the ability to open the occasional bottle of good wine to celebrate a visit by one's family or friends ought to be forgiven one as an exceptional luxury, and where would life be if it did not allow us a few weaknesses? Thus I confess that under the infectious enthusiasm of a most-loved friend, I have allowed myself to have a few cases of promising reds to be laid down for my in the Bordeaux region of France. When these wines mature, they are brought to England for me and the smiles on the faces of my friends cherishing every sip of them make all the difference in the world.

The 'carbon footprint' of the occasional luxury of this type should not bring about the end of our lovely planet. Provided one constantly watches the level of one's consumption and how it affects the lives of others, I think that the following comical celebration of the lives of most of us has a grain of justification in it. I wrote it a dozen years ago and call it Epitaph for the Common Man. After all, I want the planet for the happiness of man. A planet, no matter how lovely, would be a dead planet for me if it did not possess intelligent and enlightened life.

**Epitaph for the Common Man**
HT

It's true.
He did his share of damage to the Earth.
He caused trees to fall early,
His body heat still shakes the reeds,
His body's other emanations continue
To nibble at the ozone layer.

But he meant well:
He patted dogs,
Made children laugh,
Greeted strangers, and ...
St Peter will like this especially:
He held together the few around him.

May I leave this chapter with another quote from that lovely and modest great man, Charles Darwin. It concerns the craving that blights many a life: fame. The pursuit of fame for its own sake in today's 'celebrity society' is one certain road to unhappiness and frustration. It has its drawbacks even for those who have achieved it. In his short autobiography – which he did not write for publication, but only for his family, Darwin wrote:

> I do not mean to say that a favourable review or a large sale of my books did not please me greatly, but the pleasure was a fleeting one, and I am sure that I have never turned one inch out of my course to gain fame.[121=]

# Epilogue

*The Universe may as well revolve around the Earth, and the Earth revolve around us.*

The twelve wise men and women whom I paraded in the first part of this book are all dead, and they were, in some cases, of contrasting personalities who would turn up their noses at some others in the company. But if we could gather them around a table to ask them to come up with a list of recommendations to help us live better lives under the storm clouds of the early twenty-first century, what might they proclaim?

Clearly the more ancient ones would first need months – or rather years – of education in modern science to bring them up to the level, even, of a typical ten-year-old today. We would, I imagine at the very start, have to teach them how to 'browse the Web' or use a mobile telephone. Once they overcame the humiliation of those discoveries – especially if young children were employed to teach them – we would have to appoint over them such specialists as chemists, physicists, biologists, geologists and psychologists – not to mention teachers of modern manners – to bring them up to date with the state of knowledge today and to enable them to understand our needs. Thus the circumstances of their lengthy incarceration would have to be as idyllic as we could make them. We would have to give them a large palace, for example, in which they could roam, with extensive gardens in which to refresh their spirits.

But in ethics, in the manner of living and cooperating with others in society, they would need no lessons from us. Their good natures, their dazzling intelligence and their years of observing other human beings at close hand, would have already equipped them in that vital respect.

Unfortunately, though, we cannot summon them together to advise us as to how to lead good lives. All we can do is to try, by remote access, by examining what we know of them, to guess what their recommendations might be. So what did I, for one, think I learned from studying their lives and thoughts?

It may help if I refresh our memory of what we studied.

I think that in Socrates we detect a healthy chunk of doubt, the first step to gaining true knowledge. At the end of a distinguished career as soldier, lawmaker and teacher in Athens, he is brought in front of a large number of Jurors chosen at random from among respectable citizens and told to explain himself for airing views that are, in the view of those citizens, incorrect. He is told to repent, and to promise not to repeat his beliefs in public. He would have to be executed, otherwise. But Socrates refuses to bow to what he regards as both unjust and contrary to the best interests of those same citizens. He declares that he is really not sure of what he believes. For example, there might be gods, as the state insists, or just a single god, a creator, as he sometimes suspects. Death might also be merely a stepping stone to eternal life, as some people claim, in which case he might suddenly find himself 'in the company of Homer's heroes'. Or it might mean, on the contrary, complete oblivion, 'an eternal sleep', which would not be unwelcome. His judges are appalled and declare him a rebel, but they are not keen to kill him. They appoint only a light guard over him and urge his friends secretly to enable him to escape into exile. But he does not play their game. He refuses stubbornly. He has himself been a lawmaker, he says. How could he justify defying the laws of the state he has served for so long? Thus, despite having a wife and two young children for whom his death would be a calamity, he drinks his bowl of hemlock at the appointed hour and attains, in the spectacular manner of that death, a heroic status grander that any of Homer's heroes.

Epicurus, with his frugal way of life, but as the leader of a small community to whose full membership he admits women and slaves, is a similar personality, but is convinced that there is no afterlife. Nor are there for him any supernatural beings, no gods of any kind. He devotes himself, instead, to achieving contentment, through a simple, 'natural' existence, for both himself and those around him.

In Seneca, the Roman senator and powerful statesman, I detected the beginnings of modern humanism, but without overt emphasis on a frugal way of life, except in his own case. While he served good wines and rare foods to his guests – which he probably saw as a political necessity to ensure continued high office, he did not join in the feasts. Instead, he lived largely on dried figs and other fruit. So, under his chancellorship while Nero was a minor, he could boast that not a single innocent man had been sent to his death by the state.

Boethius was both a politician and avowed Christian. But at the end, as he awaited the king's decision whether or not to execute him for secretly corresponding with the church in Constantinople, he decided to write the mother of all Consolations, his Consolation of Philosophy, and concluded that perhaps the old pagans such as Seneca had better answers to the deepest questions of existence than had Christianity. So he left the church Fathers out of his recommendations for posterity.

Omar Khayyām, a mathematician and astronomer in the eleventh century, was a Persian, but similarly sought intellectual nourishment in the ancient Greeks and Romans. He found himself, in effect, trapped among aliens, his official fellow Muslims, and was lucky to escape the lynch mob for his daring to ask uncomfortable questions. His sparse, but philosophically rich, quatrains have inspired millions of freethinkers over the past 900 years. See if you can find a second-hand copy of my biography of him.

Spinoza tried hard to be a rationalist scientist, but did not have the tools for it. He came to the conclusion that there was only one substance of which the whole of the universe was made. He called it God/nature. Despite accusations of deep heresy, he was a deeply religious philosopher, but his divinity, God/Nature, is an unloving god, because he/she/it is too large and impersonal force to be concerned with us minions. I'm not sure even whether it is a 'knowing' god, aware even of its own presence. At best, Spinoza's deity is the God that some modern scientists such as Einstein and Hawking invoke when they fail to explain why we are here at all. By that term they mean the laws of physics or whatever it was that gave rise to the birth of the universe. See my friend Peter Atkins's confrontation of him when we visited him in the Hague in 1676.

All twelve of my beacons of inspiration were chosen because they had to struggle in life and because they succeeded in maintaining a measure of happiness or balance to their last days despite their misfortunes. But though the first half turned out to be thinkers, only two of the second half, Russell and Arendt, turned out to be so. Of the remainder, three were artists of one kind or another. They are Beethoven, Twain and Pasternak. The other, Darwin, was a scientist. The lives of all six are much more fully documented than in the case of the ancients. So we know more about them and so our judgement can be more reliable.

Beethoven's triumph over the calamity of deafness in a musician is truly of the most inspiring dimension; Twain, the American writer of humour, overcame deep depression caused by bankruptcy and the loss of two mature daughters. He survived long enough to earn more money to pay all his debts and he regained his sense of honour; Darwin struggled for the bulk of his life against an illness he caught during his voyages of discovery in South America, but managed through hard work to change our perception of ourselves with his Origin of Species, while Pasternak lived for the sake of completing his novel Doctor Zhivago to affect the course of history through undermining the intellectual credibility of Marxist ideology.

Of the remaining two thinkers, Hanna Arendt, the Jewish refugee from Nazi Germany who later became a theoretician of power and politics in the United States, was saved, above all, by her curiosity to understand. Thus she did not hate her Nazi persecutors, but concluded that they were often mere 'banal' individuals. They showed that Mankind could easily sink into barbarism if our political systems did not safeguard themselves against the ever-present threat from such individuals among us. Arendt also cultivated friendship as a source of strength and knew that it was vital to enjoy the simple pleasures of life in order to remain functional as a family member, friend, neighbour and citizen.

Finally, though I am certain in my mind that Beethoven was the greatest of all the luminaries I chose for this study – perhaps even the greatest human being who ever lived – I would pick the Englishman Bertrand Russell to befriend in preference to all the rest. This is certainly not because I was invited to travel to Wales to visit him when I was only an impressionable youth and he a towering figure in the world; nor is it because I have reason enough to believe that he would have allowed me inside his circle of adorers. I did not approve of all his politics at the time, but politics meant involvement in society to mitigate suffering and it helped to save him from depression in his 97 years of life. I believe that he will go on to inspire millions more people in the ages to come, possibly even achieving the status of a latter-day Socrates.

To sum up, I think that all the heroes I gathered together in this book sought knowledge, verifiable knowledge, for its own sake. Knowledge of the world and of our own minds made us happier within ourselves and better citizens in our communities. They advocated active involvement in the day-to-day affairs of those communities, and they knew that our minds and bodies also needed physical, as well as intellectual, nourishment to enable us to be useful citizens. They advocated, too, modest styles of life, not only because it was fairer amidst scarcities of resource, but also because material wealth often brought anxiety of its own in its wake.

I believe strongly that they all harboured a big chunk of reverence in their hearts for the universe and – particularly – for the existence of ourselves, intelligent beings, within it. But therein lies a problem, a modern problem. Men of faith have no such difficulty. By contrast, growing numbers of us secularists who do not wish to sink back into mysticism find ourselves pulled between two great magnets. On the one hand, we do not believe in a creator and cannot justify any religious feelings for dead matter that has given rise, by the laws of physics, to living beings. On the other, we feel mystical respect for all the entities we think wonderful in the world. We think we have discovered nearly all there is to find about the origins of the Universe. We know about the evolution of life on Earth. We see that the Universe is a vast – unimaginably vast – region of cold space occasionally broken up by clumps of hot suns and warm planets. We know that, precisely because of the absence of that traditional creator, there is no exterior purpose to our lives. Yet we continue to feel reverence for life and existence. How do we explain that contradiction?

What did the last, scientifically-minded of my heroes say about it? Russell, and many before him, are explicit on the question. He would say that you did not need to believe in a creator in the mould of the Judaeo-Zoroastrian god to have a sense of the sacred. He is right. Religion has been strong outside of the West and the Middle East for thousands of years without such as personal creator.

Science has, of course, not come to the end of its journey and has not, to my knowledge, answered the most basic question of all, why things exist. Nor do many think that it ever will, despite the magnificent optimism of Peter Atkins and others top scientists. At the moment, the suspicion is that what we call 'the Universe' may itself be only one of an infinite number of universes in existence. In other words, our universe of the past 13.7 billion years, frighteningly vast as it is, with its 250 billion galaxies each containing hundreds of billions of solar systems, is only a dot in the larger scheme, the so-called Multiverse, and that the Multiverse has been here for ever.

Whatever the details, I feel the Universe, and my little existence within it, are almost worthy of worship. Almost, but not quite. That is because the word 'worship' is riddled with the baggage of old-fashioned religion.

Beyond that problem, the lack of a 'greater', exterior purpose to our existence presents no obstacle to many of us moderns. The instinctual pursuit of love and happiness, together with the purposes we set for ourselves in the context of family, friendship, career and society can be more than sufficient. Indeed, they can be noble. At the very least, they give meaning to our lives. Only a subsidiary question arises: What should those purposes be, for both our own sakes and for the sake of the society of which we are a part?

I do not propose to preach here to an intelligent readership on what purposes they should set for themselves. Each one of us must determine – and we do determine, even if unconsciously – their own ethical priorities, and I believe that we are basically 'good', because the tendency to cooperate with others in the greater interests of us all has been shown to be innate to our nature.

Since I first read Boris Pasternak's Doctor Zhivago, that great novel of the Russian revolution of the early twentieth century, excerpts from several of his poems attached to the end of the book have stuck in my mind. They demonstrate, for me, as powerfully as any mass of statistics can, that social solidarity is part of our makeup. This is what makes the unsung man of the street a hero in my eyes. The following lines are from a poem called Daybreak:

They scurry out to be on time,
Leaving their food half-eaten, their tea unfinished.

I feel for each of them
As if I were in their skin.
I melt with the melting snow,
I frown with the morning.

In me are people without names,
Children, stay-at-homes, trees.
I am conquered by them all
And this is my only victory.[122]

But, dare I say it, modern scientific discoveries can go some way to fill the void that the loss of old-fashioned religion inflicts on us. Their contemplation can be as powerful as the religious experiences that some mystics are said to have experienced, and they can enable us to indulge in metaphysical allegories of a modern type. Let me make a claim that will probably strike you as absurd. What would you say if I claimed that the Earth, this small planet that revolves around a small sun on the edge of a small galaxy, really was the centre of all those universes I spoke of earlier? Since Copernicus, every school child has known the claim to be ridiculous. So let me elaborate.

According to modern physics, there is not a single fixed object in the Universe or in the Multiverse. Every entity can be regarded as either moving relative to others, or else be regarded as fixed regarding all others. In other words, it is just as correct, speaking mathematically, to say that our solar system revolves around the Milky Way galaxy, as it appears to be doing, as it is to say that the galaxy revolves around our solar system. By extension, it is possible to depict the centre of the earth as the centre of the whole Universe. Then all else will revolve around us. It is only a matter of convention. If we say 'let us assume so', it will be so.

But why should anyone wish to fix us as the centre of being, the centre of Existence? Justification comes, for me, from a contemplation of human consciousness. As far as we know, our species is the most astounding phenomenon that has come to be, so far, anywhere in the Universe or Multiverse. We have become conscious of our own existence, as well as of the existence of all other things that exist, and we have proved in our history that we can be loving, noble, creative and fun. This should allow us to be sentimental about ourselves a little, to turn to poetry and metaphor to claim that the Earth, dead material though it is, has become conscious of its own existence through us. A further assertion of imagination would enable us to go even further and say that the Universe has become aware of itself through us.

These are truly astonishing observations, and they ought to remain valid for as long as we have found no proof of other beings elsewhere who are more intelligent, and more 'good', than we are. Until then, and even then, seeing that mere dead matter can come together to produce intelligent and loving beings should be enough to send an electric tingle down anyone's spine. For me, it is akin to the visions of the divine that are claimed by mystics and seers.

Returning to the subject of this narrative, I believe that all the great men and women I have examined here sensed our specialness, and that they too were overwhelmed at times by gazing into the sky at night, by seeing what wonderful art their fellows could create, or of what acts of love and kindness they were capable. This is despite the scientific ignorance from which the more ancient of my exemplars suffered. I wanted to examine their lives, as much for myself as for anyone else who might care to read the results of my investigation.

Before the modern dawning of science, it was not possible to speculate, as we can, with any degree of confidence. Only after Darwin showed how we had evolved from lower forms by Natural Selection did it become possible to be reasonably sure that no divine hand lay behind our being here. Before Darwin, people who dared to intrude into such realms had to make leaps in the dark. No wonder that they came up with all kinds of contradictory hypotheses. If some of them did close in on our modern notions of atoms and stars, it was by pure accident and temperament, and in their heart of hearts they knew it.

A strong reason for my dozen exemplars to wish to go on living was their love of other human beings, both close to them and at large. They chose to concentrate their thoughts on the more beautiful aspects of our minds, such as our tendency to love, rather than to hate, our ability to act nobly towards those in need, our genius in creating works of beauty and, yes, even our longing for laughter and frivolity. The conversation of agreeable friends they valued among the best possessions with which a person might be blessed. After those attractions, a myriad of small things, such as to behold a sunset, to smell a fresh loaf of bread, to savour the complexity of a glass of red wine, were to them extra blessings to bind them to life, rather than to propel them towards death and nihilism.

So, when this little compilation is sent to the printers towards the beginning of 2015, the 75th year of my life on this lovely planet, I shall tell myself that I deserve a little pampering. I plan to gather my loved ones around me on that symbolic birthday, by which time my beard will hopefully be white enough to deserve full freedom to do what nature drives it to do. I shall organise a barbecue of fresh fish, caught by myself, marinated with lemon juice, chopped rosemary and a little crushed garlic, and I shall ask everyone to raise their glasses first to us all gathered there, and then to you also, both those who are, and those who will be. Goodbye.

# Appendix: Looking Back

## *Kurd's Eye View*

### Four autobiographical talks broadcast on BBC Radio 4 in August 1998

As I said in the Introduction to this work, the reader might wish to know where I came from and what kind of life preceded my presumption that what I wrote here might be of interest to anyone. Time is not right for me to write a full report on my life and inheritance. But I think the following talks that BBC Radio Four asked me to broadcast in four successive weeks in the summer of 1998 will give a sufficient account of my past. The talks received an exceptional reception from in those sections of the press that review radio programmes, much kinder than I had expected. For that reason, also, I am emboldened to believe that they may be of interest to my readers. The series was broadcast under the frivolous title of Kurd's Eye View and produced by the late and well-loved Nigel Acheson.

### Omar Khayyām And I

When the cab arrived at the hotel in Earl's Court in London in the small hours, the driver uttered a few words. But I didn't understand any of it. I held up my open palm to him with a bundle of pound notes, and he took what he thought reasonable – or perhaps not. We both smiled.

'Poor boy', he probably thought. 'He looks like a student, and he's been sent here without a word of English'.

That was October 1959, in patriarch Macmillan's Britain, a whole 39 years ago.

About 10 hours earlier, on a chilly October evening on the runway of Tehran airport, my Kurdish father, with his handle-bar moustaches, had embraced and kissed me for the first time in my memory and sent me on my way to a whole new civilisation, on board the first jet passenger airliner in the world, the crash-prone Comet 4 of the British Overseas Airways.

Tears had streamed down his cheeks, and I've not forgotten his last words: 'I'm doing this to you because the English are much more civilised than we are. I want you to learn some of their goodness and bring it here with you'.

No wonder I offered all those pound notes to the London cabby on trust.

The next day, having slept late, I stayed until lunch time at the Lexham Garden Hotel and decided to eat there, but I couldn't finish my meal. Its last course was a steaming chemical which I later learned to call 'apple pie and custard'. My father had said to me: 'You will hate their food at first. Just say "I love it, I love it, I love it" and you'll be all right'. He proved right, eventually.

Once again, I held up my open palm, this time to the hotel receptionist, and he ordered another cab. To the driver I showed a piece of paper on which was written: St Christopher's College, Gloucester Avenue, Regents Park.

I felt I could now begin to relax. As the cab wound its way through London with all its strange sights and too many buildings, I saw the end of my lonely journey drawing close, and the start of a productive new life in 'Engelestan'. St Christopher's College would be my firm place on the ground, my anchor. It would quickly teach me English and enrol me at either Oxford or Cambridge to study medicine. In a few years' time, I'd return to my people with my head held high, a fluent English speaker, with a vitally-needed professional skill, and I'd start to take up some of my father's duties as a leader of his community, whose simple hill farmers I longed to serve in those highlands of Kurdistan.

Well, that was the hope, and I had no reason to believe any of it might not come true. Yes, the Persian businessman in Tehran who'd arranged it all for my father had charged a heavy fee, but he had seemed decent enough, kind and soft-spoken, and he definitely knew his London. He even looked like an Englishman – with his intelligent, grey-blue eyes and his noble Nordic head.

The black cab eventually arrived at a row of three- or four-story buildings on the northern edge of Regent's Park. Dark and soot-laden, they were, from the neglect of the war years, but solid and honest, like the English themselves, and I held up my open palm to the driver once more. Then, carrying my large suitcase, I walked into the hall of No 8, 'No 8, Gloucester Avenue'. On its entrance was pinned a disappointingly small name-plate. 'St Christopher's College'.

There was no-one to greet me. So I walked on towards the hall, from inside which I heard some rumbling. I knocked and walked in. I found a young man and a young woman wrestling on the wooden floor. They stopped and came towards me, panting, and the young woman extended her hand:

'Hello', she said, very slowly, so that I understood some of the words. 'I am Heather, …. the cook… This is Manuel, …. the other student'.

Well, well. 'The other student'. So, we were two, and the cook would probably double up as teacher also.

Heather telephoned for 'Mr Philips', the principal, and he arrived after a few minutes in one of those post-war cars that had small windscreens divided into two, giving them the appearance of short-sighted old men who screwed up their eyes to see.

But Mr Philips was kindly enough. After years of service in India, he had returned after Independence and sunk his savings into this building to teach English to foreign students. In India, he'd been a policeman.

That night, he and Mrs Philips took me to their own house a few streets away at 30, Fitzroy Road, and set me up there after dinner. Unfortunately, Manuel and Heather had also been given rooms next to mine, and they wrestled all night.

In the following days, I grew to look forward to our communal dinners, and specially to a new dish called 'baked beans on toast'. Amazingly, even though I came from a land that produced beans and tomatoes in abundance, no-one among us had invented this tasty dish. Nor, for that matter, sliced bread to toast, even though the ancestor of modern bread wheat was domesticated in the Middle East over 10,000 years ago. But then, unfortunately, the various peoples of the Middle East had become lethargic, lost their ability to innovate, since Islamic doctrine taken hold of their minds around the turn of the eleventh century.

I must not digress, specially into weighty matters.

Things went well at first. I became fond of the Philips family, and they of me, I think. But there was no love lost between Manuel and me. He was a well-travelled, worldly young man, with small, darting eyes, brought up in Portugal and on his grandfather's lands in Africa. So he was delighted when another student arrived from Tehran and said immediately that the first thing he wanted to see was 'Soho'.

I'd, of course, not heard of that district of London and so, when they told me what it was, I was disgusted. Nevertheless, I stayed up till midnight on their return to question the Persian student on how they'd fared. 'It was wonderful', he said. 'They brought us these gorgeous, blonde women, and they let us sniff them.'

'Sniff them?'

'Yes, they let us sniff their perfume if we ordered Champagne for everyone'.

Well, thankfully not so worldly, after all. Or was it because they'd run out of money? I never found out.

As for Mr Philips, I think that serving as a policeman in India had not quite prepared him to be a good businessman. He seemed to rely only on that single shark in Tehran to send him students, and this proved inadequate. The number stopped growing beyond about 8, and, as we talked Persian all day and all evening, my English didn't make the kind of progress I needed to make. On top of that, Mr Philips had employed a couple of left-wing Welshmen as our teachers, and they told us that he was 'exploiting' us by charging our parents too much.

There were other factors, also, behind my growing unhappiness. The Welshmen told me that it would take years before I could go to university here, because I had, first, to pass a number of new examinations called 'the Advanced Level of the General Certificate of Education', and that these 'A levels' were really advanced, so tough, in fact, that in other countries they equalled the first two years of a university course. It would take a struggle to pass any of them, if ever I did.

Above all, I think, the sudden dislocation, the constant tension of my new existence, was taking its toll and I was becoming mentally exhausted. I had been uprooted from the heart of my family, where I had never had to look after myself, to be transplanted into a strange society where I had no-one to turn to, even if I managed to speak their language.

Soot-laden London, too, was particularly gloomy that winter, and a heavy weight began to depress my heart. So I allowed myself to be led by a fellow student, the son of a minor landowner from near Tehran, and we left the protection of Mr Philips's family to live on our own in a bed-sitter, back in Earl's Court Road. There, where I had first arrived in the great metropolis, I had a nervous breakdown.

...Allow me here to interrupt this story to jump backward a little, or perhaps a lot, to the eleventh century, to show you where I really, really, came from, and forward, also, to the present day, to tell you that, after almost four decades living here, it's time for me to ask, formally, that I be given the honour of becoming a fully-grown citizen.

Last May 18th, my family and I were, as far as we knew, the only people in the world who celebrated the 950th birthday of Omar Khayyam, the medieval poet and mathematician. I'm working on a biography of him and so we were aware of the anniversary.

We lifted our glasses to the great man, who loved the excitement of free debate, who was forced by a clerical fatwa of to flee for his life, a man who valued love and personal friendship as they ought to be cherished:

And when Thyself with shining Foot shall pass,
Among the Guests Star-scatter'd on the Grass,
And in thy joyous Errand reach the Spot
Where I made one – turn down an empty Glass.

...That was from Edward FitzGerald's translation of Khayyam in 1859, the little book that made such a deep impression on the English-speaking world of its time. Omar's own words in Persian had overwhelmed me in my early teens when I found him among my father's books and I have been an admirer ever since. Here was a man who wanted merely to be himself, a fun-loving, curious human being, rather than be the ideological soldier of a religion obsessed with death. They wouldn't let him be himself, and he was lucky to die in his bed.

That was in eastern Iran, where the level plains had always tempted invaders, whether Islamic Arab zealots or nomadic Turks and Mongols who quickly became zealots.

By contrast, in my highlands of the Kurdish west, Islam had mostly fallen on stony ground and foreign armies usually come to grief. Even fifty years ago during my childhood, we remained a free-spirited people whose agricultural lives had not changed significantly since the seventh century, when they had followeed Zarathustra, the ancient prophet of farmers and shepherds. One, of course, cannot be quite sure in these matters. It's possible that even then, the Kurds were heretics. The needs of their orchards and cows would have had to be placed before those of any organised religion. In fact, I dare think that eve by Khayyam's time in the eleventh century, his Persians and my Kurds were so similar in their agricultural culture that, as I sit here talking to you of him, I can almost sniff the smell of the sour-yoghurt drink that must've filled every room of his house in the city of Nishāpūr on every hot summer's day, making me a kind of 'family', or at least a servant in his lordship's household.

My father knew all this and so, when he sent me to England to study medicine, it wasn't only for the useful technical knowledge. It was primarily for the higher values of humanity, such as tolerance, which he felt the Middle East had lost, or was losing, but which Western Europe chrished.

In the intervening decades, as you know, ideological religion has been imposed on every corner of Iran, including my own, unfortunate Kurds, to the extent that the discovery of the poems of Khayyam from nearly a thousand years ago in a man's personal library is regarded nowadays as evidence of criminality.

Now, am I turning my back on my people by applying for British citizenship after nearly 40 years of living here? A majority of Middle Easterners would no doubt feel so. But let me be truthful, as Zarathustra, the prophet of my ancestors, would have ordered me to be. That majority doesn't care about Omar Khayyam – and by definition, about me – and so, in return, I no longer care about it, in the sense that I don't care what it thinks of me. Omar, on the other hand, would wish me well, I'm certain. As a free man, this is where he himself would have felt at home, and he would, also, have wanted me to say 'thank you' to the British, my hosts and gracious protectors for so long, my only true people now, without whom I would probably not be alive today.. Khayyam would want me to be proud to call myself a Briton.

## Henry II and I

The very first time I saw the Thames, I did not fall in love with it. It takes a sound mind to fall in love with a river, and I was, in the first half of 1960, at the height of a nervous breakdown. All the unsettling pressures of being plucked by my father from the heart of my family and rural Kurdish society, to be transplanted into a foreign metropolis whose language I did not know, and where I did not have a single person to whom I could turn for help, had done their work and made the world go dark before me in the middle of the day.

In the spring of 1960, I attended a course organised for foreign students by the London County Council and I was dissatisfied with the progress of my English. In the summer months, around my 20th birthday, I saved my father some precious foreign currency by working as a kitchen porter – without telling him – in a restaurant in South Kensington. By day, I was listless and preoccupied. By night, I couldn't sleep because I feared hurting myself.

Then, fortunately, I came across a wonderful Persian doctor who was studying pathology and lived in the bed-sit above mine in Earl's Court. Since we were both opposed to the Communist Part of Iran – I out of purely family allegiances, I must confess – he introduced me to Iranian student circles in London and I confided in him, eventually, about my inner gloom. He advised me to go to a smaller town for pursuing my pre-university studies and: 'to have lots of fresh fruit and exercise'. So I went to Reading, out on the old A4 Road half-way to Oxford, and there I was lucky again in my choice of lodgings. The Domzals were a refugee family from Poland. Zigmund Domzal had been a slave worker in Nazi Germany and was now the manager of a building gang. He loved talking about politics when he was not so tired as to fall asleep immediately after dinner. His bubbly wife, Chesha, had survived with her family by fleeing to Russia, and then to Iran and India, before coming to Britain. So they knew a thing or two about youths suddenly cut off from everything they loved, and they took me to their hearts. Their lovely little daughter, Basha, became a substitute for the baby sister I'd left behind in Kurdistan. I made a slow, but firm, recovery, and I fell in love with the Thames.

I bought a violin and a bicycle, and joined the local Civil Defence corpse, where I was a signalman among tea ladies and other mesmerising intellects. The giggling was exactly what I needed. On sunny Sundays, I and a fellow student, Antony Salvadoré Monaco, the son of an Italian immigrant, would cycle all the way to Woodstock, north of Oxford, for a picnic in the grounds of Blenheim Palace, or swim in the river at Pangbourne. Anthony would tell me about his sexual conquests. He was extremely worldly. Disgracefully so, really. One of his English woman friends told me I had beautiful eyes, and I ran for my life.

After a couple of years at Reading Technical College, I acquired two A-level passes, in zoology and chemistry, and two O-level ones, in physics and English. But my marks weren't good enough for any of the medical schools and, very depressed, I decided to go for chemistry, as did Anthony. It would take only three years, I said to myself, and I could return home not completely empty-handed. My father accepted the failure in good grace.

So I came to London and enrolled at Enfield College of Further Education for an external degree of the University of London, breaking the course up to save my father more foreign currency by working as an assistant research chemist at Dagenham in Essex.

But, despite enjoying the camaraderie of the research lab, my heart was not in chemistry. Instead, I drifted towards politics with my old friend, the Persian doctor, who had now become my mentor and my new family. I spent most of my time as a student activist, criticising the excesses of the monarchy in Iran, from a secular, left-of-centre position, which of course meant that I could no-longer return to Iran without trouble.

On one occasion, I narrowly escaped a brutal beating when my friend the doctor's flat was raided by Iranian naval officers on training in Portsmouth. I was not there that night, but some of the raiders were captured by the police and we took them to court. Unfortunately, my fellow students' stories did not quite tally, some having been beaten up in lavatories, others pursued on the streets. By contrast, lawyers wearing the uniforms of the Royal Navy appeared in court to lead the defence and fine-tune the lying. The muscular, Judo-playing thugs claimed that my puny friends had invited them inside their flat and then attacked them. Both sides were 'bound to keep the Queen's peace' for a year. We lost our money. The Shah paid for the other lot.

I wonder now whether my antagonising the Shah's regime was not an unconscious strategy to find an excuse not to return home. In my first months in Britain, I had found that I no-longer believed in my father's religion. I remember the day very well. I wept. In the privacy of my room on the edge of Regents Park in the spring of 1960, I knew that I was letting my people down. My father, who was – and still is – a revered leader of his ancient faith, would lose face very badly among them if it emerged that his son and heir had left the fold. Furthermore, I'd break the hearts of many of his people, some of whose elders had actually pleaded with him not to risk letting me go abroad. But he'd rejected their advice, saying that his 'flesh and blood' would never leave the creed of his ancestors.

I sometimes joke that it was the combination of the mini-skirt and the philosopher Bertrand Russell that cost me my faith. But it isn't true. The seeds of it went back to a question planted in my mind by a fellow schoolboy in my early teens about cause and effect.

Anyway, there was no going back, despite a message from a high-ranking general in the Iranian army – my mother's first cousin – that I'd be all right if I returned, provided I'd promise not to criticise the Shah any longer.

Instead, I left chemistry without completing my course, worked a few more years as a research assistant, just for the money, and then gave that up to write short stories on land-reform in Kurdistan for British women's magazines. This last flight of fancy, of course, ended the only way it could, and, having spent my meagre savings on breakfasts in Hampstead cafes posing as an author for a few months, I drifted, reluctantly, into the Persian Service of the BBC as a junior, very junior, broadcaster. I didn't know then that I'd stay there for a dozen years. I also found a girlfriend – a former principal ballet dancer from New Zealand – with whom I'd later have two wonderful, affectionate children, both at university now. I also bought a cello.

I need to interrupt the story here to do some jumping around in time to be a bit more comprehensive, because we're all firmly rooted in the past, often the distant past. I'll go back first to 39 years ago in Tehran, and then further back in England, the England of the Plantagenets of late12th century. It will make sense, I promise you.

In a literal sense, my being catapulted into Britain began in the summer of 1959 in Tehran. Having been educated in a backward province, and possibly also suffering from mild dyslexia, I'd just failed the entrance examinations of the university of Tehran and then turned down an offer from some of my father's friends to pull strings to get me in, despite my failure.

As a result, I woke up one morning in my father's Tehran house to see him kneeling beside my bed and talking to God. I think he was even crying. He told God that I was too good, too pure, to remain in Iran, that Iran would corrupt me, as it did everything else. I pretended to be asleep.

Then a debate began: To England or to France. Both had their attractions. In the end, he turned down the French on account of their lechery. They were just too sophisticated for us simple folks. On the other hand, England had become the centre of the greatest empire in history because of the uprightness of her people. Not for England all those sly, effeminate handkerchief droppings in Hollywood films. And hadn't England recently defeated the Germans and Italians and Japanese, albeit with the help of her children?

Also, had not the BBC's Persian Section always told the truth during the war, even about British defeats, whereas those thunderous Germans tried always to deceive everyone with their lies, until no-body believed them anymore?

So it was that I was sent to Britain. But what had really made Britain great? Surely not telling the truth. My father didn't know that, but I think I do, and it goes back to Henry II. Yes, you know: Henry the tyrant, who pillaged Ireland in the name of the True Faith and murdered his friend and faithful chancellor and archbishop, Thomas a' Becket, in a church.

Now, of course, Henry did not have the slightest intention of making England 'great' in the sense that interests us, in the sense of laying the foundation of the future civil society where common people would gain control over their rulers. Henry would have been horrified by the very thought of that. Nonetheless, a great deal of good did come out of his actions, even in his own lifetime.

You will recall that Henry Plantagenet, the emperor of western France, didn't quite like the Norman barons of England. They were grasping and held back too much of the taxes that were his rightful lot. But also he feared them and not forgotten what they'd done to his predecessor and enemy, the Norman King Stephen. They, and, by the way, his own mother Matilda, too, had reduced the monarch to their plaything, it becoming so bad at one point that Stephen had bestowed the eternal ownership of East Anglia and the whole of the south-east, including the rich City of London, on a psychopathic and greedy barbarian called Geoffrey de Mandeville .

So, Henry determined to be the undisputed boss. He decided to sweep aside the barons and their ally, the church, from coming between him and the lower classes of the gentry, the notables of each town and shire who held the bulk of the money, and he opened the King's Court to aggrieved subjects to bring their disputes, and bribes, to it, rather than to the barons. He also commissioned a bench of travelling judges, and instituted trial by jury, though a primitive, and controlled, form of it. Above all, he gave England the Common Law, a new body of laws that was based largely on recent thinking and the precedents of the King's Court, to liberate at least a part of the population from the barbarities of Norman chivalry, Roman punishments and Anglo-Danish custom.

By the time Henry died in 1189 to leave the throne to the absentee Richard and the decadent John, the new popular law had driven such deep roots in the consciousness of the English that it could not be uprooted again by a resurgent barony. And when that barony did force its will on John in 1215 on the plain of Runnymede, it no longer dared think that it could rule the land on its own. It had to moderate its greed to gain the support of the lower gentry, the City of London and the Archbishop of Canterbury (against the strict command of the Pope). The first steps had been taken even towards the election of notables in the shires and the municipalities. England had changed for ever.

Talking of Runnymede reminds me of a story. In the early 1980s, I went to a hotel there to interview the late Ali Amini for the Times. Amini was a former, liberal and likeable prime minister of Iran. As I took photographs of him outside the building, it occurred to me that we stood on the famous plain of Runnymede, and that it had been Amini's grandfather, the shah Mozaffareddin, who had given Iran its first constitution in the opening years of the century. I told him so, and we looked around us with new eyes. Iran's constitution had been achieved almost 700 years after Magna Carta.

I am fortunate nowadays to wake up every morning to the wide expanse of the Thames in Limehouse as it flows out to the sea, and I must say that I see in the great river a symbol of England, making me emotional each time. It's old and restrained, and it's important, economically and culturally. If I'm allowed to be eccentric a little, I might even say that this waterway has had a determining part hand in the shaping of England.

To sum it all up according to this theory: The Thames made Londinium and Londinium made England and England made Parliament and Parliament made Britain and Britain changed the world. Britain also made me, for better or worse, and that man Henry II had his part, too. Thank you, once more, then, England, and you weren't all bad, really, Henry, though, I know, the Irish wouldn't agree.

## William Shakespeare and I

The very first time I held an English text in my hands, was at Uncle Isaac's shop. This was in my little Kurdish town of Sahneh, in the mountains of western Iran, and it must have been the middle 1950's. Sahneh had, at that time, a small, but well-liked community of Jewish shopkeepers – Islam having always fallen on rocky ground among us Kurds – and, as far as I knew, Uncle Isaac was the most popular of them. My father would always stop to talk to him. Short and stocky, perhaps in his seventies, and never without his black, trilby hat, he would, invariably – in hot summer or snow-bound winter – be found just inside his dark little shop and ready to exchange pleasant tittle tattle with passers-by. He specialised in stationery, and he had struck on a good idea: recycling. He stocked bundles of pamphlets with mysterious inscriptions on one side, blank on the other, and he sold them to us children as exercise paper for a quarter of the usual price. As we always had better uses for our meagre pocket money than exercise paper, we regarded him as nothing short of a saviour.

On one occasion, a pamphlet of some 20 pages inspired me specially. I had just begun learning the Roman alphabet and tried to pronounce the title of the essay. It was a single word and it said: Hydrogen.

Oh what a wonderful word. 'Heedrogen', 'Heedrogen'. I touched it with the inside walls of my mouth and threw it around my palette, like a wine-taster, and fantasised about the world where it belonged as an everyday subject of conversation. Then my father told me that the pamphlet was in English and that the word was pronounced 'hāidrojen', not heedrogen. It was a light gas, he said, that filled airships that then blew up. Little did I know that one day I would dread the subject of hydrogen in an examination paper in a country called England.

And that reminds me: What a strange and wonderful journey my life has been. I'm a Time Traveller. From that little market town in those remote mountains, barely touched by modern life, where story-tellers still held sway as the most esteemed entertainers, where the philosophising among illiterate orchard keepers on the fringes of the town on hot summer evenings would have reminded any learned man of the Athens of Socrates, to this day of quantum mechanics, I have witnessed much on my way. This computer that memorises my words on their way to you, the jet aircraft that brought me to England, the moon landings that some people regarded as blasphemous, the telephone in your pocket, the Internet, oh what wonders!

Nowadays, anyone can have access to a dozen international news agencies from home, and I've even built a little studio in a corner of my study to which all the world's radio stations can link themselves whenever they need an interview. Think of the thousands of gallons of petrol that such 'back-to-the-cottage' workers such as myself are now managing not to pour into the air of the big cities, and imagine my thrill whenever I pull down the blinds in my room in the middle of the day in London to put me in the appropriate mood for a midnight chat over the radio stations of the Outback in Australia.

But I mustn't jump too far ahead. Where was I last week when I interrupted myself to talk about Henry II? Oh, yes, we'd reached the point in the late 1960s when I gave up chemistry to write short stories on land reform in Kurdistan for British women's magazines, failed to become a great novelist, was forced to join the BBC World Service as a junior, very junior, broadcaster in Persian, and took a girlfriend, my very first, at the age 28.

Looking back to those years, I see that almost every setback that I had in my career was exactly what I needed, only I didn't know it at the time.

This has been an important point on my mind recently as my daughter approached graduation and a job in the world. Who's to know whether any guidance we might give her would be in her best interests? Accidents play such a large part in our lives.

I also shudder when I recall how easily a foolish youth, cut off from his family and desperate to make his way, might've been led to crime. When I was still trying to sell short stories to the magazines and had fallen into arrears with my rent, my landlord knocked on the door one night with a startling proposition. His name was Dimitri. He had a number of friends who owned Greek restaurants in London and they wanted me to supply them with several hundred bottles of bootlegged gin each week.

My years as an assistant in a research lab had made me, among other things, an expert in the chemistry of gin-making, on exactly what proportion of which essential oil to add to alcohol and water to replicate a famous brand. As it happens, I don't even like gin. It was just an amusing prank with fellow technicians.

Now, an income of several hundred pounds a week which the Greeks were offering me was, of course, a fortune for a young man who paid only three pounds and ten shillings for his attic room in Hampstead. Fortunately, a little uprightness came to my rescue and I disappointed my would-be saviour. 'Dimitri', I said. 'If I were to be caught and imprisoned for this, I'd never dare to look anyone in the face ever again and talk to them about a serious social issue. They'd say: Aren't you the one who went to prison for bootlegging?'

Dimitri and his friends left with their tails between their legs, but also shaking their heads at my foolish values.

Fortunately, a fellow activist in the cause of human rights in Iran guessed my plight and asked one day whether I'd go to the headquarters of the BBC's External Services in Bush House in the Strand to voice a few sentences in Persian about the new roads that Brazil was cutting through the Amazon rain forest.

I was shocked that he worked for any foreign broadcaster. All foreign broadcasting was, to me, brazen propaganda, but he reassured me that the BBC was different. In any case, my name would not be mentioned and my family back home could not be embarrassed.

So I went along to Bush House, whose name I hadn't heard before, and I liked the programme and the general tone and quality of the news. So I asked that my name be broadcast so that my family would know I was well. My friend replied that he wasn't allowed to mention my name. 'Why not', I asked. 'Because you're only an OC'. 'What's an OC'? 'An Outside Contributor'.

I was disappointed, but at least the fee of two pounds and ten shillings went most of the way towards paying my rent to Dimitri for a whole week. And soon I was laughing. They asked me to contribute several times a week, and that enabled me to keep a girlfriend.

I stayed a dozen years at Bush House, most of the later years as a member of staff, until 1980. A year earlier, a hugely popular revolution led by a coalition of Islamic extremists, Marxists and nationalists toppled the Pahlavi monarchy, but only to replace it with a far more cruel state in the grip of a figure out of the seventh century, the ayatollah Khomeini.

Before the revolution, the Shah's government in Tehran and its supporters here blamed us, the dozen or so broadcasters in the Persian Section, for the increasing agitation in Iran and brought pressure on the Labour government to press the BBC to curb our coverage of Iranian news. It did not work. The allegations were exaggerated and a possible legal wrangle between the BBC and the British government would have caused a storm in the press. I admit that sometimes some of my colleagues who supported the uprising allowed themselves to be carried away by their emotion and referred to the Ayatollah Khomeini in reverential terms. But some others among us, including myself, intensely despised Khomeini and, we broadcast the news in exactly the same manner as elsewhere in the BBC. Furthermore, in the 37 days that the last, liberal prime minister, the late Shapour Bakhtiar tried, valiantly, to stem the tide through announcing democratic reforms, we interviewed him three times, while in all the months of Khomeini's exile in France, we talked to him only once.

As for me, I did an extra little bit of my own to stem Khomeini's rise to power. I took advantage of my father's personal friendship with the leader of the liberal opposition, the late Dr Karim Sanjabi, a Kurdish tribal chief, to beg of him not to go into coalition with Khomeini. But it was too late, Sanjabi told me on the telephone. The Shah had destroyed the organisation of the opposition and he, Sanjabi, was a general without troops. The streets had already been taken over by the fanatics. He was right.

Anyway, time came soon for me to move on, but where? I now had a family to support. Nonetheless, the urge overcame me one night. I woke up in the small hours wondering what to do. I wrote my resignation in verse in case I lost courage in the morning. It went as follows:

Dear Mark,
Next year, I'll be thirty-nine,
Time to embark on a new design.
A more ancient kind of craft,
Much more humble, much less daft
Than speaking into thin air,
Hoping someone might be there.
I hope to hear next of thee,
As Auntie's superest DG.
Goodbye, I'm going.

And yes, I'm afraid, the boss agreed. He wrote: 'My dear Hazhir, I dare say you're making the right choice'.

But what choice was I making? At that moment, it was between work and starvation. So I became desperate and thought up even more desperate schemes, except that one of them actually worked, although in an unexpected way, as has been the story of my life.

I wrote to the editor of The Times, Sir William Rees Mogg, urging him to found a news magazine for me to edit, and this at a time when the paper was losing fifteen million pounds a year in its current operations. The previous year, its management had gone on strike for eleven months in order to curb the power of the print unions, but failed.

Imagine my surprise, then, when I received a letter from the paper's foreign editor, the late Charles Douglas Home, asking me to go to see him. And yes, when I arrived, the foreign editor did allow me to sing the praises of my suggested magazine. I think it was to be devoted to world affairs only, but I am not certain now. At last, however, he spoke, and said that the paper was in absolutely no position to finance anything new. But his man in Tehran had been thrown into jail by the revolutionaries and now he had no-one there to write for him on events. Would I cover the subject, as far as possible, from here?

I struggled not to appear speechless. I said I would, but so numb was I with the new turn in my life that, when he stood up to go – borrowing his secretary's filly umbrella – I remained behind in his office and sat down with the secretary.

Charlie later became the paper's editor, a valued friend and a fellow inmate in a hospital, where he died tragically young. But that's another story. For now, I had arrived, truly arrived, in the world of journalism, and at the very top of it, at The Times of London, the oldest and most prestigious newspaper in the world.

I found myself thrown in at the most senior level of print journalism . One late Sunday afternoon in July 1980, news broke that the deposed Shah had died in Cairo and The Times summoned me to its offices in Gray's Inn Road. 'We want an OPED article placing him in the context of Persian history', they told me. 'What's an OPED article', I asked, sheepishly. 'Oh, opposite the editorials'. Pompous people. Why didn't they say 'centre page' to frighten the life out me earlier? Then they put me in a small room, gave me cup after cup of coffee to make me sweat harder, and ripped every little page out of the typewriter as soon as it was half-written. The printers would not let journalists use computers and they were impatient to go home. To make matters worse, the young lady who brought me my coffee complained that she really wanted to write books on cookery and found it hard to break into the market.

I left for home depressed, not having been able to revise what I had written, and convinced that it was the worst article anyone could have written. Fortunately, early in the next morning, it read reasonably well, and the BBC World Service, with its 39 languages, took most of its press review on the Shah from the article written by 'The Special Correspondent of The Times'. At that time, I was still bound by contract to the Persian Section and could not therefore write for anyone else under my own name.

So, as far as my English was concerned, I had travelled far from buying that pamphlet on 'Heedrogen' for exercise paper at Uncle Isaac's shop in Sahneh. From now on, I'd earn my living in the tongue of Shakespeare and, deceptively, deceptively, there were no mountains on the horizon.


## Isaiah Berlin and I

One of the most memorable evenings of my life occurred in May 1987. At a concert in London, I and a friend were waiting for the Persian singer, Shusha, to appear on the stage when I recognised the philosopher Sir Alfred Ayer sitting directly behind us. I whispered the fact to my friend and he turned to have a surreptitious look, but then he lunged backwards in rapture and almost grabbed in a tight embrace the philosopher's lady companion. They'd been boyfriend and girlfriend many years ago. and here he'd discovered her once more.

So, at the interval, I found myself enthralled by Sir Freddie, as we sipped white wine and my friend monopolised his woman. He told me that, although he was now 77 and couldn't write philosophy as fluently as he'd done once, the writing of his latest book, the biography of Thomas Pain, had been easy. I was so exhilarated that, later, I recorded the episode in my diary in verse.

I don't quite know why I'm so fascinated by philosophers. Was it that upbringing in Sahneh, my remote little market-town in the Kurdish mountains of western Iran?

Sahneh, you see, was almost pre-Socratic in many important ways in the 1940s. It even bore some physical resemblance to ancient Athens. It did not have an Acropolis or Higher Town, devoted to temples and official buildings, but it was small enough and round, and it was surrounded by a ring of orchards. Above all, it had not yet been touched by the modern world. It had no telephones and no electricity, only a few temperamental radio sets whose batteries constantly leaked. We had only a couple of motor cars.

Sahneh didn't even have a police station and, from mid-spring to mid-autumn, its social life seemed to transfer entirely to the orchards around it. A lot of people seemed unable to resist the urge to construct high, wooden platforms in their orchards to sleep on them at night, with the flimsy excuse of needing to protect their vines from wild boars that descended from the hills. I think that my fellow townsmen and townswomen just loved those long evening dinners and the discussions and story-tellings that went with them.

Now, my mother, who dreamt of her eldest son joining the ruling class of Iran one day and spoke to me only in Persian, was against my associating too much with those rude, rough Kurds, even though some of them were my father's relatives. My father wasn't keen, either. He suspected his relatives' morals. So, my two brothers and I headed for the orchards anytime we could find a good excuse.

Our favourite was Uncle Khaleel, my father's eldest maternal uncle. He was called by everyone: Kaakeh, the respectful address of elder brothers in Kurdish, and he managed my father's three orchards with his two younger brothers and their only sister, Aunty Shamsee. The darling of the family was Aunty Shamsee's illegitimate, teenage daughter, who had long, flowing brown hair, a tall, slender figure with beautiful breasts that revealed their shapes through her thins blouses. She's the only survivor of them, now, and I haven't seen her for 39 years.

Anyway, each time I and my brothers arrived in the orchards, Kaakeh would greet us with a groan – we were voracious eaters – before going away to gather a sack-full of cherries, peaches, grapes, etc., which he would then chill in a running stream for us to descend on.

In his beliefs, Kaakeh was clearly a pre-Socratic philosopher. He believed that everything could be explained in terms of natural causes. He didn't care too much for gods and supernaturals. One day, for example, my brother Feerooz quarrelled with me and swore by God that he would never ride his horse again. This was serious and Feerooz knew it better than anyone. He wailed with grief. Then along came Kaakeh, who swore by God that he would never ride Feerooz's horse, only to climb on its back immediately. We all burst into laughter and Feerooz jumped back on the horse, beaming from side to side.

By contrast, Kaakeh's younger brother, Uncle Haatee, was Socrates himself, meticulous and fussy about the precise meanings of words. His dark moods were matched only by his drooping moustaches that made him look like a Mexican robber in a bad Western. He'd become addicted to opium early in life, to relieve a toothache, he said, and he smoked it on a long pipe every evening after dinner, when he became a happy man again. He grew his own poppies, to my father's displeasure. Otherwise, he said, he'd have to buy the opium at enormous cost from Ali, the Thief.

Now, this Ali-the-Thief came down from the hills only rarely, but when he did, all the neighbouring orchards men would gather around him to hear about his latest adventure. One of his boasts was that he was the safest man to be with in the hills. 'Don't worry', he'd tell people. 'Just come with me. I know all these mountains like the back of my hand. The whole of the Iranian army is looking for me'.

He seemed to be looking and listening all the time, like a tiger in the undergrowth. He told me that the scar on his left cheek was the mark of an army bullet. His yellowish hair was bleached in streaks by the sun, and his blue eyes shone in the dark.

Back to the philosophers. The youngest of my father's three uncles, Saree, had gone blind in childhood, but remained good-looking with his glowing skin and red moustaches. I longed for him to see himself, even just once. He was the Platonist of the set. Perhaps not unnaturally for a blind man, he believed that the key to happiness was the contemplation of unchanging things, such as truth. He wasn't impudent enough, though, to put it that way.

My father, on the other hand, had to be mindful of his responsibilities in society, and of his paternal family's name. After all, had I myself not met a man they called 'the prime minister of the whole of Iran' visiting my father's father just because Grandfather had, at the age of 85, jumped from the top of one roof onto another and broken a hip? Besides, my father was much younger, and therefore more modern than his maternal uncles. So he followed Aristotle. He believed in the First Cause, which did not need a previous cause to effect it, and he believed that we were here to be virtuous, in preparation for eternal life with the First Cause.

No wonder I gave up my inheritance, although I must not mislead you. My father has a keen sense of humour and masses of humanity. Only recently, he laughed so much at a story I told him that he was forced to hand the phone to someone else, and in 1970, the only time he was given permission by the Iranian government to visit me in London, he was so moved by the great art that he saw at the National Gallery in London that he equated it to a whole country: 'Could you tell the British something from me', he asked. 'Tell them, "you who have this building, why do you think you need Northern Ireland?".

I had to rescue him from the effects of Middle Eastern propaganda and tell him that a majority of people in Northern Ireland actually wanted to remain a part of Britain. But his remark showed that he had his values right.

Anyway, a few years after arriving in England in 1959, I discovered Bertrand Russell and became an adoring fan of his, so much so that when he invited me to visit him in Wales in his last year, 1970, I declined, for fear of giving him the flu, or some other virus harmful to a 97-year-old. He died soon afterwards, nonetheless.

It occurs to me that nowadays a lot of people have become Russellites without knowing it: all those, for example, who live in what he called 'trial marriages' and others 'living in sin'.

In the past decade or so, my outlook on life has darkened somewhat, though my family and friends may not believe me when I say that. They think of me primarily as a clown. It appears to me that the life of both humans and animals is dominated by suffering. The German philosopher, Schopenhauer, of course, described it in his beautiful prose more than 150 years ago and sought refuge in the contemplation of natural and artistic beauty. I go along with that, except that I'd probably add a couple of things to the list of my consolations: for example, the company of all my family and friends – no matter how ugly – and a case of good Claret.

Later still, in the early 1990s I had the privilege of meeting another great philosopher, Sir Isaiah Berlin, and immediately took to him. He was a regular in the drawing room of the Athenaeum club in London's Pall Mall and loved to be surrounded by adoring fans and friends, among them, often, beautiful women. His booming voice still rings in my ear: 'Only fanatics and holy men have absolute values.'

He used to refer to our century as 'the most terrible in the history of the West', and no wonder. He'd witnessed the horrors of the Bolshevik take-over of the Russian revolution and, then, as a Jew, been scarred for life by the Holocaust. He was deeply attached to liberty – his concepts of 'negative and positive liberty' probably making him the greatest philosopher of his later years – and he was extremely worried, as I am, that Britain was becoming a less liberal, less western, society. He expected that the settlement here of large numbers of immigrants like myself from non-European backgrounds would eventually tear Britain apart, or at best, turn it into a country like India, where no-one dared to think aloud about any serious issue without the fear of causing a riot somewhere.

The fact that, in today's Britain, a novelist, Salman Rushdie, had to hide for his life deeply shocked him, as it still shocks me.

Such basic thinking is not welcome to the wielders of power who want only an easy life. In a decade's time, it will be someone else's responsibility to pick up the pieces.

Have you noticed that there's not a single philosopher honoured with a seat and a voice in the House of Lords? Does that not tell you something about the quality of our rulers?

The reason is not just that thinkers are often not rich enough to pour money into party coffers. Their main fault is that, by definition, they are not reliable as political supporters, as cronies.

All the thinkers I knew at the time of the Falklands war rooted for Britain. But had the Falkland Islanders wanted to be ruled by the proto-fascist junta of Argentina, I think, and I hope, that none of them would have raised an objection. Thinkers are not loyal to states in the conventional sense. They are loyal to 'Civilisation' – with a big C – however pompous that may sound.

And so I come to the end of these talks about the life of a shy little boy I once knew growing up in the remote Kurdish mountains of western Iran, who, before he'd had time to be a man, was catapulted into a different world and nearly perished from the shock.

Fortunately, I remember only the exhilaration now, and I see that my father's courage and strong social values that sent me here, were the best legacy he could have given me. True, I lost my family, in effect, when I was only 19, and my family lost a son, but great destinations often do lie only at the end of perilous journeys.

By 'great destinations' I do not mean any professional skills that I may have gained. Much more important to me, in recent years, has been the chance to drink, more widely, from the roaring river of European civilisation that, whether by chance or not, has been the brightest achievement of our species, yet.

Those untutored philosophers I left behind in the orchards of Sahneh 39 years ago never expected that, for me, one day, a foreign musician called Beethoven would be the greatest man who had ever lived. They would certainly have found my company unbearable during the writing of these talks as I listened to all the 14-and-a-half string quartets of Beethoven.

But then, they did live in the world of flying carpets and Time Lords, and the wonders of my journey and destination would really not have surprised them much.

# Recommended Reading for Pleasure

The following list is drawn up in that spirit of quiet pleasure that ought to characterise our mature years. This is not to say that enlightenment is banished from the list. Far be that abominable thought from me. No good day is ever labelled so by this temporary inhabitant of Planet Earth if it does not bring in its wake a new chunk of learning. The idea is that the two, pleasure and learning, pull forth together as two horses the same coach. So, here we go:

*History of Western Philosophy* by Bertrand Russell. Should you be exiled to a desert island and allowed to take only one book with you, this ought to be your choice. It is not the most accurate history of philosophy, but it is the most wise, as it encapsulates the genius and the judgement of one of the wisest people who have ever lived. For me, Russell was the best of them all. It is also the most entertaining history of philosophy, as well as the most inspiring. Russell had a strong sense of humour and was accepted as a master of English. Another valuable aspect of the book is that it places the philosophy and the philosopher against the background of their times, allowing Russell to be respectful and understanding. In that way, he also gives us a political, social, economic, religious and scientific history of the West. For decades, I have kept it beside my bed with the idea of using it to make me drowsy late at night. The trouble has been that it has kept me awake, making me even resent sleep as a waste of precious time, time that could be used to read more Russell.

*The Great Philosophers*, a BBC book. This series of dialogues between the philosopher Brian Magee and some of the most eloquent teachers of philosophy in our time has been most useful to me since 1987, when it was first broadcast on BBC television. The discussions examine 15 philosophers from Plato to Wittgenstein and carry the authority of a respected commentator in each case. Furthermore, the interviewees, who include the late Alfred Ayer, are often hypnotic in their charisma, intellect and wit. There are few dull moments in the whole book. Some can still be seen in their original form on the Web.

*The Autobiography of Bertrand Russell.* This book tells a history of a different kind, but with the same attributes of genius and wisdom that are exhibited elsewhere by my idol. It tells the story of the twentieth century with its two world wars and unprecedented revolutions in science and society. It moves us personally, too. Its agonies and pleasures are felt on the skin of a most sensitive person who loves deeply and is, in return, loved passionately. Russell completed it shortly before his died at the age of 97, revered, as no man had

244

ever been before, by almost the whole of humanity. The book is a roller-coaster of emotions, making you laugh and cry, sometimes in the same breath.

*Doctor Zhivago* by Boris Pasternak. If you are allowed only one volume of fiction, this ought to be it, though it is not really a work of fiction. It is largely autobiographical, or at least biographical, for it weaves into one the life stories of dozens of characters, largely those who became victims to a political revolution they had hoped would release them from tyranny and stagnation. In that sense, it too is a history of the twentieth century, but this time as seen from the eastern side of Europe. It tells the story of how a whole world was swept aside by powerful social forces and replaced by another that was run by less civilised men. At the same time, it is the story of flesh-and-blood human beings who love life and who love one another. The dozen or so poems that are appended to the end of the novel alone make this work a book to cherish. Pasternak did not write a full autobiography, but the recollections of his lover, Olga Ivinskaya, who became the model for Lara in Zhivago, comes close to telling that story. *Captive of Time: My Years with Pasternak* had to be smuggled to the West to be published. But its long-suffering author at least survived long enough to see the downfall of the tyrants who had inflicted so much pain on her, Pasternak and millions of others all over eastern Europe.

*The Leopard* by Giuseppe Tomasi di Lampedusa. This great novel is also about the sweeping away of one world and its replacement by another, one that is more frenetic and not so humane, in the eye of its narrator, a minor aristocrat. It is far less important than Zhivago, for it is only about the incorporation of Sicily into a unified Italy, but it is remarkable how many other parallels there are between the two novels. Apart from great literature, they were written at about the same time, in the years immediately after the Second World War, and they antagonised their countries' Communist parties for not paining the working class in heroic hues. Yet they were published, eventually, by the same Italian Communist publishing company, Feltrinelli. They reached a world beyond print, too, by way of glamorous Hollywood actors portraying their protagonists.

*On Being: A scientist's exploration of the great questions of existence*, by Peter Atkins. This is science-writing as lucid as it can be, and it is by one of our most brilliant professors of physical chemistry at Oxford University. As such, Atkins is at the furthest point of our knowledge of sub-atomic particles and of the structure of the Universe/Multiverse. He is optimistic that the scientific method will eventually discover why things exist at all, for at the moment we are hampered by the laws of physics not having come into being in the first trillionth of a second after the Big Bang. Peter at times sounds unkind to philosophers, but we need not take that seriously, for he enjoys playing the devil's advocate. Let me quote Philip Pullman on this, one of his smaller books: 'It presents a vision of life and death, of matter and space and time that is honest and consistent and miracle-free, except for the living and totally material miracle that is science and the scientific method. There's a level, unpretending, translucent nobility in this vision, and I admire it very much.'

*The Oxford Book of English Verse*, edited by Christopher Ricks. This tome of a book goes back to the beginnings of modern English in the 1200s and ought to adorn every bedside table. Edited in its latest incarnation by a professor of literature at the University of Boston in the United States, it leaves out the works of separatists there since the 1770s. But that is just as well. It would have been even larger, otherwise.

*A History of English Literature,* by Michael Alexander. Nor should any home be without a history of English literature and this highly enjoyable and beautifully structured big book is the perfect candidate. Written by a renowned scholar of Shakespeare and former professor of English at the University of St Andrews, the book is the result of a lifetime of experience making English literature accessible to generations of students. Michael is also a poet and a translator of verse. See his nominations in the anthology section.

*Omar Khayyām: Poet, Rebel, Astronomer.* Finally, should you wish to dip a foot into Byzantium and the Middle East around the time of the First Crusade, this work of mine may not disappoint you. A decade of effort went into it and what a surprising story it turned out. The Persian musician, mathematician, astronomer and friend of shahs almost succumbed to the wielders of fatwas and their lynch mobs, merely because he admired the ancient Greeks, rather than the men of Islam. A second edition will be issued soon (June 2015), in electronic, as well as in traditional, format.

# Acknowledgements

I am grateful to my friends, Jon Swan, now of Maine in the United States, and David Morphet, here in England, who allowed me to include some of their poems in the anthology, and to Michael (Professor) Alexander and Phyllis (Baroness P. D.) James who nominated some of their favourite poems for inclusion. Mary and Andrew Fergar, wife and son to my late BBC colleague Feyyaz Fergar, and David Perman, Feyyaz's friend and publisher at Rockingham Press, were also generous in allowing me to include several of Feyyaz's poems. I am grateful to them all.

Two philosopher friends, Peter Cave and Raymond Tallis, shared their thoughts with me on several subjects, while the distinguished scientist professor Peter Atkins of Oxford University wrote his own part in the conversation we had with Spinoza in The Hague when we visited that great man there a few months before he died in 1677.

I have quoted short passages from the writings of my early mentor Bertrand Russell. Those and similar quotations elsewhere, I believe to be in the spirit of 'fair review'. I hope that they will encourage readers to buy the original works for greater pleasure and even deeper enlightenment.

The images and plates that adorn the chapters are acknowledged individually and are nearly all in the public domain by courtesy of Wikipedia Commons. Indeed, the creators of Wikipedia itself have improved hugely the quality of their scholarship in recent years and deserve our collective gratitude. I encourage readers to contribute to the large running expenses of this vast new source of knowledge. A major attraction of an on-line encyclopaedia, such as theirs, is that it enables the searcher to jump instantaneously to other on-line sites of reference, particularly those of the universities that have exploded onto our world in the past two decades and made the work of scholars much less arduous.

My wife Christabel King has as usual been a pillar on whom my life revolves, and my 'brother' Christopher Lee continues to be a source of encouragement, joy and strength. My literary agent Sonia Land has become a friend in her own right over the years and can therefore make no mistake on my behalf.

# Endnotes

1. From his *Portraits from Memory and other Essays*, 1956, first edition, p52.
2. Roman marble bust possibly copied from a Greek bronze original, Louvre Museum, Paris. Photographed by Eric Gaba.
3. Tweaked and modernised by the author from several translations, particularly that of William James Hickie, 1853
4. Based on a translation by H. G. Dakyns, Macmillan and Co, London 1897
5. HT, Oct 2013.
6. Roman marble bust at the British Museum, photographed by ChrisO. Wikipedia Commons.
7. A painted cloister or portico where the teaching was held.
8. Diogenes Laertius apparently lived in the fourth century AD.
9. From the *Lives and Opinions of Eminent Philosophers* by Diogenes Laertius. Translated by Charles Duke Yonge, 1812-1891.
10. Ibidem.
11. VS17 in the Vatican collection of Epicurus' sayings.
12. In a letter to Menoecus, a friend.
13. Double herm of Seneca and Socrates at Antikensammlung, Berlin. Photographed by Calidius. Wikipedia Commons.
14. From the treatise De Vita Beata written for his elder brother Gallio. I have here modernised the language a little and juxtaposed the points from the translations in Seneca, by Francis Caldwell Holland, Longmans, Green And Co., London 1920. The marble bust of Seneca is a third century Roman copy of a first century original, now at the State Museum of Berlin. It is part of a double herm, with Socrates as the other half, and, judging by the close resemblance of what is known of the appearance of Socrates, its original model of Seneca may well have been commissioned by the Seneca family or a close associate of theirs while he lived. Was it a present to him, on the occasion of a birthday, for example?
15. Miriam T. Griffin, *Seneca: A philosopher* in Politics, Oxford 1976.
16. From Seneca's *Letters*, to Lucilius, towards the end of his life.
17. Vasily Rudich, *Political Dissidence Under Nero*, Routledge 1993, p150.
18. Bertrand Russell, *History of Western Philosophy*, Unwin University Books, London 1969, p273.
19. A medieval imagining of Boethius, now in the public domain.
20. Chaucer's translation of the last lines of Book II of the *Consolation*.

21. Justinian, 482-565.
22. More correctly Theoderic.
23. From Hans von Campenhausen's *The Fathers of the Latin Church*, as translated by Manfred Hoffman, London 1964, p289.
24. As a result, only fragments of the collection have survived, and these are scraps in the works of Christians who later defended their faith against his criticism.
25. H. F. Stewart, 1891.
26. From *The Consolation of Philosophy*, translated by H. R. James, 1897. The full text of this translation is available on the Web site of the University of Adelaide: http://ebooks.adelaide.edu.au/b/boethius/sonsolation
27. Ibid.
28. For example, that of the late professor P. G. Walsh's Oxford World Classics edition of 2000 or the Penguin Classics version of Professor Victor Watts, 1999.
29. Book IV, chapter IV, H. R. James.
30. Momigliano was professor of Roman History at University College London, from 1951-75. Of Jewish descent, he had previously taught at Turin University, but had had to flee Italy due to Fascist persecution.
31. Chicago University Press, 1980, p10.
32. Boethius, *The Consolation of Philosophy*, Oxford World's Classics, 1999.
33. This photograph of Khayyām's mausoleum in Nishāpūr, north-east Iran, was taken by Talinn Grigor and belongs to the Aga Kahn Visual Archive at MIT, Cambridge, Massachusetts. I am grateful to the directors of the AKVA for allowing me to print it here.
34. My translation from Khayyām's original Persian.
35. We also raise a glass to the 19th century English poet Edward FitzGerald who made Khayyām famous in the world with his 'translation' of the rub. If I am in a especially boisterous mood, we also drink to another of my heroes, the philosopher Bertrand Russell, for he too was born on May 18, though 824 years later.
36. This is a recent interpretation by astronomers of the horoscope of Khayyām's birth. For an explanation of how it was achieved, see pp. XXXII-XXXVI of *The Nectar of Grace* by Govinda Tirtha, India, 1941, re-issued by Oxford City Press, 2010.
37. According to the Institute of Physics in London. The rotation of the earth around the sun has become slightly longer since then.
38. The author, who is of medium height, has a skull circumference of only 53 cm, including, obviously, skin and hair.
39. For more of Arūzi's recollections of Khayyām, see pp 254-6 of my *Omar Khayyām: Poet, Rebel Astronomer*, Sutton, 2007.

40. An engraving in the New York Public Library Archives, now in the public domain. The caption denounces Spinoza as 'a Jew and an atheist'.

41. *Dream of Reason*, by Anthony Gottlieb, Penguin Books, London 2000. Chapter 14.

42. Ibid.

43. *History of Western Philosophy*, Fifth Impression, Bertrand Russell, London 1969.

44. *Spinoza*, Roger Scruton, Oxford, 1986.

45. *Within Reason: A Life of Spinoza*, by Margaret Gullah-Whur, London 1998. Chapter 13.

46. I am grateful to Peter for writing his own part in this pilgrimage of 1676.

47. Peter Cave of The Open University, 2014, in manuscript lent to me.

48. Literally: Each person became my friend according to their own perceptions of me. None found the secrets that hide inside me.

49. *Within Reason: A life of Spinoza*, by Margaret Gullan-Whur, London 1998.

50. A bust by Hugo Hagen based on a life-masque in 1812. Beethoven-Hauss Mueseum, Bonn. Photographed in 1898 by W J Baker. Library of Congress public domain.

51. He was born at the end of 1770, on December 16.

52. These edited excerpts are taken from the Wikipedia article 'Immortal Beloved' in February 2014.

53. Altogether, some 15 women are linked romantically to Beethoven by the gossip that has survived from those times.

54. Thayer-Forbes, p. 811, quoted by Maynard Solomon in *Beethoven*, 1998, chapter 20.

55. Much later, George Bernard Shaw revealed his Irish resentment of England by describing the decision as 'the only credible act in British history'.

56. Among my teachers had been Gillian Thoday who had earlier won London's Young Musician of the Year award. She has remained a close friend and is now Professor of Cello at the Royal Northern College of Music in Manchester.

57. Stephen also has remained a friend, though a more distant one. In 1998, Philips Classics published seven of his Beethoven performances in their series Great Pianists of the 20th Century. I recommend the album to readers. In his youth and later, I saw also how, as almost certainly with Beethoven, beautiful, musical women threw themselves on his feet and he passed by. Was I green with envy? Of course, not.

58. Years later, when I had discovered Brendel's greatness, I had the pleasure of sitting next to him at Glyndebourne on the opening night of a production of Fidelio there. This was thanks to the generosity of my agent Sonia Land

and her husband Nick who also invited my wife to the performance. On our other side sat the most musical of Britain's prime ministers, the late Edward Heath, the pleasure of whose meeting I had had in 1985, when we celebrated the bicentenary of the foundation of *The Times*. Another memory of Brendel is that he played Charlie's favourite Beethoven sonata

59. Portrait by John Collier (1850-1934) now in the National Gallery in London. Public domain photograph.

60. From his autobiography, written for his family towards the end of his life in 1881.

61. Ibid.

62. Jeremy Barlow, the musician and historian of music. We are both members of a little luncheon group of friends, known as *The Algae*, who meet monthly at the Athenæum club for lunch followed by a lecture by one of ourselves about their latest writing project or preoccupation.

63. *The Autobiography of Charles Darwin And Selected Letters*, edited by his son Sir Francis Darwin, 1892.

64. From the autobiography again.

65. In his nomination sheet of 13 December 1836 at the Athenæum, Darwin is described as 'Secretary, Geological Society & private gentleman', and his sponsors are two of the club's founders of 1824, his geological mentor Sir Charles Lyell, FRS, and his relative Sir Henry Holland, FRS. Fourteen months later, the club needed costly repairs proposed by Michael Faraday to undo the damage that gas lighting was inflicting on the club's books in its new magnificent building in Pall Mall. So Darwin and 39 others on the waiting list were drafted in by orders of the general committee, rather than being forced to wait their turns until they had accumulate sufficient numbers of supporters among the general membership. The newcomers became known as 'the 40 thieves', but they brought in immediately £842 in joining fees and £242 in annual subscriptions. For this information, I am indebted to the club's archivist Ms Jennie de Protani, MA.

66. *Darwin*, the great man's comprehensive and most enjoyable biography by Adrian Desmond and James Moore, 1991; Michael Joseph, London, p647.

67. This account of Darwin's burial hassle was first written by the author in *Armchair Athenians* and was published by the Athenæum Club to mark the occasion of the second millennium.

68. Desmond and Moore, p631.

69. This portrait is one of a series made in his last years and sold for charity. Now in the public domain.

70. *The Life of Mark Twain*, by Albert Bigelow Paine.

71. *A Pen Warmed Up in Hell: Mark Twain in Protest*, Frederick Anderson, ed.,

New York: Harper, 1972.

72. *A Book of Verse: The Biography of the Rubaiyat of Omar Khayyam*, Garry Garrard, Sutton, 2007.

73. This makes me think. Who is America's foremost humourist today. Many would say Garrison Keilor of *Lake Wobegon* fame. I would have to agree, and not just for objective reasons. He is a friend of ours and we had the pleasure of introducing his adopted Danish daughter to her future husband some 20 years ago in London. I believe that in many ways Garrison is in direct line from Twain.

74. This portrait, which I like to call 'His Lordship' and which seems to me a little unsympathetic towards Russell, was drawn for me by my friend Professor Rabbi Dan Cohn-Sherbok a few days before I was due to speak on the philosopher at a gathering of fellow members of the Athenæum club in London in April 2014. The Athenæum has the owl for its mascot. Russell was informally expelled from the club for his activism against the First World War, but re-elected after the Second.

75. The opening words of The Prologue in his *Autobiography*, London, late 1960s.

76. In a letter to Lady Ottoline Morrell, 27 August 1918.

77. I do not know where this quote occurs in his writings. But it is confirmed by my friend Peter Cave, the philosopher.

78. I do not know where this quote occurs in his writings. But it is confirmed by my friend Peter Cave, the philosopher.

79. And perhaps even ours. Recently a new chair of philosophy has been set up in his name at Cambridge. It had been planned to be called the Wittgenstein, which shows that the latter, like Heidegger, has had his fashionable day.

80. My friend Peter Cave remarks: 'A rough distinction in the 20th century was that Cambridge philos paid far more attention to science than did Oxford philos'.

81. On the same day as another great mathematician and thinker, Omar Khayyām, 824 years earlier. See *Omar Khayyam: Poet, Rebel, Astronomer*, by H Teimourian, London 2007.

82. I have not seen this possibility raised anywhere, but a little DNA analysis among today's Russells and Spaldings could settle the matter easily. Certainly Bertrand's receding chin resembled his father's, but his mother also seemed rather chinless. In the first volume of *The Amberley Papers*, by Bertrand and Patricia Russell, 1937, p558, the following short paragraph occurs in Amberley's diary of December 1873, when he, Kathrine and Spalding were in Rome: 'Th. 29. I saw Edith a short time in the morning & talked to her about complete openness in marriage in which she

entirely takes our views. After breakfast, Spalding made his confession, but I did not hear of it till the evening.' The confession apparently did not worry Amberley, for in an entry two weeks later, on January 13, 1874, he wrote: '... Kate and Spalding went to a masked ball in the evening which they did not enjoy much'. Might Spalding's confession have been that he was baby Bertrand's father? Amberley had much earlier given his consent that he be Kathrine's lover. Russell later thought that it was 'probably' a confession love for Lady Amberley. As Russell's grandmother burned all of the couple's correspondence with Spalding after their deaths, we may never find out, bar that possible DNA analysis.

83. He died from tuberculosis a year after Amberley's death.

84. Russell argued that the whole of philosophy could be deduced from logic. It was hailed as a monumental achievement in its time. Now, however, it is generally regarded as having failed, though it provided the tools and the inspiration for those who came later and surpassed it.

85. *The Life of Bertrand Russell in pictures and in his own words*, Compiled by Christopher Farley and David Hodgson, Spokesman Books, 1971, p39.

86. At the Athenæum club in London's Pall Mall, a large book commemorating members who have won the Nobel prize is given a prominent place at the top of the landing outside the grand drawing room. Russell's pages state that he was elected to the club in 1952. This is to save the club the embarrassment of admitting that it had expelled him earlier, at the end of the First World War, when he was imprisoned for his vehement opposition to that war. But when Russell was elevated in the world by the Order of Merit and the Nobel Prize in1950, the club sought him back. One of the present grandees, Brian Gilmore, who is himself a trained philosopher and a devotee of Russell, told me that Russell had not been expelled from the club officially. 'You are never expelled from the Athenæum for misbehaviour. You are persuaded to resign in order to avoid the embarrassment of being expelled.' But Brian also believes that the 'expulsion' had been justified. Russell had not been imprisoned for pacifism, but for advocating rebellion in the armed forces. That was treason, technically.

87. See the author's aide memoir *I had last night, a privilege rare / I sipped white wine with Sir Alfred Ayer.*, in the Poems of Joy section.

88. *Russell*, by A. J. Ayer, Fontana Modern Masters, London 1972.

89. Page 249, *A Short History of Philosophy*, by Robert C. Solomon and Kathleen M. Higgins, Oxford Uiversity Press, New York and Oxford, 1996.

90. A portrait in oil by his father Leonid and first printed in imperial Russia. It remains in the public domains there.

91. I say this as one who has himself written one such tome. Having published the most detailed ever biography of Omar Khayyām (over 350 pages), I often wonder to what extent I uncovered the real man. But then, Khayyām lived nearly a thousand years ago and our knowledge of his life and character is partial. Again, perhaps we are lucky that most heroes of our distant past have not left us too full a portrait of themselves, for 'no man is a hero to his butler'.

92. He was included in the delegation at the last minute and by the insistence of Stalin's secretary who suddenly appeared at the clinic where he was receiving treatment. The French leftist writers Malraux and Camus had asked for him. It is said that he did not arrange for a visit with his parents because he feared the effect of his appearance on them. Weeks of his stay in Paris were spent in hospitals and he was depressed, as well as suffering heart and muscle aches. But the way to Paris he had met his sister Josephine in Munich. See p188, *Boris Pasternak, A Biography*, by Peter Levi, Hutchinson, London, 1990.

93. My personal memory of the great man, limited though it is, accords with this suggestion of his compassion and integrity. See 'Isiah Berlin and I', the fourth part of my autobiographical talks on BBC Radio Four, in the Appendix.

94. In his clandestine memoirs after his downfall, Khrushchev claimed that he was sorry 'police methods' had been brought to bear on Pasternak. He said that he had assigned the matter to others and found out too late what had been done in his name. Ironically, his own memoirs could only be published in the West, after they had been smuggled there, just like the novel he had tried to suppress.

95. *A Captive of Time: My Years with Pasternak*, by Olga Ivinskaya, Collins/Harvill, 1978.

96. Twenty-two years younger than Pasternak.

97. As portrayed in a painting by their father Leonid in the late 1900s.

98. This stamp was issued in November 1988 by the Federal Republic of Germany to honour Arendt. The copyright of the photograph belongs to the Deutsche Bundespost on behalf of the state, but has been widely reprinted in the public media.

99. *The Origins of Totalitarianism*, chapter 10, 1951.

100. I found that the multi-volume Encyclopedia Judaica, whose first edition was being prepared while Arendt still lived and which reports on thousands of little-known figures, anathemised her name for years, relenting only in its most recent edition. Also in Boston last year (2014), I met a couple of German-speaking American Jews at a gathering of scientists who could not recall Arendt's name.

101. I am glad to report that Ted Honderich, the editor of the august Oxford Companion to Philosophy, has little time for Heidegger's philosophy. Instead, he puts Jaspers in the front rank of modern philosophers. Nor am I surprised. None of my philosopher friends understands Heidegger, due to his plethora of mystical neologisms, and Russell does not mention him at all in his *History of Philosophy*. Personally, I find him, and his Marxist, one-time student Sartre, combinations largely of charlatanry and narcissism. They will fool many people for centuries to come. It may interest the reader that Heidegger described Sartre's huge tome, *Being and Nothingness*, deeply informed by his own work as it was, as 'nothing but muck'.

102. She continued to stick by the traditional use of the term 'Man' as referring to the whole of Mankind. Not for her was the modern fad of 'he/she'.

103. Elizabeth Young-Bruehl in *Hannah Arendt: For Love of the World*, 1983.

104. See the chapter on Spinoza.

105. Suggested for inclusion here by two friends, Phyllis (P. D.) James and Prof. Michael Alesander.

106. The last line is a Russian proverb.

107. I am grateful to David Morphet for allowing me to include three of his poems in this anthology. David is a friend of many years, a former British governor of the International Atomic Energy Agency, and a present grandee of the Athenæum Club. He has published nearly a dozen collections of his poetry.

108. Suggested for inclusion here by my friend Phyllis (P. D.) James. See also her other favourite, Matthew Arnolds' *Dover Beach* in the *Poems of Loss* section.

109. Jon Swan is an American poet, playwright and journalist whose friendship has been one of the great joys of my life over the past two decades. May he continue for ever. He is in his 85th year as I write. Jon and Marianne, his Dutch-born wife, now live in Yarmouth, Maine.

110. Suggested by my friend Richard Shannon

111. Feyyaz Fergar, 1919-1993, was a multi-lingual colleague of mine in the World Service of the BBC and headed the Turkish section. Of Armenian parentage, he wrote in French, Turkish and English. This poem is from a collection called *The Bright is Dark Enough*, published by Rockingham Press in London in 1993. For more information on this most talented poet, see my obituary of him in *The Times* of April 14, 1993.

112. 28 October, 2013.

113. The opening quatrains of his 'Englishing' of Khayyām's *Rubáiyát*, as opposed to my literal translation of the same.

114. See footnote in Poems of Hope.

115. See also footnote to *Now or Then* in the Poems of Solace section. Jon wrote this joyous poem, a satire on a corner of American religious life which the great Mark Twain himself would have admired, in May 2014, when he was about 85 years old.

116. The dedication page of his autobiography, which I recommend to readers for their pure pleasure, as well as for a most moving story of the twentieth century told by one of the greatest minds that ever lived.

117. See footnote in *Poems of Loss*

118. Wall-mounted wooden telephone in the Champaign County Historical Museum, Illinois, the United States. Photograph in the public domain.

119. From the last chapter of Darwin's short autobiography written in 1881 for his family and descendants.

120. Omar Khayyām, 1048-1131. Stanza no. 9 in my translation of his rubaiyat, 2007.

121. From his *Autobiography* written for his family only, at the end of the chapter on the Voyage of the Beagle.

122. *Doctor Zhivago,* translated by Max Hayward and Manya Harari, William Collins and Co, London 1958.

# *About the Author*

**Hazhir Teimourian** was born in 1940 in Kurdish western Iran and studied classical Persian and Arabic before being sent to London to study science. There he fell under the influence of the philosopher Bertrand Russell and drifted into broadcasting in the World Service of the BBC. In 1980, he was called to The Times as a commentator on Middle Eastern politics and history and remained with the newspaper for 16 years. At times of the most intense turmoil in the Middle East, it felt as if he lived in television studios as 'presenter's friend' and became a familiar face throughout the English-speaking world. To this day, he needs a radio studio at home to cope with the demand.

Teimourian's biography of Omar Khayyām, the eleventh century poet, thinker and astronomer, was praised by the press and has been translated into several other languages. He lives in Sussex with his wife Christabel King and has two grown-up children. For more information on him, please see:

www.KhayyamByTeimourian.com or

www.LimehouseGroup.net